Studies in Black American Literature

Studies in Black American Literature

Volume II

Belief vs. Theory

in Black American Literary Criticism

edited by

Joe Weixlmann

and

Chester J. Fontenot

The Penkevill Publishing Company
Greenwood, Florida

Copyright © 1986
The Penkevill Publishing Company

ISBN 0–913283–13–4
ISSN 0738–0755

Printed in the United States of America

Notes on Contributors

Houston A. Baker, Jr., holds the Albert M. Greenfield Chair in Human Relations at the University of Pennsylvania. He is, perhaps, most well-known as the author of *The Journey Back: Issues in Black Literature and Criticism* (1980). His new book, *Blues, Ideology, and Afro-American Literature: A Vernacular Theory,* is forthcoming from the University of Chicago Press.

Amiri Baraka is Professor of English at the State University of New York at Stony Brook and the author of more than twenty books, the most recent being his *Autobiography* (New York: Freundlich Books, 1984).

W. Lawrence Hogue is Assistant Professor of English and Comparative Literature at the University of California, Irvine. The essay of his which is included in this collection is taken from his recently completed book manuscript, *To Saddle Time: Literature as Production and as a Social Institution.*

Keneth Kinnamon is Ethel Pumphrey Stephens Professor of English and Chairman of the Department of English at the University of Arkansas. With Richard K. Barksdale, he has edited the premier anthology of Afro-American literature, *Black Writers of America* (1972), and he is the author of *The Emergence of Richard Wright: A Study in Literature and Society* (1972).

Margaret B. McDowell is Professor of English at the University of Iowa. She has published books on Edith Wharton (1975) and Carson Mc-Cullers (1980) and authored numerous articles and reviews in scholarly journals, including *Black American Literature Forum.*

R. Baxter Miller is Professor of English at the University of Tennessee. He is the editor of *Black American Literature and Humanism* (1981) and the author of *Langston Hughes and Gwendolyn Brooks: A Reference Guide* (1978).

Michel Oren is Assistant Professor of English at the University of Houston—Downtown and is writing a book on contemporary American avant-garde groups. His interests include literary theory, autobiography, the grotesque, contemporary art (and anti-art) movements, and Western/Third World cultural relations.

John M. Reilly is Associate Professor of English at the State University of New York at Albany and Afro-American literature bibliographer for *American Literary Scholarship*. The compiler of *Richard Wright: The Critical Reception* (1978), he has authored numerous literary studies.

Leslie Sanders received her Ph.D. from the University of Toronto. She teaches in the Humanities and English Departments of Atkinson College, York University, in Downsview, Ontario.

Craig Werner teaches in the Afro-American Studies Department at the University of Wisconsin-Madison. He is the author of *Paradoxical Resolutions: American Fiction since James Joyce* (1982), which includes discussions of Wright, Ellison, Baldwin, Kelley, Morrison, Gaines, and fifteen Euro-American writers. Adrienne Rich is the subject of his current book-in-progress.

CONTENTS

Introduction

The essays included in this second volume of *Studies in Black American Literature* belong to the corpus of writing we encouraged in the inaugural number of the series when we indicated our preference for pieces "of a theoretical bent rather than essays which offer a 'reading' of a specific text or small body of texts." Essentially, the present volume includes three types of essays: (1) those which directly address the question of theory versus belief in Afro-American literary criticism and which suggest new ways of participating in the literary-critical enterprise, (2) those which deal with particular texts and/or authors but have clear and broad implications for the subject of the volume, and (3) those which examine the critical practice of one of the most well-known black critics of his era, George E. Kent, whose recent death has not silenced the living, multi-dimensional testimony offered in his writing to the necessary component of belief which is present in all so-called theoretical systems.

The essays which open the collection are of the first type alluded to above. In "Belief, Theory, and the Blues: Notes for a Post-Structuralist Criticism of Afro-American Literature," Houston A. Baker, Jr., details the shift in his own critical thinking and practice which occurred subsequent to the publication of his highly influential *The Journey Back: Issues in Black Literature and Criticism* (1980). The blues, he now feels, offers a "more inclusively expressive" perspective through which to understand Afro-American writing than does the symbolic/ anthropological model proposed in his 1980 study. As a dialectic which embraces the symbolic as well as the material, a blues matrix "possesses enormous force for the study of literature, criticism, and culture." W. Lawrence Hogue, in his essay on "literary production," · calls for critics to pay more attention to the conditions and institutions which affect the practice of authorship in America. His article concludes with an analysis of the strengths and weaknesses of what he considers to be the two most important new black American critical texts: Robert B. Stepto's *From Behind the Veil* (1979) and Baker's *The Journey Back*. Reading this section of the essay against the backdrop of Baker's introductory piece allows one to see that Baker has anticipated, and taken steps to remedy, the most serious charge that Hogue levels against his critical practice.

Craig Werner's "New Democratic Vistas" provides useful insights into the issues facing anyone attempting to develop a genuinely pluralistic, genuinely non-sexist and non-racist critical approach. Whether pointing out the inherent traditionalism that undergirds the professed pluralism of virtually all Euro-American critics, adapting a feminist critical model for use by Afro-Americanists, or stretching Noam Chomsky's linguistic tenets across the framework of a research genealogy, Werner's observations ring true. In "History-Making Literature," John M. Reilly examines the relationship between history and literature, especially as that issue applies to Afro-American texts. His discussion accomplishes two principal objectives. It provides a context in which to understand better the work of those who, in attempting to write Afro-American literary history, have subordinated the texts they examine to extraliterary considerations. And, by virtue of Reilly's reasoned, rooted analyses of some of these same texts, he aids in the establishment of a more effective approach to Afro-American literary study.

Essays which focus on specific texts and authors comprise the middle section of the volume. Keneth Kinnamon, exploring "Intertextuality in Two Autobiographical Works by Richard Wright and Maya Angelou," uses, and attempts to expand, the call-and-response model for analyzing black American narratives proposed in Stepto's *From Behind the Veil.* To Stepto's "pregeneric myth" of "the quest for freedom and literacy" Kinnamon would add the quest for community, a theme evident, he argues, not only in Angelou's work but in that of many black women writers. In providing the "Groundwork for a More Comprehensive Criticism of Nikki Giovanni," Margaret B. McDowell demonstrates that Giovanni's work has been subjected to more than its share of subjective criticism. Basing their responses to Giovanni's writing on a variety of skewed assumptions (predicated on politics, sexism, ignorance of the facts, even jealousy), critics, including those who have praised her work, have failed to treat it objectively. McDowell's essay documents the fact that critics often allow their knowledge of theory to go utterly by the wayside when their beliefs are deeply felt.

That reactions based on feelings unattached to theory, or on (political) theory unmediated by one's feelings, was an especially prevalent phenomenon during the Black Arts/Black Liberation era is a subject treated not only by McDowell but also by Leslie Sanders in her essay "'Dialect Determinism': Ed Bullins' Critique of the Rhetoric of the Black Power Movement." In play after play, Sanders argues, ". . . Bullins suggested that *rhetoric* was a substitute for action rather than a prelude to it and that it constituted an evasion rather than a revelation of the transformations upon which a healthier society could be predicated." Relatedly, the ideological and personal tensions of writers during the Sixties provide the subject for Michel Oren's "The Umbra Poets' Workshop, 1962-1965: Some Socio-Literary Puzzles," and Umbra is one of the many writers' groups Amiri Baraka discusses as he examines the relationship between art and social concerns in his essay "Black Theater in the Sixties." Sociopolitical activity, argues Baraka, gives art its direction; artists tend to create in response to issues raised by the masses. At times directly, but more often by implication, the essays of Kinnamon, McDowell, Sanders, Oren, and Baraka contribute to a fuller understanding of the belief/ theory matrix central to any analysis of literature, criticism, and culture.

We think that it provides a fitting coda to this volume of *SBAL* to include tributes to the life and work of George E. Kent. Kent, as both R. Baxter Miller and Houston Baker contend, was a critic of high principles — and equally great sophistication. Many have been clubbed to death attempting to run the gauntlet between Blackness and Western Culture; a good number more have survived the dash physically but incurred psychological wounds. But, as Baker tropes, Kent was an end runner, a trick player, who made the game seem easy — sometimes, as Miller notes, by reversing the rules. Kent knew that the "high ground" of Euro-American humanism and the home turf of the folk were sites on a level plane (plain). Like the critics who have contributed to this second volume of *SBAL*, Kent knew that theory and belief were kin.

While we hope that the current volume of *Studies in Black American Literature* will meet with favorable response, as the inaugural number seems to have done, we once again welcome any criticisms which our readers have to offer. As a number of the authors in this collection argue, it is principally by recognizing, and attempting to amend, our shortcomings that we make important gains within the critical arena. Suggestions of topics for future volumes are welcome as well, as are manuscript submissions on the topics already announced.

Joe Weixlmann

Chester J. Fontenot

Belief, Theory, and Blues: Notes for a Post-Structuralist Criticism of Afro-American Literature

by

Houston A. Baker, Jr.

I.

Faith may be conceived, I think, as an affective disposition toward the symbolic that serves as a ground for belief. If faith is indeed the evidence of things hoped for, the essence of things unseen, it is still not without symbolic resources for holding the "unseen" in the mind's eye of the believer. Belief and theory meet precisely at the place of such symbolic resources. Metaphor is the ground, that is to say, on which theory and belief meet. The universe of intellectual discourse that has experienced the entry of Thomas Kuhn's *The Struc-*

ture of Scientific Revolutions and that has absorbed the debates attendant upon that work's formulations surely contains ample support for the notion that all theories are but "paradigms" conceived and supported by a select community of scholars. And a paradigm is best thought of as a model or a picture — a *metaphorical* mode of appropriating masses of data to ourselves as "reality." Paradigms, like faith, are in a sense the essence of things hoped for, the evidence of things unseen. "Faith," wrote H. L. Mencken, "may be defined briefly as an illogical belief in the occurence of the improbable." Both the "illogical" and the "improbable" signal the worlds of faith, belief, theory — and metaphor.

In a sense too complex to enter fully into here, the movement of Afro-American literary study during the past several decades has represented a journey from belief to theory over the shifty terrain of metaphor and in the regions of increasing metaphorical sophistication. Some years ago, I proposed the argument that the Black Aesthetic (a dominant critical and theoretical posture among black spokespersons of the 1960s and the 1970s), in its conative assertiveness, was but a continuation of a critical line founded on idealism. The thing most needed for the realization — the wish-fulfillment, as it were — of the Afro-American critic who predicted a glorious future for the works of art that he or she studied was always absent — always merely an ideal. Only in a pluralistic and genuinely democratic society could the demands and dreams of both black writers and critics become lived realities. And that society remained but a metaphor, something hoped for and unseen. During the 1960s and 1970s, black spokespersons substituted a darker metaphor for an American democratic ideal. They conceived a Black Nation as the world in which Afro-American works of art would have successful and perdurable effects. The new metaphor and its attendant patterns of belief proved perhaps more effective for the progress of Afro-American criticism than earlier paradigms, but once the faith (which Adam Powell so adamantly urged us to keep) was lost in "blackness," little of a theoretical cast remained.

Rather than "probability," in the sense implied by Mencken, perhaps the faith that has traditionally characterized Afro-American literary study is a matter of *possibility*. What founders of our critical line and their successors in the Black Aesthetic most decisively bequeathed was a belief in the *possibility* of a strong tradition of Afro-American art and critical reflection, a tradition invulnerable to the scathing derogation of a racist society, and in tracing its lineage to sounds, rhythms, and behaviors far older than those of the verdant shores of a New World.

The master of metaphor in the Afro-American community, of course, has long since been acknowledged as the preacher, and James Weldon Johnson's preacher-as-Creator in "The Creation" captures the sense of metaphorical possibility I have in mind when he says, "I'll make me a world." Stepping out on space and conatively declaring the possibility of a signal and accomplished world of Afro-American literary art amenable to advanced modes of study and interpretation constitutes an act equivalent to that of Johnson's speaker. The movement from metaphors of possibility to possible explanatory metaphors is a journey from belief to theory. Having seized the possibility of a signal world, the task of the scholar of Afro-American literature is to elaborate metaphors that supply appropriate and adequate characterizations of the world. After idealism has willed a world into existence and secured its acknowledgment, the scholar's job is to persuasively isolate and describe features of this world by suggesting what he or she deems an adequate paradigm. Having arrived at such an articulation, however, the scholar has not left behind belief in any extended, metaphorical sense of the term.

The scholar does not take his or her paradigm as a map of reality, but as a possible guide to phenomena that he or she both perceives and half-creates. A paradigm is the most persuasively complete account available for what its proposer believes is to be seen. Like the particle physicist, the scholar is not privileged to conduct an on-site reality check vis-à-vis the phenomena that are of most interest, nor is one required to do so under the conditions of metaphorical persuasiveness that I have implied.

While the paradigm is, indeed, a model, it should not be conceived in the stick-and-colored-ball terms through which so many of us received our first instruction in molecules. Rather, the paradigm should be conceived as a trope, an unusual and defamiliarizing figure of language. The figure of the preacher is again suggestive. As he weaves his sermon, the Afro-American minister is likely to "fire arrows from God's quiver of truth" or to use a "mighty truth to break the heart of stone." He will evoke a celestial railway running from the Garden of Creation to the burning of the Last Judgment. His hand raised perilously above the heads of occupants of the mourner's bench, he will tell of the locomotive's cow-catcher wounding King Jesus in the side and releasing redemptive blood like a bold creek rising. The symbolic grounds of belief are, thus, resonantly and persuasively woven by the religious man of words. He is one who can miraculously transform a Southern landscape by interweaving a baseball pennant race with shards of Martin Luther King's orations and American patriotic gore. The mix is a heady one: "Land where my fathers died, land of the Pilgrims' pride! Land where all men have a dream, as Dr. King told us! Land of the world-famous Atlanta Braves!" When skillfully wrought, the preacher's metaphors for belief yield restless "Amens!" of assent.

Similarly, when the scholar's paradigmatic metaphors, or tropes, are appropriately wrought, assent is guaranteed. What the scholar achieves by using successful theoretical tropes — i.e., striking linguistic figures, extended and detailed to provide accounts of, say, literary works of art — is a view of "reality" in which subject and object fruitfully unite in a metaphorical bond. Scholars construct self-consistent, coherent models that both they and their audiences agree upon as the way "things" indisputably are. A disconcerting aspect of such tropological work is that what are normally regarded as "things" may, indeed, cease to exist in an empirical and observable simplicity. Bertrand Russell once wryly commented on the entailments of modern physics as follows: "The observer, when he seems to himself to be observing a stone, is really, if physics is to be believed, observing the effects of the stone upon himself." Relativistic, fluid, demanding artful interpretation — such is the world implied by Russell's observation. And such, as well, is the world of Afro-American literary art willed into existence by the metaphorical beliefs and theoretical metaphors of those who have brought us to the present, enormously exciting moment in the study of Afro-American literature and culture.

The metaphors likely to prevail in a universe of Afro-American literary-theoretical discourse are metaphors drawn from the *vernacular.* By the vernacular I want to suggest not only the majority of Afro-Americans, but, in both an economic and a political sense, the American majority. An image from a resonantly vernacular tradition of Afro-American expression serves to capture my notion of the vernacular. The picture is drawn from the black blues and sung as follows by Howlin' Wolf: "I'm a poor boy, a long way from home / Well, Lawd, I'm a poor boy, a long way from home / No spending money in my pocket, no spare meat on my bones." Citizens of the vernacular are those not numbered among the 44/100ths percent of the world that controls the major share of its capital resources. They are people like me whose epic drama is getting out of bed in the morning and making it from stormy Monday to "just one more Saturday night." By vernacular metaphors, then, I want to suggest paradigmatic explanations that account for human behavior at an "ordinary" level, if such a term can be invoked without setting off all kinds of judgmental bells. By "ordinary," I want to signal "most of us," and my dichotomy would be similar to that of a writer like Chinweizu who separates "the West" and "the rest of us." Hence, what I am after, and what I think Afro-American literary study in general must seek, are explanatory models that answer questions like: What are the nature and function of human symbolic behavior? How do various symbolic systems combine and diverge to produce expressive behavior? How do axiological constraints operate in human communities to privilege certain forms of expressive behavior? My own first model for arriving at adequate answers to such questions was drawn from the realm of symbolic anthropology. I believed that an interdisciplinary account predicated on the assumption of "Man as Speaking Subject" and employing resources of contemporary linguistic theory would illuminate the way in which Afro-American literary works of art functioned as uniquely expressive behavior that received the positive judgment of the Afro-American community. In more recent work, my metaphorical grounding has shifted from man as speaker to the text conceived of as an always/already spoken. The most adequate way, perhaps, of representing the nature of my current tropological energies is to turn now to reflections drawn from the "introduction" to my recently-completed critical study entitled *Blues, Ideology, and Afro-American Literature*.[1] Some of the more general assertions of the foregoing prefatory remarks will surely be clarified and, I hope, profitably extended by the following discussions, which begin with a rather-too-autobiographical account of my shift from a symbolic to a more materialistically-oriented critical prospect.

II.

Standing at the crossroads, tried to flag a ride,
Standing at the crossroads, tried to flag a ride,
Ain't nobody seem to know me, everybody passed me by.

"Crossroad Blues"

In every case the result of an untrue mode of knowledge must not be allowed to run away into an empty nothing, but must necessarily be grasped as the nothing *of that from which it results* — a result which contains what was true in the preceding knowledge.

Hegel, *Phenomenology of Spirit*

So perhaps we shy from confronting our cultural wholeness because it offers no easily recognizable points of rest, no facile certainties as to who, what, or where (culturally or historically) we are. Instead, the whole is always in cacophonic motion.

Ralph Ellison, "The Little Man at the Chehaw Station"

. . . maybe one day, you'll find they actually do understand exactly what you are talking about, all these fantasy people. All these blues people.

Amiri Baraka, *Dutchman*

From Symbol to Ideology

In my book *The Journey Back: Issues in Black Literature and Criticism* (Chicago: University of Chicago Press, 1980), I envisioned the "speaking subject" creating language (a code) to be deciphered by the present-day commentator. In my current study, I envision language (the code) "speaking" the subject. The subject is "de-centered." My quest during the past decade has been for the distinctive, the culturally-specific aspects of Afro-American literature and culture. Convinced that I had found such specificity in a peculiar subjectivity, the objectivity of economics and the sound lessons of poststructuralism arose to re-orient my thinking. I was convinced that the symbolic and, quite specifically, the symbolically-anthropological offered avenues to the comprehension of Afro-American expressive culture in its plenitude.[2] I discovered that the symbolic's antithesis — i.e., practical reason or the material — is as necessary for understanding Afro-American discourse as the cultural-in-itself.

My shift from a centered to a de-centered subject, from an exclusively symbolic to a more inclusively expressive perspective was prompted by the curious force of dialectical thought. My access to the study of such thought came from attentive readings of Fredric Jameson, Hayden White, Marshall Sahlins, and others. While profiting from the observations of these scholars, I also began to attend meetings of a study group devoted to Hegel's *Phenomenology of Spirit*.

Having journeyed, with the aid of symbolic anthropology, to what appeared the soundest possible observations on Afro-American art, I found myself confronted suddenly by a figure-to-ground reversal. A fitting image for the effect of my re-orientation toward the material is the gestalt illustration of the Greek hydria (a water vase with curved handles) that transforms itself into the face of an older woman. John Keats' "Ode on a Grecian Urn," with its familiar detailings of the economies of "art" and human emotions, might be considered one moment in the gestalt shift that I have in mind. Contrasting with these romantic figurations is the emergent face of a venerable ancestry. The shift from Greek hydrias to ancestral faces is a shift from high art to vernacular expression in America.

The "vernacular," in relation to human beings, signals, "a slave born on his master's estate." In expressive terms, vernacular indicates "arts native or peculiar to a particular country or locale." The material conditions of slavery in the United States and the rhythms of Afro-American blues combined and emerged from my revised materialistic perspective as an ancestral matrix that has produced a forceful and indigenous American creativity. The moment of emergence of economic and vernacular concerns left me, as the French say, *entre les deux*: suspended somewhere between anthropology and analytical strategies that Fredric Jameson calls the "ideology of form."[3]

Ideology, Semiotics, and the Material

I do not want to imply, however, in acknowledging a concern for the ideology of form, that my symbolic-anthropological orientation was untrue, in the sense of deluded or deceived. This symbolic orientation was simply one moment in my experiencing of Afro-American culture — a moment superseded now by a prospect that constitutes its determinate negation.[4] What was true in my prior framework remains so in my current concern for the ideology of form. Certainly, the mode of ideological investigation proposed by Jameson is an analysis that escapes all hints of "vulgar Marxism" through its studious attention to modern critiques of political economy, and also through its shrewd incorporation of post-structuralist thought.[5]

In the chapters of *Blues, Ideology, and Afro-American Literature,* I too attempt to avoid a naive Marxism. I do not believe, for example, that a fruitful correlation exists when one merely claims that certain black folk seculars are determinate results of agricultural gang labor. Such attributions simply privilege the material as a substrate while failing to provide detailed accounts of the processes leading from an apparent substrate to a peculiar expressive form. A faith of enormous magnitude is required to accept such crude formulations as adequate explanatory statements. The "material" is shifty ground. And current critiques of political economy suggest that postulates based on this ground can be appropriately understood only in "semiotic" terms. Hence, the employment of ideology as an analytical category begins with the awareness that "production" as well as "modes of production" must be grasped in terms of the sign. Jean Baudrillard, for example, argues a persuasive case for "political economy" as a code existing in a relationship of identity with language.[6] To read economics as a semiotic process leads to the realization that ideological analyses may be as decidedly intertextual as, say, analyses of the relationship between Afro-American vernacular expression and more sophisticated forms of verbal art. For if what is normally categorized as *material* (e.g., "raw material," "consumer goods") can be semiotically interpreted, then any collection of such entities and their defining interrelationships may be defined as a *text.*

In *Blues, Ideology, and Afro-American Literature,* however, I do not write or interpret the *material* in exclusively semiotic terms. Although fully aware of insights to be gained from semiotics, my analyses focus directly on the living and laboring conditions of people designated as "the desperate class" by James Weldon Johnson's narrator in *The Autobiography of an Ex-Coloured Man.* Such people constitute the vernacular in the United States. Their lives have always been sharply conditioned by an "economics of slavery" as they worked agricultural rows, searing furnaces, rolling levees, bustling roundhouses, and piney-woods' logging camps in America. The sense of "production" and "modes of production" that foregrounds this Afro-American labor in the United States seems an appropriate inscription of the material.

The Matrix as Blues

The guiding presupposition of my new book is that Afro-American culture is a complex, reflexive enterprise which finds its proper figuration in blues conceived of as a matrix. A matrix is a womb, a network, a rock bearing embedded fossils, a rocky trace of a gemstone's removal, a principal metal in an alloy, a mat or plate for reproducing print or phonograph records respectively. The matrix is a point of ceaseless input and output, a web of intersecting, crisscrossing impulses always in productive transit. Afro-American blues constitute such a vibrant network. They are what the French philosopher Jacques Derrida might describe as the "always already" of Afro-American culture.[7] They are the multiplex, enabling *script* in which Afro-American cultural discourse is inscribed.

First arranged, scored, and published for commercial distribution early in the twentieth century when Hart Wand, Arthur "Baby" Seals, and W. C. Handy released their first compositions, the blues defy narrow definition. For they exist not as a function of formal inscription, but as a forceful condition of Afro-American inscription itself. They were for Handy a "found" folk signified, awakening him from (perhaps) a dream of American form in Tutwiler, Mississippi, in 1903.[8] At a railroad juncture deep in the Southern night Handy dozed restlessly as he awaited the arrival of a much-delayed train. A guitar's bottle-neck resonance suddenly jolted him to consciousness, as a lean, loose-jointed, shabbily-clad black man sang:

> Goin' where the Southern cross the Dog.
> Goin' where the Southern cross the Dog.
> Goin' where the Southern cross the Dog.

This haunting invocation of railroad crossings in bottle-neck tones left Handy stupified and motivated. In 1914, he published his own "Yellow Dog Blues."

But the autobiographical account of the man called "Father of the Blues" offers only a simplistic detailing of *a progress,* describing, as it were, the elevation of a "primitive" folk ditty to the status of "art" in America. Handy's rendering leaves unexamined, therefore, myriad corridors, mainroads, and way-stations of an extraordinary and elusive Afro-American cultural phenomenon.

Defining Blues

The task of adequately describing the blues is equivalent to the labor of describing a world-class athlete's awesome gymnastics. Adequate appreciation demands comprehensive attention. An investigator has to *be* there, following a course recommended by one of the African writer Wole Soyinka's ironic narrators to a London landlord to "see for yourself."

The elaborations of the blues may begin in an austere self-accusation: "Now this trouble I'm having, I brought it all on myself." But the accusation seamlessly fades into humorous acknowledgment of duplicity's always-duplicitous triumph: "You know the woman that I love, I stoled her from my best friend, / But you know that fool done got lucky and stole her back again." Simple provisos for the troubled mind are commonplace, and drear exactions of crushing manual labor are objects of wry, *in situ* commentary. Numinous invocation punctuates a guitar's resonant back beat with: "Lawd, Lawd, Lawd . . . have mercy on me / Please send me someone, to end this misery." Existential declarations of lack combine with lustily-macabre prophecies of the subject's demise. If a "match box" will hold his clothes, surely the roadside of much-travelled highways will be his memorial plot: "You can bury my body down by the highway side / So my old devil spirit can catch a Greyhound bus and ride." Conative formulations of a brighter future (sun shining in the back door some day, wind rising to blow the blues away) join with a slow moving *askesis* of present, amorous imprisonment: "You leavin' now, baby, but you hangin' crepe on my door," or, "She got a mortgage on my body, and lien on my soul." Deprecating confessionals and slack-strumming growls of violent solutions combine: "My lead mule's cripple, you know my off mule's blind / You know I can't drive nobody / Bring me a loaded .39 (I'm go'n pop him, pop that mule!)." The wish for a river of whiskey where if one were a "divin' duck" he would submerge himself and never "come up" is a function of a world in which: "When you lose yo' eyesight, yo' best friend's gone / Sometimes yo' own dear people don't want to fool with you long."

Like a streamlined athlete's awesomely dazzling explosions of prowess, the blues song erupts, creating a veritable playful festival of meaning. Rather than a rigidly personalized form, the blues offer a phylogenetic recapitulation — a non-linear, freely-associative, non-sequential meditation — of species experience. What emerges is not a filled subject, but an anonymous (nameless) voice issuing from the black (w)hole.[9] The blues singer's signatory coda is always *atopic*, placeless: "If anybody ask you who sang this song / Tell 'em X done been here and gone." The "signature" is a space already "X"(ed), a trace of the already "gone" — a fissure rejoined. Nevertheless, the "you" (audience) addressed is always free to invoke the X(ed) spot

in the body's absence.[10] For the signature comprises a scripted authentication of "your" feelings. Its mark is an invitation to energiz-
ing intersubjectivity. Its implied (in)junction reads: Here is my body
meant for (a phylogenetically-conceived) you.

The blues are a synthesis (albeit one always synthesizing rather than
one already hypostatized). Combining work songs, group seculars,
field hollers, sacred harmonies, proverbial wisdom, folk philosophy,
political commentary, ribald humor, elegiac lament, and much more,
they constitute an amalgam that seems always to have been in motion
in America — always becoming, shaping, transforming, displacing the
peculiar experiences of Africans in the New World.

Blues as Code and Force

One way of describing the blues is to claim their amalgam as a code
radically conditioning Afro-America's cultural signifying. Such a
description implies a prospect in which any aspect of the blues — a
guitar's growling vamp or a stanza's sardonic boast of heroically back-
breaking labor — "stands," in Umberto Eco's words, "for something
else" by virtue of a systematic set of conventional procedures.[11]
The materiality of any blues manifestation such as a guitar's walking
bass, or a French harp's "whoop" of motion-seen, is, one might say,
enciphered in ways that enable to material to escape into a *named* or
coded blues signification. The material, thus, slips into irreversible
difference. And as phenomena named and set in meaningful relation
by a blues code, both the harmonica's whoop and the guitar's bass
can recapitulate vast dimensions of experience, for such discrete blues
instances are always intertextually related by the blues code as a
whole. Moreover, they are involved in the code's manifold intercon-
nections with other codes of Afro-American culture.

A further characterization of blues suggests that they are equivalent to Hegelian "force."[12] In the *Phenomenology,* Hegel speaks of
a flux in which there is "only *difference* as a *universal* difference, or
as a difference into which the many antitheses have been resolved.
This difference, as a *universal* difference, is consequently the *simple*

element in the play of Force itself and what is true in it. It is the *law of Force*" (p. 90). Force is thus defined as a relational matrix wherein *difference* is the law. Finally the blues, employed as an image for the investigation of culture, represent a *force* not unlike electricity. Hegel writes:

> Of course, given *positive* electricity, negative too is given *in principle*; for the positive *is*, only as related to a negative, or, the positive is *in its own self* the difference from itself; and similarly with the negative. But that electricity as such should divide itself in this way is not in itself a necessity. Electricity, as *simple Force,* is indifferent to its law — *to be* positive and negative; and if we call the former its *Notion* but the latter its being, then its Notion is indifferent to its being. It merely *has* this property, which just means that this property is not *in itself* necessary to it. . . . It is only with law as law that we are to compare its *Notion* as Notion, or its necessity. But in all these forms, necessity has shown itself to be only an empty word. (p. 93)

Metaphorically extending Hegel's formulation vis-à-vis electricity, one might say that a traditional property of cultural study may well be the kind of dichotomies inscribed in terms like "culture" and "practical reason." But even if such dichotomies are raised to the status of law, they never constitute the necessity or "determinant instances" of cultural study and explanation conceived in terms of *force* — envisioned, that is, in the analytic notion of a blues matrix as force. The blues, therefore, comprise a mediational site at which familiar antimonies are resolved (or dissolved) in the office of adequate cultural understanding.

Blues Translation at the Junction

To suggest a trope for the blues as a forceful matrix in cultural understanding is to summon an image of the black blues singer at the

railway junction lustily transforming experiences of a durative (un-
ceasingly oppressive) landscape into the extraordinary energies of
rhythmic song. The railway juncture is marked by transience. Its
inhabitants are always travelers — a multifarious assembly in transit.
The "X" of crossing roadbeds signals the multidirectionality of the
juncture and is simply a single instance in a boundless network that
redoubles and circles, makes sidings and ladders, forms Ys and branches
over the vastness of hundreds of thousands of American miles. Poly-
morphous and multidirectional, scene of arrivals and departures,
place betwixt and between (ever *entre les deux*), the juncture is the
way-station of the blues.

The singer and his production are always at this intersection, this
crossing, codifying force, providing resonance for experience's mul-
tiplicities.   Singer and song never arrest transience — *fix* it in "transcendent form."   Instead, they provide expressive equivalence for
the juncture's ceaseless flux.   Hence, they may be conceived of as
translators.[13]

Like translators of written texts, blues and their sundry performers
offer interpretations of the experiencing of experience. To experience the juncture's ever-changing scenes, like successive readings of
ever-varying texts by conventional translators, is to produce vibrantly-
polyvalent interpretations encoded as blues. The singer's product,
like the railway juncture itself (or a successful translator's original),
constitutes a lively scene, a robust matrix, in which endless antinomies
are mediated and understanding and explanation find conditions of
possibility.

The durative — transliterated as lyrical statements of injustice,
despair, loss, absence, denial, and so forth — is complemented in
blues performance by an instrumental energy (guitar, harmonica,
fiddle, gut-bucket bass, molasses jug, washboard) that employs locomotive rhythms, train bells and whistles, as onomatopoeic references.
In *A Theory of Semiotics*, Eco writes:

> Music presents, on the one hand, the problem of a semiotic
> system without a semantic level (or a content plane): on the
> other hand, however, there are musical "signs" (or syntagms)

with an explicit denotative value (trumpet signals in the army) and there are syntagms or entire "texts" possessing pre-culturalized connotative value ("pastoral" or "thrilling" music, etc.). (p. 111)

The absence of what Eco calls a content plane implies what is commonly referred to as the "abstractness" of instrumental music. The "musical sign," on the other hand, suggests cultural signals that function onomatopoetically by calling to mind "natural" sounds, or sounds "naturally" associated with common human situations. Surely, though, it would be a mistake to claim that onomatopoeia is, in any sense, "natural"; for different cultures encode even the "same" natural sounds in varying ways. (A rooster onomatopoetically sounded in Puerto Rican Spanish is phonically unrecognizable in United States English, as a classic Puerto Rican short story makes hilariously clear.)

If onomatopoeia is taken as cultural mimesis, however, it is possible to apply the semiotician's observations to blues by pointing out that the dominant blues syntagm in America is an instrumental imitation of *train-wheels-over-track-junctures*. This sound is the "sign," as it were, of the blues, and it combines an intriguing melange of phonics: rattling gondolas, clattering flatbeds, quilling whistles, clanging bells, rumbling box-cars, and other railroad sounds. A blues text may, thus, announce itself by the onomatopoeia of the train's whistle sounded on the indrawn breath of a harmonica or a train's bell tinkled on the high keys of an upright piano. The blues stanzas may then roll through an extended meditative repertoire with a steady train-wheels-over-track-junctures guitar backbeat as a traditional, syntagmatic complement. If desire and absence are driving conditions of blues performance, the amelioration of such conditions is implied by the onomatopieic *training* of blues voice and instrument. Only a *trained* voice can sing the blues.[14]

At the junctures, the intersections of experience where roads cross and diverge, the blues singer and his performance serve as codifiers, absorbing and transforming discontinuous experience into formal expressive instances that bear only the trace of origins, refusing to be pinned down to any final, dualistic significance. Even as they speak of paralyzing absence and ineradicable desire, their instrumental rhythms suggest change, movement, action, continuance, unlimited and unending possibility. Like signification itself, blues are always nomadically wandering. Like the freight-hopping hobo, they are ever on the move, ceaselessly summing novel experience.

Antinomies and Blues Mediation

The blues performance is further suggestive if economic conditions of Afro-American existence are brought to mind. Standing at the juncture, or railhead, the singer draws into his repertoire hollers, cries, whoops, and moans of black men and women working in fields without recompense. The performance can be cryptically conceived, therefore, in terms suggested by the bluesman Booker White who has said: "The foundation of the blues is working behind a mule way back in slavery time."[15] As a force, the blues matrix defines itself as a network mediating poverty and abundance in much the same manner that it reconciles durative and kinetic. Many instances of the blues performance contain lyrical inscriptions of both lack and commercial possibility. The performance that sings of abysmal poverty and deprivation may be recompenced by sumptuous food and stimulating beverage at a country picnic, amorous favors from an attentive listener, enhanced Afro-American communality, or Yankee dollars from representatives of record companies traveling the South in search of blues as commodifiable entertainment. The performance, therefore, mediates one of the most prevalent of all antinomies in cultural investigation — creativity and commerce.

As driving force, the blues matrix, thus, avoids simple dualities. It perpetually achieves its effects as a fluid and multivalent network. It is only when "understanding" — i.e., the analytical work of a translator who translates the infinite changes of the blues — converges with such blues "force" that adequate explanatory perception (and half-creation) occurs. The matrix effectively functions toward cultural understanding, that is, only when an investigator brings an inventive attention to bear.

The Investigator, Relativity, and Blues Effect

The blues matrix is a "cultural invention"; i.e., a "negative symbol" that generates (or obliges one to invent) its own referents.[16] As an inventive trope, this matrix provides the type of image or model that is always present in accounts of culture and cultural products. If the analyses that I provide in my new book prove successful, the blues matrix will have *taken effect* (and *affect*) through me.

To "take effect," of course, is not identical with to "come into existence" or to "demonstrate serviceability for the first time." Since what I have defined as a blues matrix is so demonstrably anterior to any single instance of its cultural-explanatory employment, then my predecessors are obviously legion. "Take effect," therefore, does not herald discovery in the traditional sense of that word. Rather, it signals the tropological nature of my uses of an already extant matrix.

Accounts of art, literature, and culture ordinarily fail to acknowledge their governing theories; further, they almost invariably conceal the *inventive* character of such theories. Nevertheless, all accounts of art, expressive culture, or culture in general are indisputably functions of their creators' tropological energies. When such creators talk of "art," for example, they are never dealing with existential givens. Rather, they are summoning objects, processes, or events defined by a model that they have created (by and for themselves) as a picture of art. Such models, or tropes, are continually invoked to constitute and explain phenomena unseen and unheard by the senses. Any single model, or any complementary set of inventive tropes, therefore, will offer only a selective account of experience – a partial reading, as it were, of the world. While the single account temporarily reduces chaos to ordered plan, all such accounts are eternally troubled by "remainders."

Where literary art is concerned, for example, a single, ordering, investigative model or trope will necessarily exclude phenomena that an alternative model or trope privileges as a definitive artistic instance. Recognizing the determinacy of "invention" in cultural explanation entails the acknowledgment of what might be called *normative relativity*. To acknowledge relativity in our post-Heisenbergian universe is, of course, far from original. Nor is it an invitation to the skeptics or the conservatives to heroically assume the critical stage. The assumption of normative relativity, far from being a call to abandonment or retrenchment in the critical arena, constitutes an invitation to speculative explorations that are aware both of their own partiality and their heuristic translations from suggestive (sometimes dramatic) images to inscribed concepts. The openness implied by relativity enables, say, the literary critic to *re-cognize* his endeavors, presupposing from the outset that such labors are not directed toward independent, observable, empirical phenomena, but rather toward processes, objects, and events that he or she half-creates (and privileges as "art") through his or her own speculative, inventive energies and interests.

One axiological extrapolation from these observations on invention and relativity is that no object, process, or signal element possesses *intrinsic aesthetic value*. The "art object" as well as its value are selective constructions of the critic's tropes and models. A radicalizing uncertainty may, thus, be said to mark cultural explanation. This uncertainty is similar in kind to the always selective endeavors of, say, the particle physicist.[17]

The physicist is always compelled to choose between velocity and position.[18] Similarly, an investigator of, say, Afro-American expressive culture is ceaselessly compelled to forego manifold variables in order to apply intensive energy to a selected array.

Continuing the metaphor, one might say that if the investigator's efforts are sufficiently charged with blues energy,[19] he is almost certain to re-model elements and events appearing in traditional, Anglo-American space-time in ways that make them "jump" several rings toward blackness and the vernacular. The blues-oriented observer (the *trained* critic) necessarily "heats up" the observational space by his or her very presence.[20]

The entailments of an inventive, tropological, investigative model such as that proposed by *Blues, Ideology, and Afro-American Literature* include not only awareness of the metaphorical nature of the blues matrix, but also a willingness on my own part to do more than merely hear, read, or see the blues. I must also play (with and on) them. Since the explanatory possibilities of a blues matrix – like analytical possibilities of a delimited set of forces in unified field theory – are hypothetically unbounded, the blues challenge investigative *understanding* to an unlimited play.

Blues and Vernacular Expression in America

The blues should be privileged in the study of American culture to precisely the extent that inventive understanding successfully converges with blues force to yield accounts that persuasively and playfully refigure expressive geographies in the United States. My own ludic uses of the blues are various, and each figuration implies the valorization of vernacular facets of American culture. The Afro-American writer James Alan McPherson is, I think, the commentator who most brilliantly and encouragingly coalesces blues, vernacular, and cultural geographies of the United States in his introduction to *Railroad: Trains and Train People in American Culture*.[21]

Having described a fiduciary reaction to the steam locomotive by nineteenth-century financiers and an adverse artistic response by such traditional American writers as Melville, Hawthorne, and Thoreau, McPherson details the reaction of another sector of the United States population to the railroad:

> To a third group of people, those not bound by the assumptions of either business or classical traditions in art, the shrill whistle might have spoken of new possibilities. These were the backwoodsmen and Africans and recent immigrants – the people who comprised the vernacular level of American society. To them the machine might have been loud and frightening, but its whistle and its wheels promised movement. And since a commitment to both freedom and movement was the basic promise of democracy, it was probable that such people would view the locomotive as a challenge to the integrative powers of their imaginations. (p. 6)

Afro-Americans — at the bottom even of the vernacular ladder in America — responded to the railroad as a "meaningful symbol offering both economic progress and the possibility of aesthetic expression" (p. 9). This possibility came from the locomotive's drive and thrust, its promise of unrestrained mobility and unlimited freedom. The blues musician at the crossing, as I have already suggested, became an expert at reproducing or translating these locomotive energies. With the birth of the blues, the vernacular realm of American culture acquired a music that, in McPherson's words, had "wide appeal because it expressed a toughness of spirit and resilience, a willingness to transcend difficulties which was strikingly familiar to those whites who remembered their own history" (p. 16). The signal expressive achievement of blues, then, lay in their translation of extraordinary technological innovativeness, unsettling demographic fluidity, and boundless frontier energy into expression which attracted avid interest from the American masses. By the 1920s, American financiers had become aware of commercial possibilities not only of railroads, but also of the black music deriving from them.

A "race record" market flourished during the Twenties. Major companies issued blues releases under labels such as Columbia, Vocalion, Okeh, Gennett, and Victor. Sometimes as many as ten blues releases appeared in a single week; their sales (aided by radio's dissemination of the music) climbed to hundreds of thousands. The onset of the Great Depression ended this phenomenal boom. During their heyday, however, the blues unequivocally signified a ludic predominance of the vernacular with that sassy, growling, moaning, whooping confidence that marks their finest performances.

McPherson's assessment seems fully justified. It serves, in fact, as a suggestive play in the overall project of refiguring American expressive geographies. Resonantly complementing the insights of such astute commentators as Albert Murray, Paul Oliver, Samuel Charters, Amiri Baraka, and others,[22] McPherson's judgments highlight the value of a blues matrix for cultural analysis in the United States.

In harmony with other brilliant commentators on the blues already noted, Ralph Ellison selects the railroad way-station (the "Chehaw Station") as his topos for the American "little man."[23] In "The Little

Man at the Chehaw Station," he autobiographically details his own confirmation of his Tuskegee music teacher's observation that in the United States:

> "You must *always* play your best, even if it's only in the waiting room at Chehaw Station, because in this country there'll always be a little man hidden behind the stove . . . and he'll know the *music,* and the *tradition,* and the standards of *musicianship* required for whatever you set out to perform." (p. 25)

When Hazel Harrison made this statement to a young Ellison, he felt that she was joking. But as he matured and moved through a diversity of American scenes, Ellison realized that the inhabitants of the "drab, utilitarian structure" of the American vernacular do far more than respond in expressive ways to "blues-echoing, train-whistle rhapsodies blared by fast express trains" thundering past the junction. At the vernacular level, according to Ellison, people possess a "cultivated taste" that asserts its "authority out of obscurity" (p. 26). The "little man" finally comes to represent, therefore, "that unknown quality which renders the American audience far more than a receptive instrument that may be dominated through a skillful exercise of the sheerly 'rhetorical' elements — the flash and filigree — of the artist's craft" (p. 26).

From Ellison's opening gambit and wonderfully-illustrative succeeding examples, I infer that the vernacular (in its expressive adequacy and adept critical facility) always *absorbs* "classical" elements of American life and art. Indeed, Ellison seems to imply that expressive performers in America who ignore the judgments of the vernacular are destined to failure.

Although his injunctions are intended principally to advocate a traditional "melting pot" ideal in American "high art," Ellison's observations ultimately valorize a comprehensive, vernacular expressiveness in America. Though he seldom loses sight of the possibilities of a classically "transcendent" American high art, he derives his most forceful examples from the vernacular: Blues seem implicitly to comprise the *All* of American culture.

Blues Moments in Afro-American Expression

In *Blues, Ideology, and Afro-American Literature,* I attempt to provide suggestive accounts of moments in Afro-American discourse when personae, protagonists, autobiographical narrators, or literary critics successfully negotiate an obdurate "economics of slavery" and achieve a resonant, improvisational, expressive dignity. Such moments and their successful analysis provide cogent examples of the blues matrix at work.

The expressive instances that I have in mind occur in passages such as the conclusion of the *Narrative of the Life of Frederick Douglass.* Standing at a Nantucket convention, riffing (in the "break" suddenly confronting him) on the *personal* troubles he has seen and successfully negotiated in a "prisonhouse of American bondage," Douglass achieves a profoundly dignified blues voice. Zora Neale Hurston's protagonist Janie in the novel *Their Eyes Were Watching God* — as she lyrically and idiomatically relates a tale of personal suffering and triumph that begins in the sexual exploitations of slavery — is a blues artist par excellence. Her wisdom might well be joined to that of Amiri Baraka's Walker Vessels (a "locomotive container" of blues?), whose chameleon code-switching from academic philosophy to blues insight makes him a veritable incarnation of the absorptively vernacular. The narrator of Richard Wright's *Black Boy* inscribes a black blues life's lean desire and suggests yet further instance of the blues matrix's expressive energies. Ellison's invisible man and Baraka's narrator in *The System of Dante's Hell* (whose blues book produces dance) provide additional examples. Finally, Toni Morrison's Milkman Dead in *Song of Solomon* discovers through "Sugarman's" song that an awesomely-expressive blues response may well consist of improvisational and serendipitous surrender to the air:

> As fleet and bright as a lodestar he wheeled toward Guitar and it did not matter which one of them would give up his ghost in the killing arms of his brother. For now he knew what Shalimar knew: If you surrendered to the air, you could *ride* it.[24]

Such blues moments are but random instances of the blues matrix at work in Afro-American cultural expression. In my study as a whole, I attempt persuasively to demonstrate that a blues matrix (as a vernacular trope for American cultural explanation in general) possesses enormous force for the study of literature, criticism, and culture. I know that I have appropriated the vastness of the vernacular in the United States to a single matrix. But I trust that my necessary selectivity will be interpreted not as a sign of myopic exclusiveness, but as an invitation to inventive play. The success of my efforts would be effectively signaled, I think, by the transformation of my "I" into a juncture at which readers of my book could freely improvise their own distinctive tropes for cultural explanation. A closing that in fact opened on such inventive possibilities (like the close of these remarks) would be appropriately marked by the crossing sign's inviting "X." That deconstructive "X" might mark a middle ground on which belief and theory converge in productive and creditable explanations of America.

NOTES

1.   (Chicago: University of Chicago Press, 1984).

2.   Though a great many sources were involved in my re-oriented cultural thinking, certainly the terminology employed in my discussion at this point derives from Marshall Sahlins's wonderfully lucid *Culture and Practical Reason* (Chicago: University of Chicago Press, 1976). Sahlins delineates two modes of thinking that have characterized anthropology from its inception. These two poles are: "symbolic" and "functionalist." Sahlins resolves the dichotomy suggested by these terms through the middle term "cultural proposition," a phrase that he defines as a cultural mediating ground on which the material and symbolic, the useful and the ineffable, ceaselessly converge and depart.

3.   The "ideology of form" as a description of Jameson's project derives from the essay "The Symbolic Inference; or, Kenneth Burke and Ideological Analysis," *Critical Inquiry*, 4 (1978), 507-523. Surely, though, Jameson's most recent study, *The Political Unconscious: Narrative as a Socially Symbolic Act* (Ithaca, New York: Cornell University Press, 1981), offers the fullest description of his views on ways in which cultural texts formally inscribe material/historical conditions of their production, distribution, and consumption.

4.   The Hegelian epigraph that marks the beginning of these remarks, taken from the *Phenomenology of Spirit,* offers the best definition I know of "determinate negation."

5.   I have in mind Louis Althusser's and Etienne Balibar's *Reading Capital* (London: NLB, 1977) as well as Jean Baudrillard's *For a Critique of the Political Economy of the Sign* (1972; trans. St. Louis, Missouri: Telos Press, 1981) and *The Mirror of Production* (1973; trans. St. Louis, Missouri: Telos Press, 1975). By "post-structuralist" thought, I have in mind the universe of discourse constituted by *deconstruction.* Jacques Derrida's *Of Grammatology* (1967; trans. Baltimore, Maryland: The Johns Hopkins Press, 1976) is, perhaps, the locus classicus of the deconstructionist project. One of the more helpful accounts of deconstruction is Christopher Norris's *Deconstruction: Theory and Practice* (London: Methuen, 1982). Of course, there is a certain collapsing of post-structuralism and political economy in the sources cited previously.

6.   See *For a Critique of the Political Economy of the Sign.*

7.   In *Of Grammatology,* Derrida defines a problematic in which *writing,* conceived as an iterable *differe(a)nce,* is held to be *always already* instituted (or, in motion) when a traditionally designated *Man* begins to speak. Hence, *script* is anterior to speech, and absence and *differe(a)nce* displace presence and identity (conceived of as "Intention") in philosophical discourse.

8.   The story appears in Handy's *Father of the Blues,* ed. Arna Bontemps (New York: Macmillan, 1941), p. 78. Other defining sources of blues include: Paul Oliver, *The Story of the Blues* (London: Chilton, 1969); Samuel B. Charters, *The Country Blues* (New York: Rinehart, 1959); Giles Oakley, *The Devil's Music: A History of the Country Blues* (New York: Harcourt Brace Jovanovich, 1976); Amiri Baraka, *Blues People: Negro Music in White America* (New York: Morrow, 1963); Albert Murray, *Stomping the Blues* (New York: McGraw-Hill, 1976); and William Ferris, *Blues From the Delta* (Garden City, New York: Anchor, 1979).

9.   The description at this point is coextensive with the "de-centering" of the subject mentioned earlier. What I wish to effect by noting a "subject" who is not *filled* is a displacement of the notion that knowledge, or "art," or "song," is a manifestation of an ever-more-clearly-defined individual consciousness of *Man.* In accord with Michel Foucault's explorations in his *Archaeology of Knowledge* (1969; trans. New York: Harper and Row, 1972), I want to claim that blues are like a discourse that comprise the "already said" of Afro-America. Blues' governing statements and sites are, thus, vastly more interesting in the process of cultural investigation than either a history of ideas or a history of individual, subjective consciousness, vis-à-vis blues. When I move to the "X" of the trace and the body as host, I am invoking Mark Taylor's formulations in a suggestive deconstructive essay toward radical Christology called "The Text as Victim," in *Deconstruction and Theology* (New York: Crossroad, 1982), pp. 58-78.

10.   The terms used in "The Text as Victim" are "host" and "parasite." The words of the blues are host-like in the sense of a Christological/Logos-as-Host. But without the dialogical action of the parasite, of course, there could be no host. Host is, thus, parasitic upon a parasite's citation. Both, in Taylor's statement of the matter, are *para-sites*.

11.   The definition of "code" is drawn from *A Theory of Semiotics* (Bloomington: Indiana University Press, 1976). All references to Eco refer to this work and are hereafter marked by page numbers in parentheses.

12.   *Phenomenology of the Spirit*, trans. A. V. Miller (New York: Oxford University Press, 1977). While it is true that the material dimensions of the dialectic are of primary importance in my current study, it is also true that the locus classicus of the dialectic, in and for itself, is the *Phenomenology*. Marx may well have stood Hegel on his feet through a materialist inversion of the *Phenomenology*, but subsequent generations have always looked at that uprighted figure — Hegel himself — as an authentic host.

13.   Having heard Professor John Felstiner in a session of the 1982 Modern Language Association Convention present a masterful paper defining "translation" as a process of preserving "something of value" by keeping it in motion, I decided that the blues were apt translators of experience. Felstiner, it seemed to me, sought to demonstrate that *translation* was a process equivalent to gift-giving in Mauss's classic definition of that activity. The value of the gift of translation is never fixed because, say, the poem is always in a transliteral motion, moving from one alphabet to another, always renewing and being *renewed* in the process. Translation forestalls fixity. It calls attention always to the *translated*'s excess — to its complex multivalence.

14.   One of the most inspiring and intriguing descriptions of the relationship between blues voice and the sounds of the railroad is Albert Murray's lyrical exposition in *Stomping the Blues*.

15.   Quoted in Oakley, *The Devil's Music*, p. 7.

16.   I have appropriated the term "negative symbol" from Roy Wagner's monograph *The Invention of Culture* (Chicago: University of Chicago Press, 1975), p. xvi.

17.   My references to a "post-Heisenbergian universe" and to the "particle physicist" were made possible by a joyful reading of Gary Zukav's *The Dancing Wu Li Masters: An Overview of the New Physics* (New York: Morrow, 1979).

18.   Zukav writes: "According to the uncertainty principle, we cannot measure accurately, at the same time, both the position *and* the momentum of a moving particle. The more precisely we determine one of these properties, the less we know about the other. If we precisely determine the position of the particle, then, strange as it sounds, there is *nothing* that we can know about its momentum. If we precisely determine the momentum of the particle, there is no way to determine its position" (p. 111). Briefly, if we bring to bear enough

energy to actually "see" the imagined "particle," that energy has always already *moved* the particle from its *position* (which is one of the aspects of its
existence that one attempts to *determine*) when we take our measurement.
Indeterminancy thus becomes normative.

19.   The "blues force" is my translational equivalent in investigative
"energy" for the investigative energy delineated by Heisenberg's formulations.

20.   Eco employs the metaphor of "ecological variation" in his discussions of the semiotic investigation of culture to describe observer effect in the
mapping of experience (see *A Theory of Semiotics*, p. 29).

21.   (New York: Random House, 1976). All citations refer to this edition
and are hereafter marked by page numbers in parentheses.

22.   See fn. 8 above.

23.   The Chehaw Station is a whistle-stop near Tuskegee, Alabama. It
was a feature of the landscape of Tuskegee Institute where Ellison studied music
(and much else). His essay "The Little Man at the Chehaw Station" appears
in *American Scholar,* 47 (1978), 24-48. All citations refer to this version and
are hereafter marked by page numbers in parentheses.

24.   *Song of Solomon* (New York: Knopf, 1977), p. 337.

Literary Production:
A Silence in Afro-American Critical Practice

by

W. Lawrence Hogue

Recent advances in modern linguistics, along with developments in semiotics, structural anthropology, and Michel Foucault's concept of discursive formations, have eroded many of the assumptions and presuppositions traditionally associated with literature. This erosion has proven fundamental. Literary modes and categories inherited from the past no longer accommodate the reality experienced by a new generation of literary scholars and intellectuals. The traditional concept of realism has proved inadequate. The proposition that the writer is the "creator" of something "original" has come under serious attack.

The previously unquestioned assumption of the text's literariness — that is, that the text possesses certain qualities which place it above the matrices of historical conditions — has been undermined profoundly. Definitions of artistic beauty, greatness in literary texts, and literary worth and value have been deemed ideological. The conjecture that the writer writes to tell the "truth" has been denounced vehemently. Lastly, and, perhaps, most importantly, the once acceptable assumptions that critical practice is an innocent activity and that the literary text is inextricably owned by and exclusively associated with the discipline "literature" have been almost completely quelled.

These advancements and developments have produced new critical and theoretical options for those seeking to assess and explain Afro-American, other minority, and other self-conscious and avant-garde texts — whose ideological formations are different from or exist outside of the ruling ideological formation. (Here and throughout this essay, the term *ideological formation* refers to the total set of relations that unites the practices which give rise to a formalized system.)

Developments in semiotics and Michel Foucault's concept of discursive formations produce critical practices which shift their concerns and focus from a juridical to a theoretical status. In normative critical practices, the text, Pierre Macherey observes, is subordinated to an "external principle of legality," an "aesthetic legality [that] has a juridical rather than a theoretical status; its rules merely restrain the writer's activity. Because it is powerless to examine the work on its own terms . . . [normative] criticism resorts to a corroding resentment."[1] In its theoretical status, critical practice is a certain "form of knowledge."

These developments produce critical practices which shift their focus from the world of creation, the scene of charismatic authorship to a specific productive process, to a set of operations that transforms a given language into something new. The text becomes a textual system which transposes one or more systems of signs into another. This textual system is composed of a dispersion of its statements or facts, its gaps and silences. The fact that the text permits certain statements and excludes others exposes its ideological biases and shows the way in which it functions as a cultural object with social impact that can be calculated politically.

Thus, the ruling ideological formation — through its various political, cultural, educational, economic, and social institutions, practices, and apparatus — constructs a network which engages in its own reproduction, which distributes certain ideological awarenesses into aesthetic, scholarly, sociological, and historical texts. These awarenesses have a certain will or intention to repress, to control, to manipulate, or even to incorporate ideological differences.[2]

In any literate society there exist various distinct modes of literary production, which Terry Eagleton defines as "a unity of certain forces and social relations of material production."[3] Most literary productions belong to the dominant formation's cultural apparatus. The dominant literary establishment includes the specific institutions of literary production and distribution — editors, publishing houses, bookstores, and libraries. It also encompasses a range of secondary support institutions including literary academies, English departments, literary criticism, the concept of literature, literary journals and review magazines, and granting and awarding agencies. The function of these secondary institutions is more directly ideological, since they are concerned with the definition and dissemination of literary "standards," "criteria," and "assumptions."

The concept of literature generates the ideological biases of the ruling ideological formation. The current definition of literature began taking shape during the latter half of the eighteenth century. With a Latin root, *littera,* literature was, in effect, a condition of reading: of being able to read and of having read. It was close to the modern sense of literacy. But, in its modern form, the concept of literature shifts from learning and reading to "taste" or "sensibility" or "discrimination."[4] These terms become the unifying concepts of literature. They comprise a signifying practice which produces the organization into which forms of imaginative writing are compressed. These forms, in turn, have come to produce a signification of reality which entails a particular ordering of concepts within, and by means of, language; they reflect a historically and ideologically produced way of viewing literary texts. Thus, in its current conception, literature becomes attached to national traditions. In its attachment to national traditions, literature becomes ideological; it becomes a construct whose function is to reproduce aspects of the nation state's ideologies, In short, literature is, as Terry Eagleton has noted, a construction "fashioned by particular people for particular reasons at a certain time."[5]

Editors, publishers, critics and reviewers, who function as a kind of conduit for many of the dominant society's cultural, ideological, and intellectual wishes, impute literature with a defined literary experience. In presiding over the dominant society's literary taste, these critics and editors are instrumental in keeping certain ideas, social habits, myths, moral conventions, stereotypes, meanings of literary experience, and certain prejudices alive publicly — usually under the pretense of not wanting to upset the status quo, or offend the public. In executing the cultural and intellectual wishes of the ruling literary establishment, these editors, reviewers, and critics publish and review favorably those literary texts which meet the extant ruling literary standards, criteria, and tastes.

Furthermore, critics and reviewers seek the establishment's defined "meaning" of the literary experience, in all texts that come to their attention. They evaluate literary texts by pointing out their contributions to knowledge and explaining the ways in which they reproduce the values and stereotypes of the dominant ideological formation. They certificate those texts which have been judged to speak the discourse better; they repress non-conformist texts, subjects, and perspectives as being inferior aesthetically for their inability to approximate established criteria — thereby effecting certain silences in literature. In short, they determine what is a "good" or "bad" literary text in accordance with the degree to which it effectively reproduces certain values and codes of the dominant society. The entire mode of literary production is really no more than a branch of the dominant society's social ideologies.

My intention is not to put forth the simplistic argument that only those literary texts which reproduce the dominant ideological formation's priorities are published. Institutions — English departments, editors, publishers — and writers contain and possess many values, meanings, and traditions which are antithetical to the state's priorities. But these values, meanings, and traditions are compatible with specific forms of discourse which allow the ideological formation to appropriate them. They must speak a particular language or accept certain genres, conventions, and values that will not permit certain meaning and positions to be articulated within these forms of discourse.[6] In short, not only can what one says reproduce the ideological formation, but the way, the style, the codes one uses to say something can also be appropriated to reproduce the dominant ideological formation.

Critical practice, then, is not scientific; it is a preeminently political exercise. It works upon and mediates the reception of literary texts. It is an active and ongoing part of the ideological apparatus as it produces certain cultural objects whose "effects" function to reproduce values of the ideological formation. As a series of interventions within the uses to which so-called literary texts are to be put within the canon or tradition, critical practice sends out signals as to the worth and value of literary texts.

Publishers, in particular, play a crucial role in reinforcing the ruling establishment's standards and criteria by catering to the normative, hypothesized reader. In *The Sociology of Literature,* Robert Escarpit contends that with the rise of the middle class in eighteenth-century England, literature ceased to be the privilege of men of letters.[7] It shifted its focus and concerns from the aristocracy to the bourgeoisie, who demanded a literature which suited its own standards, that reproduced its values.

With this large, middle-class audience, the publisher then found himself — and still does — caught between the writer's desire, on the one hand, and the public's demands on the other. Attempting to accommodate both, the publisher influences his writer in the interest of the public by giving advances for the production of particular kinds of books, and he influences the public through censoring and advertising in the interest of the writer. In short, the publisher tries to induce a compatible writer-public relationship. But, as Maria Corti explains, the publisher fails to make a distinction between the "effective, virtual reader" and the "hypothesized reader."[8]

A consequence of the publisher's appeal to the mass "hypothesized reader" is that marginal and "other" groups are not seen as constituting a real or specific audience worth catering to. The oversight contributes to the weeding out, the repression of non-conformist literary texts. Also, this induced writer-public relationship coerces writers with non-conformist perspectives and ideologies into writing for the "hypothesized reader." When a writer is forced to write for an alien reader, a "sort of detachment results which," Robert Escarpit observes, "may allow the author to have an ideology different from that of his readers and to have to decide on the meaning not only of his own work, but of literature itself."[9]

These signals from reviewers, critics, and publishers affect the ways in which texts are perceived by other institutions within the dominant literary establishment: i.e., English departments, consumers, distributors, granting agencies, and awarding agencies. These signals explain the reason that English departments teach, and awarding agencies praise, those literary texts which generate certain values, conventions, and meanings of literary experience, subjects, and perspectives.

The literary establishment's signifying process shows that any critical practice which is conscious of the social function of literature must include an examination of the composition and expectations of the reading public which views the literature, of the context through which the literature is transmitted to that public, of the role of criticism (review magazines) and censorship (editors, publishing houses) mediating between writer and reader, and of the ways in which the structure of a text, the choice of genre, and the institution of literature as a whole may be related to social conventions.[10] In reinserting the signifying process into the social process as a whole, critical practice allows the reader to see not just the way in which a literary text is "made" but also the manner in which culture, as well, is produced and *invented* — rather than being "natural," absolute, or eternal.

Most traditional Afro-American critical practices are silent concerning the way in which literary texts are "made," produced. They are silent regarding the way in which the production of Afro-American literary texts is tied to the reproduction of the dominant ideological formation's values and regarding the fact that literature, in its present state, is a social institution which functions to generate the values of the ruling social order. In an article entitled "Generational Shifts and the Recent Criticism of Afro-American Literature" (*Black American Literature Forum*, 15 [1981], 3-21), Houston A. Baker, Jr., delineates three dominant Afro-American critical practices which defined or "made" Afro-American literature in the past forty years. Baker argues that the critical practice which defined Afro-American literature during the 1940s and 1950s was what he terms "the poetics of integration." The assumptions and criteria for this practice were established by Arthur P. Davis in the 1940s and reached their hegemony with Richard Wright in 1957. In the "Introduction" to *The Negro Caravan* (1941), Davis writes:

> The editors . . . do not believe that the expression "Negro Literature" is an accurate one, and in spite of its convenient brevity, they have avoided using it. "Negro Literature" has no application if it means *structural peculiarity*, or a Negro school of writing. The Negro writes in the forms evolved in English and American literature. . . . The editors consider Negro writers to be American writers, and literature by American Negroes to be a segment of American literature.[11]

Davis reiterates this assimilationist critical practice in his paper "Integration and Race Literature," which, as Baker informs us, he presented to the first Conference on Afro-American writers sponsored by the American Society of African Culture in 1959:

> "The integration controversy is another crisis, and from it we hope that the Negro will move permanently into full participation in American life — social, economic, political, and literary."[12]

In his essay "The Literature of the Negro in the United States," first published in 1957, Richard Wright views the Supreme Court case *Brown v. The Board of Education* as the beginning of the end of racial discrimination in the United States. Wright augurs that Afro-

American literature will become indistinguishable from the literature
of the dominant American society: "At the present moment there
is no one dominant note in Negro literary expression. As the Negro
merges into the mainstream of American life, there might result actually a disappearance of Negro as such."[13] With such a strong-willed
determination to "merge into the mainstream of American life," to
write "in the forms evolved in English and American literature," both
Davis and Wright accept uncritically the ruling literary establishment's
fundamental assumptions about literature. They accept uncritically
the literary establishment's criteria for producing literary texts — including Afro-American texts. They assume that "English and American literature[s]" have universal standards and criteria which the
Afro-American writer must reproduce if he or she is to write "good"
literature. For example, in his review of *Their Eyes Were Watching
God*, Richard Wright states that "Miss Hurston seems to have no desire whatever to move in the direction of serious fiction. . . . The
sensory sweep of her novel carries no theme, no message, no
thought."[14] In not questioning the ideological production of literature, Wright fails to understand that "serious fiction" is always relative
and ideological.

   In his essay on recent Afro-American literary criticism, Baker contends that a group of Afro-American writers, intellectuals, and critics
who had a different ideological and philosophical disposition towards
American egalitarianism than those who espoused the "poetics of
integration" emerged in the 1960s: ". . . the emerging generation
set itself the task of analyzing the nature, aims, ends, and arts
of those hundreds of thousands of their own people who were as-
saulting America's manifest structures of exclusion" (p. 5). The
critical practice which accompanied this new ideological orientation
was one of cultural nationalism, one which had its own "structures
of exclusion." The formation of this critical practice had its origins
in Langston Hughes' writing in the 1920s and its culmination in Amiri
Baraka's cultural nationalism of the 1960s and Addison Gayle's black
aesthetic of the 1970s. This black nationalist critical practice defined
the worth and value of Afro-American texts in accordance with their
accurate reflection of an ideologically defined nationalist Afro-Amer-

ican historical "reality" — i.e., the extent to which they presented positive Afro-American images and paradigms. In *The Way of the New World: The Black Novel in America*, Addison Gayle uses these black aesthetic criteria to determine the worth and value of Afro-American texts from William Wells Brown's *Clotel, or the President's Daughter* (1853) to Ernest J. Gaines's *The Autobiography of Miss Jane Pittman* (1971). Gayle praises those novels — like Delany's *Blake*, Chesnutt's *The Marrow of Tradition*, McKay's *Banana Bottom*, Killens' *And Then We Heard the Thunder*, and Gaines's *Miss Jane Pittman* — which reproduce the values and conventions of the cultural nationalist world view.

The black aestheticians also repress those Afro-American texts which cannot be appropriated to serve their ideological and literary needs. For example, Gayle criticizes those Afro-American texts — like Johnson's *The Autobiography of an Ex-Coloured Man*, Wright's *Native Son*, and Ellison's *Invisible Man* — which define the Afro-American within the ideological space of the dominant society.

In having no bones about using literature to further his political ends, Gayle, along with Hughes and Baraka, understands the political function of literature. He knows that it implies a particular form of politics, that all literary theories presuppose a certain use of literature. In reproducing the culture of Afro-America and generating the group's ideology, Gayle's black aesthetic understands that literature is a social institution which functions to keep certain myths, values, conventions, and stereotypes before the reading public.

But Gayle's black aesthetic theory of literature is silent completely on the manner of Afro-American literary texts' production. It is silent on the way in which ruling literary establishments, throughout American literary history, have affected and promoted those Afro-American texts which reproduce the dominant society's definitions and stereotypes, and repressed those Afro-American texts which reject the dominant society's ideology. In ignoring literature as a production, Gayle cannot show that literature, along with the images of the Afro-American it projects, is not innocent but is a social institution which reproduces the values of the dominant society.

Within the past five years, two major Afro-American critical texts —

Robert B. Stepto's *From Behind the Veil* (1979) and Houston A.
Baker's *The Journey Back* (1980) — emerged to establish new critical
perspectives for defining Afro-American literature.   Stepto's *From
Behind the Veil: A Study of Afro-American Narrative* is a "history
or fiction of the historical consciousness of an Afro-American art
form — namely, the Afro-American written narrative."[15]   It works
from three basic assumptions.   First, it assumes that Afro-American
culture has its own store of "pregeneric myths," "shared stories or
myths that not only exist prior to literary form, but eventually shape
the forms that comprise a given culture's literary canon" (p. ix).   For
Stepto, the primary Afro-American pregeneric myth is the "quest
for freedom and literacy."   Secondly, *From Behind the Veil* assumes
"that once the pregeneric myth is set in motion in search of its literary
forms, the historian of Afro-American literature must attempt to
define and discuss how the myth both assumes and does not assume
the properties of genre" (p. ix).   Lastly, Stepto assumes that "if an
Afro-American literary tradition exists, it does so not because there
is a sizeable chronology of [Afro-American] authors and texts, but
because those Afro-American authors and texts collectively seek their
own literary forms . . . bound historically and linguistically to a shared
pregeneric myth" (pp. ix-x).

In the book's first section, Stepto delineates four types of slave
narratives — the eclectic, the integrated, the generic, and the authenticating.   This section completes itself by describing the way in which
Booker T. Washington's *Up From Slavery* and W. E. B. Du Bois'
The Souls of Black Folk reproduce the generic and authenticating
slave narratives.

The book's second section demonstrates the way in which certain
"major" contemporary Afro-American narratives reproduce these
same delineated Afro-American written narratives.   Johnson's *The
Autobiography of an Ex-Coloured Man* reproduces the generic and
authenticating narratives of Washington and Du Bois.   Richard Wright's
Black Boy reproduces Frederick Douglass's *Narrative,* and Ellison's
Invisible Man reproduces both Washington's and Douglass's.

As Stepto points out in his preface, *From Behind the Veil* is different or innovative because he attempts to "avoid writing yet another
survey of Afro-American literature that systematically moves from

texts to non-literary structures and passively allows those structures to become the literature's collective 'history'" (p. x). *From Behind the Veil* is also valuable because it frees Afro-American texts from the matrix of the dominant American literary establishment and places them in an Afro-American matrix in which they can be received and judged more favorably. In establishing an Afro-American matrix, Stepto understands that the worth and value of literary texts are defined within cultural contexts rather than by some universal standard. *From Behind the Veil* isolates a pregeneric Afro-American cultural myth and uses it to define an Afro-American literary tradition and to establish criteria that can be used to determine the worth and value of Afro-American texts.

But the mere fact that Stepto selects "the search for freedom and literacy" rather than another Afro-American myth, such as communal struggle, indicates that his choice is ideological. In not exposing the ideological motives for selecting the pregeneric myth, Stepto deludes the reader into believing that "the search for freedom and literacy" is *the* pregeneric myth, that it objectively represents the Afro-American historical real, and that all Afro-American writers share this pregeneric myth. But, the Afro-American pregeneric myth is not innocent; it is bound culturally and historically. Its acceptance by the ruling literary establishment is contingent upon whether the ruling literary establishment or the ruling ideology can appropriate it.

Making salient the ideological nature of the pregeneric myth forces the reader to raise other questions about Stepto's *From Behind the Veil*. What is the relationship between Stepto's pregeneric myth and certain myths of the dominant ideological formation? What role has the dominant literary establishment played in promoting Stepto's pregeneric Afro-American narratives? The "major" Afro-American narratives selected by Stepto reproduce many of the dominant establishment's values. Booker T. Washington's *Up From Slavery* reproduces the dominant society's myth of the Protestant work ethic. Wright's *Black Boy*, Johnson's *The Autobiography of an Ex-Coloured Man*, and Ellison's *Invisible Man* chronicle the dominant society's myth of the rugged individual's quest for freedom. In short, Stepto's pregeneric myth, along with the Afro-American narratives and literary tradition he selects to generate it, reproduces many of the dominant society's conventions, stereotypes, and values and, therefore, can be appropriated easily to generate the dominant society. Stepto's pregeneric myth, like the ruling literary establishment, represses and subordinates those Afro-American narratives — like Delany's *Blake*, Bontemps' *Black Thunder*, Hurston's *Their Eyes Were Watching God*, Brooks' *Maud Martha*, and Reed's *Mumbo Jumbo* — that produce and reproduce Afro-American myths which counter those of the dominant society.

Houston A. Baker, in *The Journey Back: Issues in Black Literature and Criticism*, like Stepto, identifies myths and linguistic structures from the Afro-American historical past and uses them to construct an Afro-American literary tradition. Also, Baker, like Stepto, ignores the fact that Afro-American myths, stereotypes, and cultural objects are made, are produced and, therefore, have political and ideological functions.

In *The Journey Back*, Baker examines the ways in which texts written in English "preserve and communicate culturally unique meanings."[16] After describing the place occupied by works of black literature in black American culture, Baker delineates the manner in which writers like Hammon, Wheatley, the slave autobiographer Vassa, Wright, Ellison, Baldwin, Baraka, and Brooks "journey through difficult straits" and in the process preserve, in language, the details of their voyages. Through the black writer's work, argues Baker, "we are allowed to witness, if not the trip itself, at least a representation of the voyage that provides some view of our emergence" (p. 1). As with Stepto's book, the value of Baker's *The Journey Back* lies in the fact that it turns to an Afro-American cultural context to establish criteria for interpreting Afro-American texts, for determining the cultural worth and value of Afro-American texts. *The Journey Back* is also effective in identifying certain Afro-American paradigms and linguistic structures that give contemporary Afro-Americans a certain political sense of their "emergence."

But in failing to deal with language as being culturally biased, with the production of cultural objects, and with each black writer's "representation of the voyage," Baker fails to reveal the force of meaning of a culture and its literature. First, in arguing that Afro-American writers can preserve, in language, the Afro-American historical real, Baker assumes that language is transparent. But language is socially and historically produced; it is saturated with cultural and historical codes. This means that the shape of a group's or a culture's reality is homologous to the structure of the culture's language. To assume that language is transparent is to ignore the role that language plays in our understanding people, social history, culture, and the laws by which a society functions.

Secondly, in assuming that the black writer's "journey back" and his representation of the voyage is a reflection, rather than an ideological representation, of the Afro-American historical real, Baker falls into an antiquated and heavily critiqued realism. According to realism, reading is always more or less transitory. It is considered as a brief crossing from expression to the self, from representation to the world, from words to things, and from language to reality. But in light of the fact that language is not transparent and, as Foucault has informed us, that all discourses — including literary texts — permit and exclude, it becomes difficult to accept Baker's supposition that the writer's "journey back" mirrors Afro-American social reality. Rather, the "journey back" is an ideological representation of the Afro-American social reality.

Furthermore, Baker's "anthropology of art" not only ignores the black writer him- or herself, but also his or her awarenesses — be they political, racial, or sexual — and the way in which these awarenesses affect the writer's production of the "trips" and voyages of the journey back. But, more importantly, Baker's "anthropology of art" is silent on the role played by the dominant cultural apparatus and Afro-American critical practices in producing and repressing, and therefore determining the shape of, Afro-American texts. Therefore, it is unsurprising that Hammon, Wheatley, and Vassa — whose work reproduces many of the conventions and values of the dominant society — represent Afro-American literature in the eighteenth century. Baker writes: "On a first view, 'acculturation' seems to explain everything: Hammon's progress toward Christian orthodoxy, Wheatley's engagement with the God and muses of her white overlords, Vassa's detailing . . . of his education as a gentleman" (p. 19). If Baker's "anthropology of art" were not silent on production, he would raise questions about those aborted and repressed Afro-American texts which do not give acculturationist representations of Afro-America in the eighteenth century. But, more importantly, he would know that the written narratives that report these "journeys backs" are not innocent, but are produced for particular cultural and ideological purposes.

This critique of Stepto and Baker, who identify and generalize certain Afro-American myths and linguistic structures, can serve as a model for understanding the limitations and possibilities of thematic Afro-American critical studies. As I have stated earlier, the value of these Afro-American critical studies lies in the fact that they identify dominant themes, myths, cultural patterns and forms which enhance a greater comprehension of Afro-American culture. The identification of these themes and myths gives the reader greater insight into the way in which Afro-Americans make sense out of their existence. But Afro-American myths and definitions are not natural: they are produced. And any use of these myths in ignorance of the nature of their production can lead to an entrapment.

With an awareness of the role literary production plays in the definition of Afro-American literature, we can begin to see that literature is one of the social institutions within society, or even within oppressed social groups within society. Its function is to generate a group's world views or ideologies. It is to provide indices or coherent myths for social subjects as they seek equilibrium. But, when a group is not in control of its literary productions, as is the case for Afro-Americans, it must become aware of the ways in which the group which is controlling Afro-American literary productions is using them. It must be concerned with the question of whose interests those productions serve.

NOTES

1.   *A Theory of Literary Production* (London: Routledge and Kegan Paul, 1978), p. 16.

2.   See Edward W. Said, *Orientalism* (New York: Pantheon Books, 1978), p. 12.

3.   *Criticism and Ideology* (London: NLB, 1976), p. 45.

4.   See Raymond Williams, *Marxism and Literature* (Oxford: Oxford University Press, 1977), p. 48.

5.   *Literary Theory: An Introduction* (Minneapolis: University of Minnesota Press, 1983), p. 11.

6.   See Eagleton, *Literary Theory*, p. 200.

7.   (London: Frank Cass, 1971), p. 49.

8.   *An Introduction to Literary Semiotics* (Bloomington: Indiana University Press, 1978), pp. 53-54.

9.   *The Sociology of Literature*, p. 59.

10.   See William Mills Todd, III, "Introduction," in *Literature and Society in Imperial Russia, 1800-1914,* ed. William Mills Todd, III (Stanford, California: Stanford University Press, 1978), p. 1.

11.   (1941; rpt. New York: Arno Press, 1969), p. 7.

12.   In *The American Negro Writer And His Roots, Selected Papers From the First Conference of Negro Writers, March, 1959* (New York: American Society of African Culture, 1960), p. 40.

13.   "The Literature of the Negro in the United States," rpt. *Black Expression,* ed. Addison Gayle, Jr. (New York: Weybright and Talley, 1969), pp. 227-228.

14.   "Between Laughter and Tears," *New Masses,* 5 October, 1937, pp. 23, 25.

15.   (Urbana: University of Illinois Press, 1979), p. x.   Future citations from the book appear parenthetically in the text.

16.   (Chicago: University of Chicago Press, 1980), p. xii.   Future citations from the book appear parenthetically in the text.

New Democratic Vistas:
Toward a Pluralistic Genealogy

by

Craig Werner

The great poems, Shakspeare [sic] included, are poisonous to the idea of the
pride and dignity of the common people, the lifeblood of democracy. The
models of our literature, as we get it from other lands ultramarine, have had
their birth in courts and grown in castle sunshine.

—Walt Whitman[1]

I think all theories are suspect, that the finest principles may have to be modified,
or may even be pulverized by the demands of life, and that one must find, therefore, one's own moral center and move through the world hoping that this center
will guide one aright.

—James Baldwin[2]

What emerges . . . is something one might call a genealogy, or rather a multiplicity of genealogical researches, a painstaking rediscovery of struggles together with the rude memories of their conflicts. And these genealogies, that are the combined product of an erudite knowledge and a popular knowledge . . . could not even have been attempted except on one condition, namely that the tyranny of globalizing discourses with their hierarchy and all their privileges of a theoretical *avant-garde* was eliminated.

—Michel Foucault[3]

I.

Cultural Solipsism, the Wild Zone, and the Distrust of Theory

The repudiation of theoretical systems, especially those originating in Europe, is one of the constituting struggles shaping the American genealogy. Whether couched in the theological argument of Samuel Baldwin's *Armageddon: Or, the Existence of the United States Foretold in the Bible,* the botanical observations of Thomas Jefferson's *Notes on Virginia,* or the anti-feudal prophecy of Whitman's *Democratic Vistas,* American discourse consistently dismisses external theoretical systems as inadequate to the richness, real or potential, of the American experience. From the Puritan vision of the "City on the Hill" through William Carlos Williams' writings on the "American meter," numerous American writers have envisioned new modes of perception, expression, and social organization "organically" embodying the unprecedented multiplicity of their natural and social environments.[4] Seen in relation to this genealogy, Baldwin's repudiation of theory seems quintessentially American.

Seen in relation to the "rude memories" of the Afro-American community, however, Baldwin expresses an even more profound distrust of theory than does Whitman, who in fact metamorphoses into one aspect of the problem. Despite their theoretical commitment to multiplicity, even the most insistently anti-theoretical "classic" American writers remain largely oblivious to the fact that their responses to European theory assert an equally limited Euro-American male experience. Their "organic" theories of American culture, from an

Afro-American or a woman's perspective, frequently signify little more than an exchange of one form of theoretical oppression for another. Implicitly asserting that their own group's experience carries greater significance or resonance than that of other groups, the early American theorists contradicted, usually unknowingly, their own organic beliefs and perpetuated a form of what I shall call "cultural solipsism." Afro-American writers responding to the pluralistic ideals of Euro-American rhetoric have nevertheless maintained an acute consciousness of its internal contradictions. When Benjamin Banneker echoes Jefferson's own arguments in his response to the racist implications of *Notes on Virginia,* he underlines the structural similarity of Jefferson's thought to that against which Jefferson himself had rebelled; just as French scientific theory denied the reality of American wildlife, so Jefferson denies the reality of the Afro-American intellect.[5] Similarly, Frederick Douglass's speech of July 5, 1852, accuses white America of slipping into modes of thought and action indistinguishable from those of the British prior to independence.[6] In each case, ostensibly democratic theories evince little knowledge of Afro-American experience.

These deeply rooted contradictions in Euro-American thought inevitably exert an influence over contemporary theoretical discourse. Several major movements in literary theory explicitly reject pluralism, calling into question the epistemological importance of social and political relationships. Carried out almost entirely within academic institutions dominated by Euro-American males, these movements embrace avant-garde European theories and rarely claim any relevance to the social concerns of groups not involved actively in the avant-garde.[7] More disturbing are those contemporary theorists who identify themselves as pluralists yet conduct their inquiries in a manner that perpetuates the old contradictions. Even such a humane and insightful critic as Wayne Booth falls victim to this trap in *Critical Understanding: The Powers and Limits of Pluralism* (Chicago: University of Chicago Press, 1979), an analysis of the underlying assumptions of the critical tradition in which he works. Despite his professed pluralistic beliefs, Booth discusses the tradition solely as the creation of Euro-American males. The only critics Booth discusses at length are Ronald

S. Crane, Kenneth Burke, and M. H. Abrams; he fails to mention a single Afro-American critic and refers to Virginia Woolf, whose *A Room of One's Own* concerns many of the issues he raises, only in passing. This severely circumscribed data base both creates the false impression that Booth shares the avant-garde indifference to the problems of the dispossessed and guarantees that his conclusions will reflect the same underlying contradictions as those of Whitman and Williams.

Repeated confrontation with the limitations of Euro-American male theory has encouraged an Afro-American awareness of the dominant-group/muted-group dynamic described by feminist critic Elaine Showalter.[8]   Basing her analysis on the work of anthropologists Edwin and Shirley Ardener, Showalter presents a model relevant to the situation of both Afro-Americans and women confronting a culture that renders them invisible. Showalter's model represents the experience of the dominant group (Europeans, Euro-Americans, males) as a solid circle and the experience of the muted group (Americans, Afro-Americans, women) as a dotted circle:

Showalter's gender-oriented gloss of the diagram parallels W. E. B. Du Bois' description of "double consciousness" and can be applied easily to the relationship of Euro- and Afro-Americans: "Much of muted circle Y falls within the boundaries of dominant circle X; there is also a crescent of Y which is outside the dominant boundary and therefore . . . 'wild.' We can think of the wild zone of women's culture spatially, experientially, or metaphysically. Spatially it stands for an area which is literally no-man's-land, a place forbidden to men, which corresponds to the zone in X which is off-limits to women. Experientially it stands for the aspects of the female life-style which are outside of **and unlike those of men;** again, there is a corresponding zone of male experience alien to women. But if we think of the wild zone metaphysically, or in terms of consciousness, it has no corresponding male space since all of male consciousness is within the circle of the dominant structure and thus accessible to or structured by language. In this sense, the 'wild' is always imaginary; from the male point of view, it may simply be the projection of the unconscious. In terms of cultural anthropology, women know what the male crescent is like, even if they have never seen it, because it becomes the subject of legend (like the wilderness). But men do not know what is in the wild."[9]   If we consider Afro-Americans as a muted group in Euro-American culture, this suggests several observations.

First, Euro-American writers who implicitly deny the existence of an autonomous Afro-American culture generate theories, propagated by legend and encoded in the dominant language, which "justify" the social oppression of Afro-Americans; this in turn discourages or precludes the expression of experiences associated with the wild zone. Secondly, because they identify "reality" with the contents of their own circle, dominant-group members frequently present their legends and theories as "universal" or "objective" and dismiss expressions of the wild zone as "limited" or "subjective."[10]   Thirdly, this discourages dominant-group members from exploring the world, external or internal. By repressing all experiences which they associate with the wild zone, dominant groups close their theoretical systems to new energy, condemning both both dominant and muted groups to an essentially inorganic articulation of experience. Inevitably, any theory generated entirely in response to dominant-group experience, however "organic" or "pluralistic" in intent, reduces wild-zone experiences to superficially comforting stereotypes, dependent functions of dominant-group needs. Unless they challenge the structural hegemony of dominant-group experiences, all theories will simply perpetuate the solipsistic culture of the past.[11]

One of the most penetrating Afro-American critiques of cultural solipsism, Ralph Ellison's *Invisible Man* illustrates several important aspects of Showalter's formulation. In simple terms, invisibility stems from the distortion of a particular experience or aspect of the personality by perceptions originating in the external environoment. The individual experiences most likely to be rendered invisible are those associated with the wild zone. From Mr. Norton to Brother Jack, dominant-group individuals perceive experience primarily in relation to themselves. When they "see" the narrator's (or Tod Clifton's or Trueblood's) "difference," they create solipsistic legends that reduce the wild zone to a dependent function of their own psychological or political needs; they then use the legends to strengthen their own position of privilege. As a result, when he confronts the white skin of the men at the Battle Royal or the science of the Brotherhood, the invisible man must either repress all knowledge of the Afro-American wild zone and play the stereotyped role prescribed by the dominant-group solipsism or risk exclusion from the dominant-group circle, including the area $(X + Y)$ shared by the dominant and muted groups. The resulting life in the wild zone involves the experience Ellison refers to as "falling outside of history."[12] Although this experience may seem momentarily liberating, it devolves gradually into a peculiarly inchoate state, exemplified by Rinehart, which curtails communcation, even with members of the muted group, who continue to accept the solipsistic language of the dominant group. Taken to its logical conclusion, then, Showalter's formulation suggests that a society predicated on cultural solipsism offers only a choice between the invisibility of self-denial and the invisibility of exile.

Although it is not my purpose presently to pursue this issue, this formulation of the constituting tension between dominant-group theory and muted-group experience suggests the serious consequences of using any structure derived entirely from a single group's experience to articulate another group's reality. In fact, the very formulation of a dichotomy between "theory" and "belief" may inadvertently perpetuate just such a situation.[13] Although it is not inherent in the terms themselves, academic discourse has traditionally perceived theory as somehow separate from, and usually superior to, belief. Claiming that they are interested in incorporating the full reality, these "objective" or "universal" theories in reality mask a deep commitment to the beliefs shared by dominant-group members. Although Euro-American males reacting against European theories which have rendered them invisible frequently label their values "American" rather than "universal," the implications for muted groups remain the same. Any experience not capable of articulation in terms established by the dominant group can automatically be excluded from further consideration. As a result, most muted-group challenges to dominant-group theory are dismissed as trivial or marginal; they are consigned to the wild zone from whence they came.[14]

Given this absurdly circular, but thoroughly vicious, discourse, it is not surprising to find Baldwin's skepticism concerning theory as a pervasive element in Afro-American literary criticism. Faced with "standard" studies of American literature (including those of Roy Harvey Pearce, R. W. B. Lewis, Richard Chase, Leo Marx, and James E. Miller) that render Afro-Americans entirely invisible, critics as diverse in background as Sterling Brown, Larry Neal, Barbara Smith, and Robert Stepto refuse to endorse the standard theories and seek to expand the experiential base of critical discourse.[15] Articulating a pervasive attitude of the Afro-American tradition in regard to dominant-group theory, George Kent repudiates the idea of a "pre-existing Western universal," endorsing instead a "legitimate universalism" based on the writer's ability to enforce "the illusion that the vibrations from the space her imagination has encircled are captured and focused with all the power and significance which the raw materials afforded."[16] Essentially, Kent envisions universalism as a function of experience, a perspective that subverts the authority of the universal — even the "legitimate universal," which is itself simply an "illusion" subject to alteration. This recognition of the inherent subjectivity of any statement of universality subverts the establishment of a dichotomy between theory and belief. Acknowledging the origins of abstraction in concrete experience, theorists working within this sensibility feel little need to mask or repress the deeply held beliefs conditioning their perceptions. Far from invalidating the resulting theories, this approach encourages an acceptance of alternative belief systems and alternative senses of the universal. By eliminating the need, and ultimately the desirability, of an objective theory capable of encompassing all experiences, this approach paradoxically offers some hope for a more inclusive pluralism than that generated within the Euro-American male tradition.

Why, given this deep skepticism, discuss literature in relation to theory at all? Why not simply carry out guerilla attacks on solipsistic theories? My response is twofold. First, to predicate all action on dominant-group theories and attitudes, even on the repudiation of these theories, involves a constant psychological involvement with dominant-group thought processes that can easily result in inadvertent alienation from the wild zone. Given this pressure to acquiesce to invisibility, theoretical models of a "pure" pluralistic process encourage awareness of the threats to personal or group integrity posed by solipsistic discourse. Secondly, a theoretical model that attempts to relate seemingly disparate guerilla approaches can help individuals working in a particular area to understand and benefit from other approaches. In essence, pluralistic theory can help resist attempts by the dominant group to fragment, particularize, and ultimately trivialize the muted group. By acknowledging the origins of theory in belief, clearly articulating the beliefs and accepting the provisional status of the theory, the pluralistic critic committed to resisting cultural solipsism can attempt to "hard-wire" his or her theory in a way that discourages applications violating one's underlying beliefs.[17]

The theory presented in this essay rests on my belief in values I shall refer to as *Integrity* and *Extension,* values deeply rooted in both the Afro- and Euro-American traditions. Integrity involves recognition of the full experience of all individuals and groups, including those experiences usually consigned to the wild zone. Serving to protect what Foucault calls the "rude memories of struggles," the relatively unmediated experience supporting genealogical research, this recognition is a necessary precondition for extension, which involves the desire to draw on and contribute to the experience of other groups and individuals. Extension can be seen as an attempt to protect the integrity of the individual and group against entropy, the tendency of systems to run down and ultimately die when cut off from outside sources of energy.[18] If cultural solipsism manifests entropy by forcing experience to remain within the dominant-group circle, extension seeks to expand the circle and to offer access to new sources of energy. Seeking the "erudite knowledge" necessary to Foucault's genealogies, extension recognizes diverse integrities (to the greatest extent possible in their own terms) and expands the experiential resources available for coping with the problems arising from the contact of diverse groups in a pluralistic culture. By advancing a theoretical model, first in ideal form and then in relation to the actualities of cultural solipsism, I wish to re-member the roots

and branches of my own genealogy, conjoining Foucault and Robert
Johnson, Adrienne Rich and Robert Stepto, Willa Cather and George
Clinton, Thomas Pynchon and James Baldwin in a funk pluralization
of Whitman's vistas.

II.

Vocabulary, Dialect, Language: A Pluralistic Model

The underlying structure of an ideal pluralistic theory designed to
acknowledge diverse integrities can be imaged in the following model:

Universal
↑
Language
↑
Dialect
↑
Vocabulary
↑
Experience

This model suggests an ideal process in which individual experience,
including the experiences associated with the wild zone, shapes the
individual vocabulary, which involves all available types of expression,
verbal and nonverbal.[19]   These vocabularies in turn shape dialects
based on the shared experiences of groups (racial, sexual, regional,
occupational, familial) which in turn shape a pluralistic cultural language that remains accountable to the generative experiences.   Ultimately these languages (American, Asian, African) shape a conception of a legitimate universal.   The ideal structure described above
reverses the idealization process of culturally solipsistic theories, which
argue that experience — cultural and personal — should be shaped
in accord with a pre-existing set of ideal standards.   Labeling these
idealizations "universal" allows the denial of any cultural ("pagan,"
black, lesbian) or individual experience not in accord with the uni-

versal. Conversely, the pluralistic idealization is constructed to acknowledge equally all disparate integrities. Any idealization not
validated by the experience of the "lower-level" [20] group should be
recognized as an aspect of one of the generative dialects rather than
solipsistically asserted as a cultural language or universal.

A first step toward relating this pluralistic idealization to reality
involves the recognition that languages, dialects, vocabularies, and
"universals" are not fixed in their forms. As Noam Chomsky observes,
idealizations of fixed forms simply provide a way of conceiving the
actual complexity of discourse: "Certainly, it is true that no individual
speaks a well-defined language. The notion of language itself is on a
very high level of abstraction. In fact, each individual employs a
number of linguistic systems in speaking. How can one describe such
an amalgam? Linguists have generally, and quite properly, proceeded
in terms of an idealization: Let us assume, they say, the notion of a
homogeneous linguistic community. Even if they don't admit it,
that is what they do. It is the sole means of proceeding rationally,
so it seems to me. You study ideal systems, then afterwards you can
ask yourself in what manner these ideal systems are represented and
interact in real individuals."[21] To begin, realistic use of the idealized
forms dictates a recognition of their involvement in complex social
processes. In fact, as Gregory Bateson observes, the understanding
of any complex phenomenon, especially one involving a constant
reevaluation of "fixed" concepts, alternates between a focus on form
and a focus on the process through which the form is observed and
revised.[22] A given form of expression (integrity) is always subject
to modification and adjustment in response to external feedback
(extension). Any given pluralistic idealization, therefore, can claim
only a provisional validity. A more adequate model of the pluralistic
model, adapting a diagram originally presented by Bateson, incorporates both form and process:

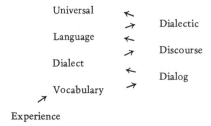

This idealization of the pluralistic process rests on the assumption (a naive assumption that will be qualified later in this essay) that each individual experiences life in a "pure" form not mediated by pre-existing conceptual systems and would be capable of generating a vocabulary expressing the full complexity of that experience. No limits should be imposed on the definition of experience, which would encompass thought and action, internal and external realities; and no limitations should be imposed on the vocabulary, which includes the full range of articulation and expression. For purposes of convenience, I shall present this ideal structure in terms of the written and spoken word, though gestural, musical, and iconographic vocabularies play an equally important role in actual expression. In this ideal situation, no individual could challenge the validity of another individual's vocabulary or impose his or her vocabulary on the other's experience. Individual vocabularies would alter and increase with new experiences, affirming and developing individual integrity.

Secure in their integrity, individuals would then engage in dialog, the most personal form of extension, expressing their experiences to one another and generating "shared vocabularies" or dialects. To the extent that individuals share experiences, they would agree on the meanings of particular words, establishing a base for further dialog. When disagreements on the meaning of a particular word arose, each individual would extend him/herself in an attempt to understand the experience of the other that generated the difference in vocabulary. To the extent that an experience can be fully understood, this would enable each individual to extend his or her own vocabulary and, ideally, attain literacy in new dialects. Inevitably dialects, even those derived through an ideal pluralistic process, lack the precision of individual vocabularies. Nevertheless, they are extremely important in that they establish a form (always subject to adjustment) in which everyday communication can be carried out without the large expenditure of energy needed for ideal dialog.[23] Because these everyday dialects derive from intense dialog, however, they incorporate respect for the integrity of diverse individuals. Dialect groups may reflect many different types of shared experience: racial (black English), professional (academic English), regional (Southern English), even recreational (sportstalk). As Chomsky comments: "It is evident that the language of the ghettos is of the same order as that of the suburbs."[24] Obviously any individual may be fluent in a number of dialects, none of which, within the pluralistic process, can claim superiority over any other, since all derive from shared individual vocabularies. The size of a dialect group may be as small as two (see, for example, Thomas Pynchon's portrayal of Enzian's parents in *Gravity's Rainbow*) or as large as the terms of a particular experience dictate.[25] Marcus Garvey's pan-Africanist program, for example, can be seen as an attempt to form a dialect group of many millions.

Garvey's movement could equally well be viewed as an attempt to formulate a cultural language; in fact, the conceptual distinction between large group dialects and cultural languages is primarily a matter of convenience of terminology. The dialects of Northern and Southern blacks can be seen as parts of an Afro-American language or an Afro-American dialect, which in turn can be seen as coming together with an Afro-Caribbean dialect or language (derived from Jamaican, Cuban, etc. dialects) to form a pan-African language or with the Euro-American dialect(s) to form an American language. The important point regarding large dialects or languages is that they attempt to realize the pluralistic ideal in an institutional context. In a process structurally analogous to dialog, representatives of dialect groups come together in social discourse, generating "shared dialects" or cultural languages. Whatever the languages or dialects involved, no group, secure in the integrity of its dialect, should feel tempted to deny the integrity of any other group. The language derived from pluralistic discourse reflects the shared wisdom of diverse groups. As in the case of dialect formation, the process of discourse encourages dialect groups to extend themselves to new experiences, ultimately enriching both their dialect and the "common language" available for future discourse.[26] The ideal result would be the creation of truly democratic institutions taking form from, and always subject to, modification by the generative discourse.[27]

The language emerging from these adjustments of dialect to dialect and vocabularly to language are frequently (and, ideally, tentatively) fixed in institutional forms — dictionaries, legal codes, curricula, etc.

Even in theory, however, this institutional fixing of form introduces several new problems for the pluralistic ideal. Ideal institutional discourse would be carried out by representatives of dialect groups, speaking in a "common voice" encoded in the group dialect. Their grasp of the experience of the dialect group and the intricacies of the dialect must be unshakeable; in effect, the representative becomes a griot or sage. When entering into discourse, the representative must recognize that his or her dialect represents a consensus involving numerous individual experiences. In addition, he or she must be willing to pursue a deep knowledge of diverse cultural and historical experiences as a prerequisite of extension to other groups. Further, the representative must understand the distinction between his or her personal vocabulary and group dialect. This is particularly important in regard to the resolution of disagreements. Whereas an individual engaged in dialog can at least attempt to confront directly the experiential roots of the difference and alter his or her vocabulary immediately, the task of the representative is more complex. The representative cannot simply agree to "change" the dialect. Rather, he or she must return to the community with an expanded vocabulary and, through the process of dialog, attempt to extend the dialect. Though slow, the process is necessary to the integrity of the dialect; no leader would be able to violate group integrity for personal gain. As a result, when representing a dialect, an individual inevitably speaks with less flexibility and precision than when speaking in his or her vocabulary.

At this point, I wish to reconsider the concept of "pure experience" on which the ideal pluralistic process is based. In reality, of course, no individual generates a vocabulary directly from experience. Rather, he or she adapts the existing languages and dialects in a vocabulary expressing the subtleties of his or her experience. To the extent that existing dialects and languages reflect an ideal pluralistic process, however, they will articulate common experiences likely to be shared by new members of the community. Therefore, pluralistic languages and dialects expedite rather than frustrate the expression of individual vocabulary, enabling individuals to accept the legitimate impression of past experience. Incorporating this concept of impression into the ideal pluralistic process results in the following model:

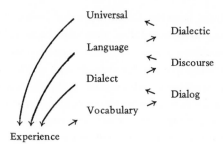

The lower-level loops would typically provide the deepest impressions since they reflect more specific levels of experience.[28]

The presence of the loop extending from the universal to experience raises the question of the "universal" as it relates to the pluralistic ideal. Because at each stage of the pluralistic process those expressions not shared by each group are eliminated from the more abstract form, a universal derived from the dialectic between diverse cultural languages would not be more applicable to one group than another. Chomsky expresses the linguistic dimension of this question in describing what he calls the "universal grammar": "Let us define 'universal grammar' (UG) as the system of principles, conditions, and rules that are elements or properties of all human languages not merely by accident but by necessity — of course, I mean biological, not logical necessity. Thus UG can be taken as expressing 'the essence of human language.' UG will be invariant among humans."[29] Literally incarnate in every human being, these invariant universals, which would be expressed only in provisional form, would probably involve basic drives or relationships dictated by human physiology. In linguistic terms, as Chomsky argues, this implies that the physiology of the brain and of our perceptual apparatus places a limitation on *possible* human languages. Extremely abstract in content, the universal is, paradoxically, extremely concrete inasmuch as it is embedded in all individual vocabularies, group dialects, and cultural languages. Comparing diverse traditions of folklore and myth, which express both the wisdom of dialect and language groups, and deeply felt psychological needs, may' provide some sense of a legitimate universal.[30] In order to approach the pluralistic ideal, however, it is absolutely essential that no judgment concerning the universal be propagated by members of any one language group. The integrity of each cultural language, which on this level of abstraction is essentially fixed since it takes decades or centuries for alterations in individual vocabulary and/or group dialect to influence the structure of folklore and myth, would need to be respected fully in conceiving the universal. Given this respect, the universal would actually be universal; no theoretical expression of the universal would perpetuate the distinction between dominant and muted groups. Each culture would be free to express its integrity, extend its richness to others, and accept their extension in return. Ole Miss would grant George Clinton an honorary Ph.D., and Gilbert Sorrentino would play the Apollo. The crowds would be mixed.

III.

Solipsism, Oppression, Repression

In addition to imaging an ideal process, the model presented above can be used to explain the ways in which dominant-group theories and actions discourage pluralism. Reorienting the pluralistic model to reflect traditional Euro-American male conceptions of the universal provides a model of the actual workings of cultural solipsism:

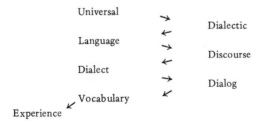

Any dialect or vocabulary not in accord with the dictates of the solipsistic universal or language may be excluded from the processes imaged on the right-hand side of the model. "Pagans" can be ignored in discussions of the "higher values" within the discourse of Christianity; the black dialect (which becomes a pejorative term indicating departure from a correct standard English) can be denied entry into the institutional discourse that defines the "American" language; individuals disagreeing with the inherited traditions of their community may be declared insane. Creating a dominant-group/muted-group relationship, this reversal of the pluralistic process enforces invisibility by refusing to recognize the reality of the wild-zone experiences not validated by the culturally solipsistic language.

From a pluralistic perspective, however, these solipsistic languages are not languages at all, but simply dialects run amuck. Essentially, the dialect of the dominant group (bourgeois Euro-American males) or a "language" formed from the intersection of dominant groups (whites, males, lawyers, academics, businessmen) is elevated to universal.[31] Members of the dominant group, typically unaware of the unstated premises of their behavior, then, proceed as if by serving their own interests they are serving the ultimate good.[32] This in turn distorts all levels of the communication process. An individual insisting on his or her personal vocabulary when engaged in dialog excludes other vocabularies, implicitly denying the reality of the generative experiences.[33] A similar insistence on a particular dialect as the basis of social discourse — that of the Southern white planters during slavery, for instance — denies the experience of entire dialect groups — poor whites or blacks banned from voting by "literacy" tests and property requirements. Ultimately cultural solipsism perpetuates itself since any muted-group individual wishing to participate in social discourse must adopt the culturally solipsistic language. Since this language excludes all vocabulary derived from the wild zone it creates, the muted-group individual adopting the language can do little to alter the langauge in a pluralistic manner. The wild zone enters discourse only indirectly, as imaged in the stereotypes of muted-group "difference" propagated by the dominant group.[34] Exercising its control of social, legal, and economic power, the dominant group may enforce its dialect through openly oppressive measures: lynch mobs; literacy tests; police violence; discrimination in employment, education, and housing. On occasion these measures may contribute to programs explicitly intended to destroy dialect-group integrity. In her discussion of totalitarian movements, Hannah Arendt presents an argument echoed by Malcolm X in his analysis of Euro-American racism. Emphasizing the denial of experience required for participation in totalitarian discourse, Arendt describes the irreconcilable conflict between culturally solipsistic languages and pluralistic dialects:

> Totalitarian movements are possible wherever there are masses who for one reason or another have acquired the appetite for political organization. Masses are not held together by a consciousness of common interest and they lack that specific class articulateness which is expressed in determined, limited, and obtainable goals. The term masses applies only where we deal with people who either because of sheer numbers, or indifference, or a combination of both, cannot be integrated into any organization based on common interest.[35]

Obviously, any group not admitted into the organization (party, racial group, church) is subject to enslavement, imprisonment, or direct violence. Even for those with access to the organization, the price of admission is a complete denial of the wild zone. No assertion of the "limited and obtainable" goals of a dialect group participating in pluralistic discourse will be tolerated in a solipsistic totalitarian context.

Active oppression, however, is neither the most common nor the most effective technique of totalitarianism, which is simply an extreme form of cultural solipsism. As it exists in the United States, cultural solipsism operates almost entirely through ostensibly democratic processes. Capitalizing on cultural forces eroding the strength of identification with dialect groups, the dominant group embeds its dialect in the texture of everyday experience (in schools, media, etc.) in ways that encourage muted-group members to form vocabularies reflecting the dominant solipsism. As Chomsky observes, the dominant group creates the illusion of open discourse by establishing premises for discourse and then allowing relatively open access to the process within the premises. Chomsky comments:

In a democratic system of propaganda no one is punished (in theory) for objecting to official dogma. In fact, dissidence is encouraged. What this system attempts to do is to fix the limits of possible thought: supporters of official doctrine at one end, and the critics — vigorous, courageous, and much admired for their independence of judgment — at the other. . . . But we discover that all share certain tacit assumptions and that it is these assumptions that are really crucial. No doubt a propaganda system is more effective when its doctrines are insinuated rather than asserted, when it sets the bounds for possible thought rather than simply imposing a clear and easily identifiable doctrine that one must parrot — or suffer the consequences. The more vigorous the debate, the more effectively the basic doctrines of the propaganda system, tacitly assumed on all sides, are instilled. Hence the elaborate pretense that the press is a critical dissenting force — maybe even too critical for the health of democracy — when in fact it is almost entirely subservient to the basic principles of the ideological system.[36]

Refusing to acknowledge the origin of these premises in its own dialect, the dominant group treats the resulting discourse as if it incorporates all legitimate dialects. Especially in a context in which the premises and their limitations can be enforced by oppressive measures (McCarthy hearings, anti-abolitionist violence, refusal to publish subversive texts), this forces the invisible individual to repress — or more insidiously to refuse to articulate even for him/herself — all aspects of vocabulary (and therefore of experience) that would demand a wider frame of discourse. As Arendt recognized, this renders democratic institutions almost entirely impotent in a solipsistic (totalitarian) cultural context:

> The success of totalitarian movements among the masses meant the end of two illusions of democratically ruled countries. . . . The first was that the people in its majority

had taken an active part in government and that each individual was in sympathy with one's own or somebody
else's party. On the contrary, the movements showed that
the politically neutral and indifferent masses could easily
be the majority in a democratically ruled country, that
therefore a democracy could function according to rules
which are actively recognized by only a minority. The
second democratic illusion exploded by the totalitarian
movements was that these politically indifferent masses
did not matter, that they were truly neutral and constituted no more than the inarticulate backward setting for
the political life of the nation. Now they made apparent
what no other organ of public opinion had ever been able
to show, namely, that democratic government had rested
as much on the silent approbation and tolerance of the
indifferent and inarticulate sections of the people as on
the articulate and visible institutions and organizations
of the country.[37]

The clear implication of this analysis is that simply accepting solipsism
as the basis of reality and tolerating the invisibility of self *or* other
ultimately creates a context in which the movement from democratic
illusion to totalitarian oppression is possible.

Adjusting the model to reflect the interaction of the repressive and
oppressive aspects of cultural solipsism results in the following model:

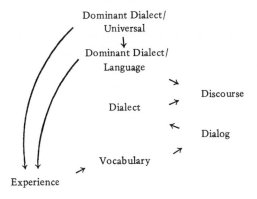

In addition to presenting its dialect as universal, the dominant group in essence rejects the importance of process, especially on the more abstract levels. To the extent that the repression imaged in the left-hand loops succeeds, the language derived from the ostensibly pluralistic process will match that imposed by the dominant group. To the extent that differences emerge in the process, they will be admitted into discourse, but the results of the discourse will not be reflected in the language that provides the terms for articulation of experience, counteracting any legitimate impression derived from a relatively pluralistic, though similarly conditioned, dialect. Oppression becomes necessary only when a dialect group insists that the results of discourse be incorporated into the language. As Afro-Amerian writers have long realized, the interaction of oppressive and repressive forces in fact serves to distort even the more concrete levels of the pluralistic process. Although the proliferation of "black" usages indicates the insufficiency of the solipsistic language fixed in form by dictionaries and the educational system, the Afro-American dialect, recognizing the dangers of violent oppression, frequently reinforces the repressions of the solipsistic language; in effect, this creates a third repressive loop (from dialect to experience) and denies dialog in the same way that the solipsistic language ignores discourse. In Richard Wright's "The Ethics of Living Jim Crow," for example, Wright's mother, acutely aware that further violations may bring down serious violence on Richard, beats him for refusing to act in accord with white expectations when he fights several white boys. By perpetuating stereotypes of black docility and/or criminality derived from the dominant-group language, the muted group effectively embeds the denial of experience in its own dialect. Carried to its most extreme, this process leads to the development of vocabularies that reinforce the solipsistic language, adding a fourth loop to the diagram of repression. Wright's description of white voices in his head controlling his behavior in *Black Boy* indicates the impact of this self-repression on individual psychology.[38]   At its most effective, this combination of oppression and repression enables the dominant group to enforce cultural solipsism without any direct contact with the wild zone of muted-group experience.

Even when most effective, however, the culturally solipsistic process involves substantial risks for members of the dominant group. By rendering muted-group members invisible — alienating them from, or forcing them to live entirely within, their wild zone — the dominant group creates internal frustrations that may well result in seemingly random violence, such as that described in *Native Son* and in the prologue to *Invisible Man*. Even when this violence is internalized, as in Toni Morrison's *The Bluest Eye,* manifestations of the frustration reinforce the dominant-group image of invisible individuals as simultaneously less competent and more dangerous than dominant-group members. This in turn can be used to justify culturally solipsistic theories, a process ultimately increasing the frustration that leads to the random violence.[39] In addition, this repression has an analogous effect on the experience of *individuals* within the dominant group who in some ways face even stronger pressure to deny their wild zones. Unable to admit the reality of wild-zone experience in others (and sometimes using these experiences to justify oppressive social actions), the dominant-group individual will be tempted to ignore any similar experience in himself. Men deny the "feminine" emotions that render women unfit for participation in discourse; whites repress knowledge of the heart of darkness they identify with the barbaric black savage. The resulting repression both discourages literacy in other dialects (extension) and creates internal frustration by denying aspects of personal integrity. Creating a wild zone of the individual dominant-group member — an invisibility made more difficult to recognize by the fact that the solipsistic language is also the individual's own dialect in a fixed form removed from the process of dialog — can lead to a psychological disintegration or aggressive violence. Structurally, of course, these responses parallel those found in invisible groups. The violence, however, manifests itself differently. Whereas the invisible-group member is most likely to express his or her violence in an attempt to force entry into social discourse, the dominant-group member can channel his or her violence into enforcing the oppression of the muted group that externalizes the internal wild zone. Cultural solipsism, however effectively or indirectly propagated, ultimately victimizes both dominant- and muted-group members.

James Baldwin's observation of the psychological and social implications of this victimization serves both as summation of the solipsistic reality and reminder of the pluralistic ideals of integrity and extension:

> The racial tensions that menace Americans today have little to do with real antipathy — on the contrary, indeed — and are involved only symbolically with color. These tensions are rooted in the very same depths as those from which love springs, or murder. The white man's unadmitted — and apparently, to him, unspeakable — private fears and longings are projected onto the Negro. The only way he can be released from the Negro's tyrannical power over him is to consent, in effect, to become black himself, to become a part of that suffering and dancing country that he now watches wistfully from the heights of his lonely power and, armed with spiritual traveller's checks, visits surreptitiously after dark.[40]

IV.

A Genealogical Approach to Afro-American Literature

The application of this theoretical structure to what Foucault calls "genealogical researches" requires a double vision simultaneously focusing on the tension between the pluralistic ideal and solipsistic reality and on the complex interaction of the "personal" (vocabulary) and the "political" (language) in all experience. The strategy expressed by the Center for Enviornomental Structure's handbook *A Pattern Language* provides a good orientation on the genealogical sensibility: ". . . no pattern is an isolated entity. Each pattern can exist in the world, only to the extent that it is supported by other patterns: the larger patterns in which it is embedded, the patterns of the same size that surround it, and the smaller patterns which are embedded in it . . . when you build a thing you cannot merely build that thing in isolation, but must also repair the world around it, and within it, so that the larger world at that one place becomes more coherent, and more whole; and the thing which you make takes its place in the web of nature, as you make it."[41] Viewing the ideal pluralistic structure as the desired pattern — the thing the critic attempts to embed in the web of reality — suggests several specific critical strategies. First, the critic should strive to recognize the position of the literary experience under consideration (genre, text, author, passage) in relation to patterns existing in the solipsistic context. Secondly, he or she should attempt to determine which specific actions/interpretations/critical methodologies will contribute most effectively to an assertion of integrity and extension within that context. Conceptualizing the problem and the ideal in relation to the same theoretical model checks against losing sight of either focus and helps to determine the crucial level of action in a specific situation.

In relation to the genealogical sensibility, specific texts can be usefully approached as "fixed forms" of authorial vocabulary derived from what Foucault calls the "rude memories of conflict," and reflecting the pressures of the solipsistic cultural context.[42] Entering into a process of dialog with his or her own vocabulary, the critic must attempt to understand as fully as possible the experience generating the textual vocabulary. The critic may then employ his or her "erudite knowledge" (in this case embedded in the theoretical model) to relate the dialect derived from the critical dialog to the web of patterns. Recognizing that most theoretical discourse takes place in an academic dialect, the genealogical critic should grant primacy to the "popular knowledge," referring all "erudite" theoretical observations back to a multiplicity of individual vocabularies.[43] As a result, the burden of what W. E. B. Du Bois called "double consciousness" shifts from muted-group individuals (who will in any case experience it within the solipsistic culture) to those admitted into social discourse. Extending Baldwin's comments on the necessity of white identification with blackness to apply to the relationship between literary critic and the experience behind a textual vocabulary results in an interesting perspective on Du Bois' famous passage:

> It is a peculiar sensation, this double consciousness, this sense of always looking at one's self through the eyes of others, of measuring one's soul by the tape of a world that looks on in amused contempt and pity. One ever feels his twoness, — an American, a Negro; two souls, two thoughts, two unreconcilable strivings; two warring ideals in one dark body, whose dogged strength alone keeps it from being torn asunder. The history of the American Negro is the history of this strife, — this longing to attain self-conscious manhood, to merge his double self into a better and truer self. In this merging he wishes neither of the older selves to be lost.[44]

When read from the position of the dominant group (American, erudite critic) rather than of the muted group (Negro, textual experience), this passage suggests that double consiousness may provide a path to a "better and truer self," extended to incorporate the wild zone normally denied with "amused contempt." Maintaining double consciousness provides a check on the tendency of dominant-group critics to deny aspects of the literary experience to support their (inadvertently) solipsistic theories.

Experiencing the "otherness within" as liberating — a form of extension that offers escape from cultural solipsism — the genealogical critic, secure in a strengthened integrity, will gradually develop literacy in diverse dialects and vocabularies. This in turn will increase the critic's ability to understand the relationship between these forms and the dominant cultural solipsism, to contribute to the dialog leading to pluralistic dialects in his or her immediate context, and to encourage the assertion of these dialects within the culturally solipsistic context. This assertion may involve either the "militant" assertion of the dialect's integrity or adaptation of masking strategies to subvert the dominant group's ability to impose its dialect. In part because of its complex historical experience of double consciousness, the Afro-American literary tradition presents a particularly rich field for the critic interested in contributing to research on a pluralistic American genealogy. Among the probems requiring an in-depth consideration beyond the scope of this essay are: (1) the nature of "experience," especially as encoded in "pregeneric" forms, and the problem of articulating the individual vocabulary; (2) the complex structure of particular dialects, which combine pluralistic derivation and protective repression; (3) the distinctive structures of the Afro- and Euro-American dialects; (4) the strategies available for Afro-American participation in institutional discourse; (5) the contribution, realized and potential, of Afro-American writers to the American cultural language; (6) the nature of the "legitimate universal"; and (7) the development of "meta-" perspectives incorporating the full vocabulary/dialog/dialect/discourse/etc. process and ultimately leading to an increased sense of the limitations of *all* idealizations of experience. A brief overview of several cases involving these issues provides some indication of potential directions for future genealogical research.

Inquiries into the generation of Afro-American vocabularies reflecting the "rude memory of conflicts" will inevitably be concerned with what Robert B. Stepto calls "pregeneric" sources, texts not consciously taking form from the cultural language institutionalized in literary genres.[45] Oral histories, folk traditions, diaries, and some slave narratives provide the most direct possible access to "pure" vocabularies, in part because many such sources were never intended for any audience outside the wild zone. The preservation and/or recovery of such sources, however, is of crucial importance to pluralistic genealogy. In addition to expanding the range of vocabularies available to the cultural language, such sources check against solipsism in critics who may unconsciously base their theoretical erudition solely on generic texts constructed with conscious reference to the dominant cultural language. Stepto's *From Behind the Veil* and Zora Neale Hurston's *Mules and Men* exemplify different approaches to the use of pregeneric materials to assure the accountability to experience of erudite discourse concerning the shape of the Afro-American dialect.

The shaping of individual vocabulary, of course, is not simply a historical problem. Both Ralph Ellison's vision of "hibernation" and James Baldwin's of "excavation" emphasize the need for a return to "pregeneric" apprehension of individual experience, including an awareness of the ways in which experience is conditioned by cul-

tural solipsism. Understanding the impact of the solipsism is a necessary prerequisite to a deeper comprehension of "pure" individual
experience. To the extent that the individual succeeds in his or her
excavation, that person will have increased access to the internal wild
zone, which will no longer be veiled by the solipsistic language. This
in turn allows the individual to generate a truly integral vocabulary.
Numerous Afro-American texts portray this process of excavation.
One of the most explicit is Baldwin's *Go Tell It On the Mountain*;
"The Threshing Floor" section portrays John Grimes' repudiation of a
sequence of internalized repressive images, and his subsequent attempt
to generate a vocabulary expressing his experience in the silence of
the wild zone. Because John's new vocabulary incorporates elements
and images derived from the sufferings of the saints, his excavation
assumes a second function as part of a dialog leading to a pluralistic
Afro-American dialect.

The internal complexity of the existing dialect, which, as noted
in Section III, combines elements of solipsistic repression and pluralistic
derivation, is itself a major conceern of genealogical research. Countee
Cullen's "Heritage" presents a classic confrontation with one aspect
of the dialect; his awareness of the repressive solipsistic dialect that
declares Africa a savage paradise conflicts with his desire for an integrity that includes the wild zone he associates with his body and
his stolen racial past. The culminating image of the black Jesus can
be viewed as an attempt to infuse his experience of repressed rage
into the passive dialect. Reflecting clearly the conflict between vocabulary and the repressive elements of dialect, Hurston's *Their Eyes
Were Watching God* demonstrates the way in which Janie is forced to
act in accord with a black woman's dialect derived from her grandmother's experience. Given the complex repressions embedded in the
Afro-American dialects as they are experienced in a solipsistic culture,
it is hardly surprising to find works such as Sterling Brown's "Ma
Rainey," Audre Lorde's "Need: A Choral of Black Women's Voices,"
and Langston Hughes's "The Negro Speaks of Rivers" that attempt
to portray or involve the reader actively in a dialog leading to a pluralistic dialect.

Research such as Stepto's *From Behind the Veil* and Amiri Baraka's

Blues People which clarifies the integrity of the Afro-American dialect greatly facilitates the comparative study of group dialects necessary for developing a sense of a truly pluralistic language. Similarly, works on American Literature such as Pearce's *The Continuity of American Poetry* or Lewis's *The American Adam* which contribute to cultural solipsism when presented *as* that language are in fact extremely insightful analyses of the Euro-American male dialect. Once these dialects are recognized as dialects, the genealogical critic can contribute to the pluralistic discourse by comparing the assumptions of two dialects regarding a given process or relationship. The Euro-American male modernist dialect, for example, typically views performance as, to quote Richard Poirier, "an exercise of power," an assertion of the individual vocabulary fixed in a text.[46] When most effectively realized, this performance style results in a profound reevaluation of vocabulary by individuals in the audience. In contrast, the Afro-American dialect typically interprets performance in relation to the call-and-response dynamic. Rather than asserting his or her power, the performer employing this dialect solicits audience affirmation of shared experience, thereby acknowledging the integrity of the dialect. Such an understanding of the conflicting premises of the dialects helps to explain the comparatively high value placed on shocking or original imagery in Euro-American modernism, and the emphasis on what Stephen Henderson calls the "mascon" image in Afro-American poetry.[47] This in turn helps clarify the frequently unarticulated premises used in determining the institutional literary canon, which normally reflects the assumptions of a single dialect. Similar comparative studies can be made to clarify tensions involving differing Afro-American dialects. Alice Walker's *In Search of Our Mother's Gardens,* for example, insists on the integrity of the dialect of black women against cultural solipsism of both Euro- and Afro-American males. Pat Parker's *Movement in Black* in turn asserts a lesbian dialect within that of Afro-American women. In each case, comparative studies based on in-depth dialect analyses can be employed to widen the base of experience involved in social discourse.

The assertion of muted-group dialects involves confrontation with institutional forces that create certain responses which, viewed only in relation to the pluralistic ideal, appear to embody a solipsism paralleling that of the dominant group. The dialect of the "Black Arts Movement," for example, appears to deny the integrity of groups or individuals ranging from the Euro-American oppressors to "integrationists" such as Ralph Ellison to the many Afro-American women who refuse to accept the "integrity" of black manhood. Seen in relation to the dominant cultural solipsism, however, the Black Arts Movement asserts a racial integrity in areas of discourse previously accessible only to those Afro-Americans employing the dominant language. Establishing an inflexible dialect, the Movement sought to avoid the potentially divisive effects of vocabularies influenced by solipsistic repression, preferring instead to attack the source of the cultural solipsism by forcibly demanding entrance into discourse. If successful, such strategies alter the cultural language, which in turn decreases the power of the repressive forces. Ultimately this should enable the formation of pluralistic dialects. By fixing a form relatively free from the most obvious racist repressions, "simplistic" texts such as some of Baraka's black nationalist poems can provide an image (though, given their solipsistic tendencies, not the reality) of a pluralistic dialect; this in turn ideally inspires new efforts to counteract the prevailing solipsism. A genealogical analysis of the Black Arts Movement, therefore (or of structurally similar movements such as the Southern Agrarian Movement) would consider its impact on both individual vocabulary and on institutional discourse. The militant assertion of dialect favored by the Black Arts Movement can be seen as one manifestation of the "protest" tradition concerned primarily with the oppressive mechanisms expressed by the right-hand side of the theoretical model, a tradition that includes such texts as David Walker's *Appeal,* Frederick Douglass's *Narrative,* Claude McKay's "If We Must Die," and Nathan Heard's *House of Slammers.* One important current in this protest tradition consists of passing narratives such as James Weldon Johnson's *Autobiography of an Ex-Coloured Man* and Nella Larsen's *Passing,* which focus on the inability of the solipsistic cultural language to articulate the wild zone of even the most thoroughly assimilated and repressed Afro-Americans.

Paradoxically, the complex psychological processes required of

Johnson's and Larsen's characters as they attempt to pass from muted to dominant group resemble those of the trickster figures who exemplify the primary alternative to the protest strategy. The genealogical critic approaching either strategy, therefore, should remain aware that differences in immediate emphasis may veil a shared dialect based on common experience. Since effective masking requires apparent acceptance of the dominant-group language, including those aspects of the language that prescribe a particular role for the invisible individual or group, a "masked" text will almost always appear superficially more repressed than a protest text. Nevertheless, by speaking in the voice expected by dominant-group readers or critics, an Afro-American writer may attain a hearing for subversive messages embedded beneath the conventional surface. Charles Chesnutt's manipulation of Plantation Tradition stereotypes in *The Conjure Woman* and Ishmael Reed's use of metafictional techniques in *Mumbo Jumbo* serve to advance Afro-American perceptions in generally indifferent or hostile areas of discourse. Just as the militant strategy risks perpetuating a reactive solipsism, this strategy risks inadvertently reinforcing the solipsistic language.

While the genealogical critic should recognize the risks involved with both the protest and masking strategies, he or she should also acknowledge their impact on the American cultural language. Berndt Ostendorf's exploration of the psychological implications of Euro-American parodies of Afro-American culture and Charles Sanders' demonstration of the profound influence of the minstrel shows on the structure of T. S. Eliot's *The Waste Land* suggest the importance of the largely ignored question of Afro-American influence on Euro-American discourse.[48] Most approaches to the topic originating in the protest tradition concentrate on the nature of the Euro-American distortions of Afro-American experience. While this analysis of the solipsistic context remains indispensable as a base for further inquiry, a complementary focus on the Afro-American contribution to pluralistic discourse is necessary to the ideal focus of genealogical double vision. In fact, Afro-American writers have provided some of the most powerful images of the pluralistic ideal, providing an obvious focus for future inquiry. Du Bois' *The Souls of Black Folk* envisions

and attempts to create an ideal pluralistic language recognizing the
integrity of the sorrow songs alongside that of the Euro-American
poetic tradition. Similarly, Toni Morrison's *Song of Solomon* treats
the integrity of the Afro-American dialect as a given and asserts its
place in the cultural language without apology, creating a rich pluralistic language shaped by Greek and African, as well as Euro-, Afro-
and Native American, experiences.

Genealogical research concerning the place of the universal in the
Afro-American literary tradition could begin with an examination of
the relationship of myth to more concrete experience. The impact
of myth on individual consciousness (Ralph Kabnis in *Cane*); the relation of myth to folklore and popular culture (Sterling Brown's
"The Odyssey of Big Boy," "The Ride of Wild Bill," and "Cabaret");
the solipsistic distortion of myth (Gwendolyn Brook's "Sermons on
the Warpland"); the generation of counter-mythologies (Audre Lorde's
The Black Unicorn); and the attempts to expand the experiential
base of the dialectical process (Melvin Tolson's *Harlem Gallery,* and
Robert Hayden's religious poetry) are among the areas of research
potentially contributing to the understanding of the legitimate universal. Ultimately, these researches should contribute to the reevaluation of expressions of the universal such as Joseph Campbell's "monomyth" which, despite its attempt to incorporate extremely diverse
cultural languages, in fact imposes a male dialect on female experience, as works such as *Their Eyes Were Watching God* and *The Color
Purple* imply.[49] The inherent danger of focusing on the higher levels
of the pluralistic process lies in potential alienation from the integrity
of individual experience. Inadvertent solipsism can insinuate itself
into cross-cultural discourse in particularly elusive ways, as Stanley
Diamond demonstrates in his generative genealogical work *In Search
of the Primitive.*[50] As with research into dialects, the genealogical
critic concerned with mythology should take special pains to check
all "erudite" analyses against the pregeneric experiences they theoretically explain.

Finally, genealogical research concerns itself with apprehending
the full complexity of the web of patterns, drawing freely on useful
models without theoretical constraint. Extending the principle of

double vision, genealogical "meta-vision" ultimately attempts to recognize the integrity of the literary experience and to contribute to pluralistic dialog and discourse, referring each perception to as many other experiences as possible. While perhaps not identical, the personal and the political, from this perspective, engage in a complex call-and-response. On a basic level, this essay is itself a response to the pluralistic call of texts such as Ellison's *Invisible Man,* Hurston's *Their Eyes Were Watching God,* David Bradley's *The Chaneysville Incident,* and Brown's "Ma Rainey," which themselves incorporate models of the call-and-response between "the rude memories of struggle" and their erudite expression, creating and critiquing the genealogies I have attempted to conjoin. Reflecting the richness and multivalent ambiguity of a complex experience shaped by both pluralistic idealism and solipsistic oppression, the vocabularies, dialects, and languages of Afro-American literature provide a series of democratic vistas on a blackness as integral and extensive as the whiteness of Melville's whale.

NOTES

I wish to acknowledge the support for this essay provided by a 1982 National Endowment for the Humanties Summer Stipend and by a 1983 award from the University of Wisconsin-Madison Graduate School Research Committee. I would also like to acknowledge the vital role which a 1981 National Endowment for the Humanities Summer Seminar at Yale University directed by Robert B. Stepto played in the development of the ideas in this essay and to acknowledge the invaluable criticisms provided by students in my classes at the University of Mississippi from 1979 to 1983.

1.   "Democratic Vistas," in *Whitman: Poetry and Prose,* ed. Justin Kaplan (New York: The Library of America, 1982), p. 955.

2.   *Notes of a Native Son* (New York: Bantam Books, 1964), p. 6.

3.   *Power/Knowledge: Selected Interviews and Other Writings* (New York: Pantheon Books, 1980), p. 83.

4.   The most thorough investigation of the origins of the American insistence on organic aesthetics remains F. O. Matthiessen's chapter on "The Organic Principle" in *American Renaissance: Art and Expression in the Age of Emerson and Whitman* (New York: Oxford University Press, 1941), pp. 133-

175. Particularly useful investigations of particular aspects of the issue include
Sacvan Bercovitch's chapter on "The Myth of America" in *The Puritan Origins
of the American Self* (New Haven, Connecticut: Yale University Press, 1975),
pp. 136-186, and R. W. B. Lewis's "Prologue: The Myth and the Dialogue" and
"The Case Against the Past" in *The American Adam: Innocence, Tragedy, and
Tradition in the Nineteenth Century* (Chicago: University of Chicago Press,
1955), pp. 1-27.   William Carlos Williams' *In the American Grain* (New York:
New Directions, 1956) is perhaps the most direct restatement of the sensibility
of "Democratic Vistas" to appear in the twentieth century.

5.   Benjamin Banneker, "Letter to Thomas Jefferson," in *Black Writers
of America,* ed. Richard Barksdale and Keneth Kinnamon (New York: Macmillan, 1972), pp. 50-52.

6.   Frederick Douglass, "Oration, Delivered in Corinthian Hall, Rochester, July 5, 1852," in *Black Writers of America,* pp. 89-101.

7.   The most extreme cases of this tendency can be seen in the work of
critics who predicate their theories entirely on Euro- and phallo-centric sen-
sibilities, as Harold Bloom does in *The Anxiety of Influence: A Theory of Poetry* (New York: Oxford University Press, 1973).   Jonathan Culler's chapter
"Reading as a Woman," in *On Deconstruction: Theory and Criticism after
Structuralism* (Ithaca, New York: Cornell University Press, 1982), pp. 43-64,
makes an intelligent and suggestive attempt to demonstrate the underlying
relevance of recent theory to previously excluded groups.   Despite his emphasis
on the deconstruction of hierarchies, however, Culler considers *no* Afro-American texts or writers, thereby perpetuating the illusion that an adequate theoretical approach can be derived solely from a Euro-American data base.   In
fact, critics such as Henry Louis Gates, Jr., in "The 'Blackness of Blackness':
A Critique of the Sign and Signifying Monkey," *Critical Inquiry,* 9 (1983), 685-
723, and Robert Stepto, in *From Behind the Veil: A Study of Afro-American
Narrative* (Urbana: University of Illinois Press, 1979) have demonstrated the
real potential for the application of aspects of contemporary theory to the
criticism of Afro-American literature.   Nonetheless, the pressure to "authenticate" (to use Stepto's term) all critical positions by employing the language of
avant-garde discourse strikes me as a manifestation of what I shall discuss below
as "cultural solipsism."   It seems to me particularly important that critics involved with Afro-American literature resist this pressure or risk contributing to
the effective silencing of their own voices.   Gates and Stepto demonstrate one
way of checking the urge for authentication by emphasizing those elements
of theory clearly anticipated by the Afro-American folk tradition.

8.   "Feminist Criticism in the Wilderness," in *Writing and Sexual Difference,* ed. Elizabeth Abel (Chicago: University of Chicago Press, 1982), pp.
9-35.   Feminist theorists are inevitably concerned with many of the same issues
that concern those working in the Afro-American tradition.   At present a deep
division remains between Afro-American and feminist theory, an unfortunate

situation that in effect forces each group to recapitulate the entire process of the other even when useful formulations with at least some relevance are already available. Employing conceptual models such as Showalter's provides one way of moving beyond the situation in which Afro-Americanists perceive feminists as part of the Euro-American cultural circle and feminists, remembering the over-emphasis on black "manhood" during the 1960s and early 1970s, perceive Afro-Americanists as essentially male.

9. "Feminist Criticism in the Wilderness," p. 30. The idea of a muted group language has been discussed at length in numerous places. Two of the most powerful of these discussions are Amiri Baraka's essay "Expressive Language," in *Home: Social Essays* (New York: Morrow, 1966), pp. 166-172, and Sheila Rowbotham's chapter "Through the Looking Glass," in *Woman's Consciousness, Man's World* (New York: Pelican, 1973), pp. 26-46, in which she discusses the "underground language of people who have no power to define and determine themselves" (p. 32).

10. See Mary Daly's discussion of the techniques of "trivialization," "particularization," "spiritualization," and "universalization" used by dominant groups to dismiss muted-group expressions in *Beyond God the Father: Toward a Philosophy of Women's Liberation* (Boston: Beacon Press, 1973), pp. 4-6.

11. See Susan H. Leger's "The Strange Impossibility of Feminist Criticism," *Massachusetts Review*, 24 (1983), 330-336, which expresses many of the reservations I feel concerning the expression of "alternative" perspectives in the terminology of the mainstream. Similarly, Daly refuses to orient her discussion explicitly in regard to the phallocentric theological tradition.

12. *Invisible Man* (New York: Random House, 1952), p. 328.

13. See the recent debate on the issue of theory and belief that began with Steven Knapp and Walter Benn Michaels' essay "Against Theory," *Critical Inquiry*, 8 (1982), 725-789. Although I am sympathetic with Knapp and Michaels' basic perspective on recent developments in critical theory, it seems to me that they have accepted the definition of theory proposed by the dominant culture and that the current debate is concerned primarily with new attempts to fix a definition of theory that will once more be used to reinforce the interests of the dominant group in establishing the premises for academic discourse. It bears noting that eight of the nine participants in the *Critical Inquiry* exchange are male and none asserts the relevance of any critical perspective originating outside the Euro-American male academic community.

14. See Daly, pp. 4-6.

15. Among the "classic" studies that omit all mention of Afro-American writers are Lewis's *The American Adam*, Pearce's *The Continuity of American Poetry* (Princeton, New Jersey: Princeton University Press, 1961), Marx's *The Machine in the Garden* (New York: Oxford University Press, 1964), Chase's *The American Novel and Its Tradition* (Garden City, New York: Doubleday/Anchor, 1957), and James E. Miller's *The American Quest for a Supreme Fiction*

(Chicago: University of Chicago Press, 1979). To note only two of the important omissions such a solipsistic focus involves, it seems clear that W. E. B. Du Bois and Charles Chesnutt are both actively concerned with the technological developments that concern Marx while Melvin B. Tolson clearly participates in the Whitman tradition discussed by both Pearce and Miller. Among the central Afro-American responses to the solipsism of this tradition are Sterling Brown's *Negro Poetry and Drama* (Washington, D. C.: Associates in Negro Folk Education, 1937); Larry Neal's "The Black Arts Movement," in *The Black Aesthetic* (Garden City, New York: Doubleday/Anchor, 1972), pp. 257-274; Stepto's *From Behind the Veil*; and Barabara Smith's *Toward a Black Feminist Criticism* (Trumansburg, New York: Out & Out Books, 1977).

16.   *Blackness and the Adventure of Western Culture* (Chicago: Third World Press, 1972), p. 112. Significantly, Kent's definition is derived from his experience of the work of a woman, Gwendolyn Brooks.

17.   This ideal is, of course, impossible to realize fully, just as it is impossible to recognize the full range of beliefs conditioning one's own statements. Nonetheless, it seems useful to attempt to realize the ideal if for no other reason than to encourage responses that bring unrecognized beliefs to light.

18.   For an excellent discussion of the utility and limitations of the concept of entropy as a cultural metaphor see Thomas Schaub's *Pynchon: The Voice of Ambiguity* (Urbana: University of Illinois Press, 1981), pp. 5-31.

19.   It seems clear that in some cases the vocabulary of the wild zone will involve a deeply felt silence. As Foucault observes in *The History of Sexuality* (New York: Vintage Books, 1978), p. 23, forced articulation can serve to subject wild-zone experiences to the control of the dominant language: "The obligation to confess is now relayed through so many different points, is so deeply ingrained in us, that we no longer perceive it as the effect of a power that constrains us."

20.   I am aware of a tendency to perpetuate hierarchical perceptions in some of the language used in this essay. All such implications are unintentional, reflections of my inevitable participation in the solipsism of the Euro-American male tradition that has conditioned my perceptions.

21.   Noam Chomsky, *Language and Responsibility* (New York: Pantheon Books, 1979), p. 54.

22.   *Mind and Nature: A Necessary Unity* (New York: Bantam Books, 1979). Bateson's chapter "From Classification to Process" provides (on pp. 214-218) the underlying structure of the model presented in this essay.

23.   For a suggestive discussion of the actual mechanics of the dialog process see Erving Goffman's *The Presentation of Self in Everyday Life* (Garden City, New York: Doubleday, 1959).

24.   *Language and Responsibility*, p. 55.

25.   In *Gravity's Rainbow* (New York: Viking, 1973), Pynchon describes

the communication between Enzian's parents, one black and one white, as follows: "By the time he left, they had learned each other's names and a few words in the respective languages — afraid, happy, sleep, love, . . . the beginnings of a new tongue, a pidgin which they were perhaps the only two speakers of in the world" (p. 351).

26.   The image of the common language which is both accessible and shared derives from the title of Adrienne Rich's *The Dream of a Common Language* (New York: Norton, 1977).   For a complex discussion of the relationship between this ideal language, which in terms of my model would probably be referred to as a dialect, and the solipsistic cultural context, see Rich's essays "Women and Honor: Some Notes on Lying" and "Disloyal to Civilization: Feminism, Racism, Gynephobia," in *On Lies, Secrets, and Silence* (New York: Norton, 1979).

27.   For discussions of the actual mechanics of the discourse process, see Richard Sennett's *The Uses of Disorder: Personal Identity and City Life* (New York: Vintage: 1970) and Murray Edelman's *Politics as Symbolic Action* (New York: Academic Press, 1971).

28.   In actuality, a fourth loop should be extended to reflect the tendency of individuals to articulate their experiences in terms of the vocabulary they have generated to articulate previous experience.   Since in ideal terms, however, no such preconditioning should exist, I have omitted the loop from this diagram to clarify the dynamics under discussion.

29.   *Reflections on Language* (New York: Pantheon Books, 1975), p. 29.

30.   I find this aspect of the ideal model the most difficult to conceive and to articulate, in part because I think very little of the necessary process of developing a conception of the legitimate universal has actually been carried out.   My extremely tentative conception of the legitimate universal derives primarily from physiologically oriented studies such as Chomsky's *Reflections on Language* and Julian Jayne's *The Origins of Consciousness in the Breakdown of the Bicameral Mind.*   Approaches reflecting psychology and comparative mythology seem to me potentially useful, although to date they seem deeply limited by various solipsistic biases.   Among the works that have influenced my thought on the subject are C. G. Jung's *Two Essays on Analytical Psychology* (Princeton, New Jersey: Princeton University Press, 1966), which includes his discussion of the "The Archetypes of the Collective Unconscious," pp. 90-113; Bruno Bettelheim's *The Uses of Enchantment: The Meaning and Importance of Fairy Tales* (New York: Knopf, 1976); and Joseph Campbell's *Hero With a Thousand Faces* (New York and Cleveland: World, 1956).

31.   It is important to remember that the elevated dialect may itself have been derived in a roughly pluralistic manner within the dominant group.   Frequently this derivation is used as evidence that the solipsistic language or universal is itself pluralistic in derivation.

32.   The following discussion of the oppressive and repressive aspects of cultural solipsism obviously draws heavily on the Marxist conceptions of ideology and, more specifically, of the relationship between superstructure and base.   Although I disagree with the author's assertion that Marxist criticism provides a critical language incorporating all other dialects, Terry Eagleton's *Literary Theory: An Introduction* (Minneapolis: University of Minnesota Press, 1983) provides an intelligent overview of the ways in which cultural solipsism operates in contemporary literary culture.   Nonetheless, I hesitate to authenticate my perceptions through the use of a Marxist dialect for essentially the same reasons I hesitate to authenticate them through use of a deconstructionist dialect.   A good deal of Marxist literary discourse, as Eagleton recognizes, attempts to simplify the literary experience by establishing a fixed form for the evaluation of diverse textual experiences.   Some major Marxist critics, most notably Bertolt Brecht, in his essay "Against Georg Lukacs," *New Left Review,* No. 84 (1974), pp. 39-53, present strong cases for a much more flexible, and at least potentially pluralistic, Marxist aesthetic.

33.   This decision to acknowledge the reality of the experience of others is by no means necessary. It does, however, seem to me necessary to maintaining social and psychological coherence.   See Hazel E. Barnes' *Humanistic Existentialism: The Literature of Possibility* (Lincoln: University of Nebraska Press, 1959) for what I find to be the best overview of the extremely complex philosophical issues involved in making such a decision.

34.   See Berndt Ostendorf's *Black Literature in White America* (Totowa, New Jersey: Barnes and Noble, 1982) for a discussion of the psychology involved in such muted-group presence.   Two classic works on the nature of the stereotypes projected on Afro-Americans by the dominant culture are Sterling Brown's *The Negro in American Fiction* (New York: Atheneum, 1969) and Jean Fagan Yellin's *The Intricate Knot: Black Figures in American Literature, 1776-1863* (New York: New York University Press, 1972).

35.   *The Origins of Totalitarianism* (New York: Harcourt Brace Jovanovich, 1973), p. 310.   For an Afro-American analog to Arendt's perceptions, see Malcolm X's discussion of the destruction of the African and Afro-American sense of "common interest" in *The Autobiography of Malcolm X* (New York: Grove Press, 1965), pp. 174-178.

36.   *Language and Responsibility*, pp. 38-39.   For a more extensive discussion of the mechanisms of control employed in a variety of political-economic systems, see Charles Lindblom's *Politics and Markets: The World's Political-Economic System* (New York: Basic Books, 1977).

37.   *Origins of Totalitarianism*, p. 312.

38.   Wright describes the repressive experience as follows: "As I talked I felt that I was acting out a dream. I did not want to lie, yet I had to lie to conceal what I felt. A white censor was standing over me and, like dreams forming

a curtain for the safety of sleep, so did my lies form a screen of safety for my living moments" (*Black Boy* [1945; rpt. New York: Harper and Row, 1966], p. 280).

39.   For a powerful development of this concept, see Clay's speech in the second act of Amiri Baraka's *Dutchman* (New York: Morrow, 1964), p. 36, which portrays murder as the inevitable result of Afro-American acceptance of the Euro-American language.

40.   *The Fire Next Time* (New York: Dell, 1963), p. 129.

41.   Christopher Alexander, Sara Ishikawa, Murray Silverstein, et al., *A Pattern Language: Towns, Buildings, Construction* (New York: (Oxford University Press, 1977), p. xiii.

42.   It should additionally be noted that any given text may be viewed both as a manifestation of or a confrontation with a specific problem.

43.   Robert Hemenway describes one process for "checking" erudite perceptions in his excellent essay on the relationship of folklore to the criticism of Afro-American literature "Are You a Flying Lark or a Setting Dove?" in *Afro-American Literature: The Reconstruction of Instruction,* ed. Dexter Fisher and Robert B. Stepto (New York: Modern Language Association, 1978), pp. 122-131.

44.   *The Soul of Black Folk* (1903; rpt. Greenwich, Connecticut: Fawcett, 1961), pp. 16-17.

45.   *From Behind the Veil,* pp. ix, 3-31.

46.   *The Performing Self* (New York: Oxford University Press, 1971), pp. 45-48.

47.   *Understanding the New Black Poetry* (New York: Morrow, 1973), pp. 3-42.

48.   See Ostendorf's discussion of the minstrel show in *Black Literature in White America* and Charles Sanders' "*The Waste Land*: The Last Minstrel Show?" *Journal of Modern Literature,* 8 (1980), 23-38.

49.   My awareness of the phallocentric bias of Campbell's monomyth and, specifically, of the importance of Hurston's and Walker's works in recognizing that bias has been greatly increased by Malin Walther, an undergraduate student at the University of Wisconsin — Madison.

50.   *In Search of the Primitive: A Critique of Civilization* (New Brunswick, New Jersey: Transaction Books, 1974).

History-Making Literature

by

John M. Reilly

I.

It has been the fate of the Afro-American writer to be preoccupied
with setting history straight. Slavery and racism, enforcing a sense
that collective experience is the result of willful actions by others,
have burdened writers, much as other Blacks, with the dreadful thought
that they are creatures of history whose freedom to interpret reality
is as questionable as their chance of shaping it.[1] Other things occur
in such early Afro-American texts as the slave narratives, but valida-
tion of the writer's authority and verification of the details within

his or her narration by repetition and corroborative devices was for
many prose writers the most apparent technique of their work, because definition of Afro-American humanity in the records of the
American nation was the justification of literature. Moreover, as
Darwin Turner has observed, the need to satisfy a predominantly
white audience that for its own reasons demanded immediate histor-
icity continued until nearly the present day to restrict writers to
"self-consciously validated re-creations of Black history,"[2] re-creations meant to achieve their effect by describing the condition of a
people objectified by history.

Inevitably literature written amidst oppressive social conditions
and aiming to be read by an audience disposed to doubt its authenticity assumed a documentary mode. Barbara Foley has argued that
the need for Black literature to justify its historical vision has had
significant literary results: "Many writers have converted this negative
requirement into a postitive asset, producing nonfictional works that
interpret American reality with passion and controlled artistry." What
is more, Foley continues, the power and verisimilitude evident in the
nonfiction carries over into the works of Afro-American authors who
have used the materials of Black experience in fiction, either by imitating reality in presenting events and characters potentially occurring in
the historical world, or by imitating a type of text — such as the
journal, chronicle, or biography — normally accepted as the model
of a "true" report.[3] No question about it, the Afro-American writer
has made the most of the rhetorical situation, and, in the process,
insinuated by the evidence of textual invention a suggestion that the
writer, at least, is more than the creature of history.

Despite our eager recognition of the blues-like accomplishment in
making the best of a situation, acknowledging the creative energy involved leaves unanswered the question that has directed the course
of Afro-American writing like fate. What is the relationship between
history and literature to be? Is history a completed sequence of objective events, while a text that refers to history may argue that when
those events took place Blacks were also present? The clear implication of documentary writing and the rhetorical devices of authentication would seem to be that the writers employing these methods prob-

ably perceive history as distinct from literature, having an existence prior to the texts designed to verify the appearance of Blacks in history's midst.

Typically, pondering the meaning of history yields a declaration that it is cyclical in nature, evidences failure or fulfillment, displays improvement in the human condition, or some other such ontological description. The patterns devised to give the details of human experience coherence occur in discourse, and one is tempted to say that these patterns are the form given to history by human agency, rather than history itself, until one recalls that nearly all we know of the direction of events derives from discourse piled upon discourse, document upon document, interpretation upon interpretation. Together they comprise a collection of propositions, assertions, and counterarguments that in its enormity makes summation difficult, certitude probably impossible. This shifting and never completed association of inscriptions, arguments, tales, reports, and hearsay is what we know of the past. In practice, then, if not by stipulation, the texts proffering descriptions and explanations of the historical world become the substance of history, much as the theories in scientific discourse designed to explain the natural world become the subject of the investigation and testing that constitutes scientific practice.

It is not necessary to deny the existence of historical data, or to elevate products of thought to an ideal state, in order to accept the ancient notion that history is a branch of literature. There is ample precedence in the writing of the students of historical consciousness for asserting that "history constructs its objects, and that its objects are objects of language, rather than entities of which words are in some way copies."[4] The presumed concreteness of historical representation is a result, says Hayden White, of the fictive capability of the historian:

> Historical documents are not less opaque than the texts studied by the literary critic. . . . In fact, the opaqueness of the world figured in historical documents is, if anything, increased by the production of historical narratives. Each new historical work only adds to the number of possible

texts that have to be interpreted if a full and accurate
picture of a given historical milieu is to be faithfully drawn.
The relationship between the past to be analyzed and historical works produced by analysis of the documents is paradoxical; the more we know about the past, the more difficult it is to generalize about it.[5]

Such self-consciousness about the epistemological operations of historians enables the metahistorian to investigate the presuppositions
that inform the efforts to solve historical problems. It can be equally
helpful to the literary historian.

The idea underlying metahistory that historical representation must
be understood in terms of its own system rather than by its congruence
with the real world has its counterpart in the recognition by literary
critics that fiction creates its own objects. The reality of a novel, poem,
even autobiography exists in a specificity and coherence that are
products of imagination. The cautionary note in this is familiar: the
work of literature must not be confused with the reality either of
the exterior world or of the author, for to do so is to deny the text
its epistemological status, its special function as an instrument of
literary cognition. Still, there are times when the qualities of specific
works of literature induce, if not neglect of the admonition to dis-
tinguish the structures of a text from the materials appropriated to its
purposes, then relegation of literariness to a secondary place reserved
for the discussion of literary devices.

Study of the historicism of Afro-American literature is a prominent
example of subordination of the text to other considerations. The
weight of collective experience that has dominated the consciousness
of Black writers has proved especially determining in the intellect of
those who have attempted an Afro-American literary history. Judicious
appraisals and sensitive remarks certainly can be found in the essays
and books that attempt comprehensive treatment of Afro-American
writing, but sophisticated examples of *literary* history are rare, first
of all because the surveys ordinarily are conceived almost entirely in
reference to other sorts of schemes than literary. Hugh M. Gloster's
Negro Voices in American Fiction (Chapel Hill: University of North

Carolina Press, 1948) seems an obvious illustration in its reduction of literary works to elementary sociological remarks, an activity that continues, especially in classrooms, to represent itself as literary study even now. Much more able and valuable treatments of Afro-American literature, however, are in their own ways excursions into complementary modes of survey rather than histories of texts; thus, Vernon Loggins' *The Negro Author: His Development in America* (New York: Columbia University Press, 1931), for all of its valuable detail on eighteenth and nineteenth century authors and their chief works, is controlled by the search for, and apology for the absence of, deliberate Black art that will match the achievements of folk literature; and despite the excellence of insight in Carl Milton Hughes' *The Negro Novelist: A Discussion of the Writings of American Negro Novelists, 1940-1950* (New York: Citadel, 1953), pattern cannot surface from beneath the details of reception and context. A prominent feature of the essay in Afro-American literary history is what Houston Baker terms the conative mode — a critic's attempt to will into being successful literature.[6] Benjamin Brawley, working from the "observation," in *The Negro Genius,* that "the temperament of the American Negro is primarily lyrical, imaginative, subjective; and his genius has most frequently sought expression in some one of the arts,"[7] provides an example of the conative mode founded on a premise that simply evades historiographical problems by substituting race for history. Despite other variety, the most prevalent assumption among those who think about Afro-American literary history — whether in articles, books, or classroom presentations — is that the success of literature can be discerned in its utility as social documentation, an assumption to which is sometimes joined severe judgment of works composed, it is presumed, before Afro-American authors had the option to choose art over combative writing. In other words, works of literature are dissolved into their referents.

The second consequence of working with texts that display so openly their authors' sense of the burden of collective experience is the belief among critics of those texts that history — so evidently the property of others beyond literature — shows itself to be unconditionally objective. Since the presence of historical reference has made the design of inquiry seem so self-evident, Afro-American literary historians have tended not to ask questions about their own practice, even when it tends to contradict equally valued principles of practical criticism, such as the idea that literature cannot simply be equated with alternate realities; and the discipline has been the poorer for it. In its state of innocent positivism Afro-American literary history will not acknowledge its own nature as fictive creation, like other sorts of history. Nor, oblivious to its own possibilities, can it properly state the *literary* issues that must be considered in regard to historically preoccupied Afro-American writing. We must get beneath the suppositions that have sustained the practice of literary history for the sake of the discipline and to examine one of its potentially most intriguing subjects — the way that Afro-American authors have sought not so much to reflect or report, as to *make* history.

Let it be clear that an end to methodological innocence is not to be attained by denying either the relevance of Afro-American literature to the lives of its readers or to the role it plays in overcoming racism. Moreover, literature cannot be removed from the arena of history. If the Scylla of literary history is a too simple equation of a text with events and things outside of it, then the Charybdis would be an over-correction of the simple identification by advancing a proposition that literature exists independently of other manifestations of culture and historical experience. The complex forms of literature are conceived and sustained linguistically like all other instances of discourse. Literary texts, thus, have no particularly privileged significance due either to the processes by which they originate or to the means by which they communicate. The models of reality expressed in the socially created medium of language show no inherent difference because they are fictional or nonfictional, formulated as metaphor or as declaration. The models are conceived and conveyed in language, with literature occupying its place on the linguistic continuum as one among other sub-systems. Moreover, communication by a literary text occurs as a transaction with an audience that, so to speak, completes the text by assimilating its signs and patterns through the grid of shared linguistic skills and cultural fields; thus, literature by its very nature coexists with other instances of social life as part of the institution of language within broader social life.

It follows, of course, that history, so far as its interpretation and communication are concerned, also originates in language and offers its descriptive and documentary texts to reception by an audience in the same way that literature does. The relationship between the two, then, consists in the exchange of patterns of linguistically shaped thought, an exchange that proceeds through reinforcement of historical models, by their reconception in new texts, and by the attempt to substitute new categories and narratives for old.

To avoid the errors in assumption that can beset the Afro-American literary historian, inquiries must be cast in a way that preserves a sense of that exchange, so much the more so when the focus is upon the preoccupation with history itself in literature. Investigation aimed at discovering the historical accuracy of a literary work will not do, except as an observation of documentary intent, because it disregards the linguistic character of the text; and single-minded concentration upon the linguistic structures threatens in its own way to misrepresent the text by desocializing it. If the relational and generative quality of literature is not to be dismissed, works of literature must be seen as their writers' efforts to appropriate the world to language and mind, just as technology and social organization represent the effort to appropriate the world physically. "Art," writes Robert Weimann,

> was, and is, part of the more comprehensive dialectic by which the appropriation of objectivity and realization of subjectivity are mutually intertwined. . . . In the process of appropriation of the natural means and the social forms of human existence, labor and art and consciousness all interact. They are reflections of, and factors in, the never-ending endeavor of men to understand and control (and to affect by playing, and making images of) the destiny of their social existence.[8]

Through investigation of the forms of writing that appropriate the world, we enter not only a narrative, but also, however dimly, we gain access to the consciousness of writers and their audiences. The observable successes and failures of texts in their dynamic play show us the writers in history attempting to make it subject to human thought and, therefore, will. Obviously enactment of literary texts understood in this way has great importance for Afro-American literary history, for it establishes literature as part of the mass movement Richard Wright described in *12 Million Black Voices* as "moving into the sphere of conscious history."[9]

Illustration of appropriation of the world to a writer's subjective conception of history naturally appears with the beginnings of Afro-American prose literature, *A Narrative of the Uncommon Sufferings and Surprising Deliverance of Briton Hammon . . .* (Boston, 1760). Into the brief length of his narrative Hammon crowds an account of a near shipwreck, captivity among hostile Indians, jail in Havana, and enforced service aboard three different ships. An introductory note to the reader says that it is apt for one in Hammon's enslaved condition to relate only matters of fact as they occur to his mind. Certainly brevity would seem to permit little more than matter of fact, but the facts emerge from memory in a mind in which the relation of events forms the pattern of God's Providence preserving Hammon through twelve years of suffering and, at last, arranging for him to find his original master and return from the Indies to New England. The matters of fact occurring in Hammon's mind are emplotted under the aspect of American Colonial values according to which wordly trials betoken the power of a transcendent deity to direct lowly human life. Apparently whenever recorders of fact seek to render their relationships, the writing becomes imaginative, the experience nearly, if not completely, literary.

Reading Hammon's brief narrative also suggests the procedure for literary historical investigation. The work is culturally determined, but that is a conclusion reached through observation of the structures of the text — for example, the episodic movement in time/space of the natural world enclosed by the eternally fixed benevolence of God. It is not a judgment to be made from the distance of study in "historical backgrounds" or "ideas in literature." The complex structures of literature, even literature purporting to be nothing other than factual, provide the substance of study and, thus, provoke further investigations.

A subject for further investigation has already been suggested by note of the Afro-American writer's preoccupation with history: How is history mediated in the works of Afro-American literature? A comprehensive answer cannot be expected now, but perhaps I can at least indicate the importance of the inquiry by rehearsing the approaches to conscious history manifest in some historically preoccupied texts.

II.

No literature ever made greater claim to fidelity to fact than did the nineteenth century American slave narratives. Actual life stories and specific information about the conditions slaves suffered were expected to be their first level of popular appeal. A second was probably the adventurous plot of escape. The weight of fact could be counted on to show the necessity to end the dreadful system, but at the same time abolition was argued by subjective evidence emerging from the patterns of fact: a mind judging, a career beginning when the fugitive reached free territory, a human being declaring that regardless of what a reader may have heard about Blacks the way they really are is certified by the existence of the narrative, a work of literature. Though there is a great difference between the narrative of Briton Hammon and a representative nineteenth century slave narrative by, say, Frederick Douglass, there is also evident in the writings of each a common motive in their application of imagination to the facts of their lives — the one discerning the agency of his God to deliver him from suffering, the other calling upon agency presumed to inhere in his fellow man for deliverance from bondage.

In 1845 when Frederick Douglass published the first of the three narratives he was eventually to compose about his life's experiences, perhaps he was as sure as Hammon had been that he had discerned the significant pattern among facts; however, certainty was not to last for Douglass. Neither the legal system nor politics was ever likely to abolish slavery, and popular moral persuasion was an unpredictable force at best. Perhaps, then, violence might be the appropriate means to end slavery, but how might it come about and how might victory for abolition be assured?   If war were too uncertain, then perhaps Blacks should seek to emigrate from America. In those *ante-bellum* days it was impossible to be sure what course of practical action to take or cause to espouse, and imaginative literature embodying the uncertainty of its creators became problematic in its own way.

If writing becomes imaginative when authors render facts into significant relationships, in conditions of uncertainty imaginative narrative will be a hypothesis rather than a declaration, a search for possibility more than an affirmation of discovered truth. While much of Black abolitionist writing partakes of tentativeness when read carefully, the fullest range for hypothesis occurred in fiction and in one outstanding work, *Blake, or the Huts of America* . . . by Martin Robison Delany.[10]   *Blake* is as specifically objective in some ways as are the fugitive slaves' autobiographical narratives. Both the novel and the narratives record circumstances immediately recognizable as characteristic of nineteenth century American slavery, but Delany is free to imagine not only the relationships among events but the events themselves. He, thus, can direct his book from the start to the problem of finding a plausible resolution to slavery.

The direction Delany will take becomes evident early in the story. The slave Henry Holland returns to his master's plantation after a business trip to find that his wife has been sold in his absence. He then announces a position that seems to need no period of preparation before it is stated in all its bluntness, and truth: "'You do your mightiest, Colonel Franks, I'm not your slave, nor never was and you know it!   And but for my wife and her people, I never would have stayed with you till now . . . . but now the tie is broken! I know that the odds are against me, but never mind!'" (p. 19). The reader extracts from Henry's speech the basic contradiction of slavery, a person is at once human and the object of a theory of property. The significance of the exposed contradiction is pointed up by the master, who says of the speech that "'It's rebellion! A plot — this is but the shadow of a cloud that's fast gathering around us!   I see it plainly, I see it!'" (pp. 19-20).

Calling Henry's speech conspiracy and rebellion, the Colonel evidently recalls Vesey, Prosser, and Turner and indicates that this novel will present slavery as caste conflict without the elaboration of argument surrounding the subject in political debate. Equating verbal defiance with physical rebellion the master announces the novelist's contention that servile insurrection is a plausible means of liberation and that words, even this novel, are a consistent part of insurrection.

Though the novel *Blake* is less restricted than autobiographical narratives, it carries to conclusion the logic inherent in the narratives. Delany carefully documents the hardship and brutality of slavery in his fiction just as the fugitive slaves did for their audiences, even to the extent of footnoting passages in imitation of their texts. Similarly, the novel takes pains to strip away the hypocritical doctrine that often justified slavery. "'It is all a matter of self-interest with me,'" says one of the fictional slaveholders, "'and though I am morally opposed to slavery, yet while the thing exists, I may as well profit by it, as others'" (p. 64). Given such views, what is more plausible than rebellion? Certainly not moral persuasion.

The logic of slave narratives is also extended by the career of Henry subsequent to his defiance of Colonel Franks and his flight from the plantation. He embarks upon a dangerous journey, as do the protagonists of all slave narratives, but Henry's journey is not to the freedom promised by arrival in a free state. Instead this *picaro* journeys throughout the South, speaking eloquently of abolition to audiences composed of slaves, the only certain agents of change.

Though the novel is simplified by its author's dropping the political and social arguments on the slavery issue, it does not become unmediated documentary. Nearly everywhere Delany moves Henry in the fictional plot he is welcomed by slaves as if they awaited him and knew his mission beforehand. He carries to the conspirators he recruits a secret he imparts in a whisper. The secret is never revealed to the reader, but it is said to be a principle known to all nature. It cannot be a principle of organization, for Henry tells the slaves that one or two conspirators on each plantation will suffice to spread discontent and plan sabotage. By elimination of alternatives the secret emerges from the text as the ideal of enlightened consciousness, the necessary counterpart to resolution of will and the source of the novelist's imagined history.

As he progresses, Henry assumes many different names representing many different rebellious individuals, and in time he passes to Africa and Cuba too. In Africa and on the middle passage Henry recruits additional conspirators who, together with slaves in America, represent continuity of heritage and experience. This receives additional force from the revelation that the man introduced as Henry Holland and taking on so many different names in his travels truly is Henrico Blacus, a native African in whose career can be seen the symbol of the Black diaspora.

Cuba, where the novel reaches its conclusion, was the object of dreams of North American slaveholders who would extend their empire by annexing the island to the United States, and it is literarily the author's example of an Afro-American society in which rebellion might occur. Writing about the United States Delany had knowledge gained firsthand. Cuba he knew only through reading; yet, because Cuba could possibly be free from the American government and the influence of its slavery politics, it met the requirements of his historical imagination. In posing the possibility of a self-determining Black nation in Cuba Delany expresses what must be called utopianism. Utopianism need not issue in a full-fledged literary model of a good life, any more than statements such as "all men are created equal" result in a just society, but both equality and Delany's imagined conspiracy are utopian in the sense that they state principles for creating a new social order and repudiating the repressive power of historically present social circumstances.

Delany can exploit the symbolic potential of his protagonist's career, but he cannot detach his novel completely from received facts. Continually he feels compelled to return to documentary detail as if he were compiling an illustrative summary of the conditions of life under slavery. His imaginative problem shows most clearly as the novel moves toward its close. The final dozen chapters of the novel now extant prolong the preparations for insurrection and interrupt the progress of events with false alarms and digressions to such an extent that it seems likely that if the missing six chapters of *Blake* are ever recovered, we will find they contain little more than a bare outline of rebellion and almost nothing of its consequences. Delany's utopian impulse spends itself imagining the removal of oppression before it can flower in portrayal of free life.

Unlike Harriet Beecher Stowe, whose literary form and conception of history permitted resolution, Martin Robison Delany in the counterpart to *Uncle Tom's Cabin* can hypothesize but not conclude. Stowe's conviction that history is domestic romance was strong enough to permit her the appropriate sentimental closure for her genre, but Delany is uncertain how to plot his story, because he cannot see clearly the pattern of Afro-American history. On the one hand it may have the powerful objective force of the documentary passages in the slave narratives he imitates, but on the other hand there might be the possibility, adumbrated in the slave narratives, that it will develop the plot of utopian romance. The conflicted form of *Blake* has room for the development of a heroic and a symbolic character, but the outcome of his career remains as uncertain as the times in which Delany wrote.

For Arna Bontemps, writing three-quarters of a century after Delany, slave rebellion became commentary upon the Black condition in the United States rather than its possible cure. Reading "almost frantically" in the collection of slave records and narratives at the Fisk Library Bontemps determined in the early 1930s to adapt the accounts of Gabriel Prosser's rebellion of 1800 to the purposes of fiction. For factual substance he relied on sources such as the *Calendar of Virginia State Papers* and contemporary press accounts to carefully reconstruct the systematic preparation of Gabriel's insurrection and explain the strategy the conspirators of Richmond hoped to employ to establish an autonomous Black state. So specific is the detail and so exemplary the rational preparation of Gabriel's plot, especially when compared to the uprisings led by Denmark Vesey and Nat Turner which Bontemps rejected as subjects for his fiction, that *Black Thunder*[11] might serve as a handbook for guerilla organization.

As desirable or provocative as insurrectionary organization might have been to Delany's imagination, Bontemps cannot allow such detail to become his theme, because for the 1930s rebellion was not a

plausible historical hypothesis.   The maintenance of cultural continuity was, however, an appropriate purpose.   Bontemps says he was attracted by the theme of time in the story of Gabriel.   The uprising depended first upon patience, and then, when the moment came to act, it depended upon the fortunate choice of a date when weather and the expectations of white slave owners – or rather their lack of expectations – were favorable to the effort.   The misfortune of heavy rainfall prohibiting the assembly of conspirators threw the rebellion of 1800 into defeat and turned the mind of the novelist of 1934 to the thought that Afro-American history swings like a pendulum from proud hope to shattered dream.   Writing in an introduction to the 1968 reprint of *Black Thunder* Bontemps entertains the idea that in the death of Martin Luther King, Jr., the pendulum had swung once more toward failure.   Yet the novel does not leave the impression of discontinuous hope and despair.   Imaginative reconstruction of Gabriel's military preparations recreates as well the motives for rebellion, motives that do not take pendulum swings but persist as the character old Bundy says: "'I wanted to see y'-all do something like Toussaint done.   I always wanted to be free powerful bad'" (p. 34).
  · Among the sources Bontemps consulted for his novel he must have found reference to the legend that Gabriel had bought his freedom at the age of twenty-one and used his free status to travel about enlisting confederates.   When the revolt aborted, the legend continues, Gabriel hid aboard a ship bound for the island of San Domingo, was betrayed, and brought to trial, and at his execution made an inspiring speech that gave rise to a song called "Gabriel's Defeat."[12]   Actually Gabriel lived and died a slave, gave no speech that survives, and left no discoverable legacy in song.   Bontemps adheres to documentary actuality not legend, but still he accomplishes what the legend does. He vivifies Gabirel's spirit of resistance and hope.   Under interrogation in the novel Gabriel has this exchange with a prosecuting attorney:

> "Did you imagine other well-fed, well-kept slaves would join you?"
>
> "Wouldn't you j'ine us, was you a slave, suh?"
>
> "Don't be impudent.   You're still a black –"
>
> "I been a free man – and a gen'l, I reckon." (p. 213)

In combination with references to the beginnings of what was to become the underground railroad, the congruity of the slaves' aspirations to the philosophy of the Enlightenment, and above all the strength of Gabriel's character, this is sufficient speechmaking to create from the stuff of historical records a literarily effective symbol.

Comparison of *Blake* and *Black Thunder* is inevitable. The abundant similarities of detail and the common use of a heroic manner of description arise from the possibilities of the common subject matter. On the level of fundamental conception, however, the two novels differ strikingly. For Delany, as we have seen, slave rebellion is historical prediction, a hypothesis derived from study of the conditions of slavery undertaken in a time when it seemed important to consider insurrection as a means to bring Afro-Americans to historical consciousness and agency. Bontemps, on the other hand, had hindsight. The rebellions failed their military and political purposes, and their example had negligible effect upon general consciousness at the time. Still, Bontemps shares Delany's motive to discover possibility in history. It is the search for possibility, rather than reportage or protest that distinguishes the Afro-American writers' engagement with history. However else they may differ in their views of events and institutions the Afro-American authors speak in the potential mood.

A further similarity also marks the occurrence of history in Afro-American writing, especially the fiction. Particular events are singled out as significances around which life is organized. As the works of Delany and Bontemps indicate, one such event is the slave rebellion. Historians debate the prevalence of rebellion, arguing whether or not the circumstances of North American slavery permitted effective organized resistance. Writers take up the incidents of insurrection as the means to explore the potentiality for slaves, who are placed in the role of objects to the power of the slaveholders, to become their own subjects and makers of history. In its attenuation Delany's account of the preparations for the fictional rebellion suggests more than failure to achieve a satisfying episode with which to conclude the novel. If rhetorical effect had been his major interest, he might easily have produced for his two audiences an inspirational and admonitory victory that would fittingly conclude the career of the heroic Blake.

In one sense realism would not allow the ending, because Delany had insufficient evidence that slave rebellions would succeed, unless they were part of a comprehensive guerilla strategy as they had been in Haiti, or as John Brown planned for America. Such considerations did not curtail Harriet Beecher Stowe, whose premise for the removal of slavery was much less realistic, so it is clear that Delany's problem was not history so much as the plot in which he conceived it. Experience undermined Delany's confidence to make a romance in which evident good triumphs over clearly identified evil.

Experience conceived as a prolonged period of subjection in history intruded upon Arna Bontemps' creative consciousness before the creation of *Black Thunder*; therefore, he tried to emplot his fiction as tragedy. The conflict between slave and master that incited rebellion becomes aggravated in the fall of Gabriel. Blacks cannot escape the pendulum of history, though there is also knowledge that, while rebellion fails, its struggle brings about an epiphany of the persistence to seek freedom.

Other events given privileged places in the epistemes of Afro-American writers include Reconstruction, or more commonly its betrayal, and the great twentieth century migration north. Like the slave rebellion these events are disruptive moments that can show a protagonist in the relative freedom of uncertain destiny. They are events of supreme importance to Afro-America but secondary considerations to white American culture; thus, they comprise a first level of definition for Afro-American literary works.

III.

This variance of Afro-American historical awareness from that of white America demands counter-plotting. For example, the post-Reconstruction period in white popular story appears as an era of sectional reconciliation, but for Afro-America the dénouement to the Civil War was not played as it ought to have been. Blacks became a secondary factor in the political struggle between Republicans attempting to extend their power into the South and Democrats demanding home rule that would be secure from the threat of popular democracy. In the circumstances, "reconciliation" became the plot of a *white* drama performed by the practical politicians who concluded the bitter Presidential election of 1876 by withdrawing from the South the troops who alone could have enforced racial justice. Reconciliation depended upon repression of the newly freed Blacks and their exclusion from an effective role in the economy. Writers of fiction necessarily sought a form in which to describe redress. There was Sutton Griggs reviving utopianism in *Imperium in Imperio* (Cincinnati: Editor Publishing Company, 1899), and, as with the treatment of slave rebellions, there occurs also the use of plots from tragedy and romance by authors seeking the possibilities of history.

A representative tragedy may be found in Charles W. Chesnutt's *The Colonel's Dream*.[13] The novel is constructed as a visitor's tale with Henry French, a New York businessman, returning to his Southern home for rest after an exhausting series of business deals. French, formerly a Colonel in the Confederate Army, represents the possibility of reconciliation not only in his past and present occupations, but also by the company of his motherless son, who brings the perspective of innocence to the site of old conflicts.

The cause of revitalizing his home town soon appeals to the Colonel's business initiative, so he buys back his old home from a Black barber and sets about to reopen a cotton mill in town. He plans to run the mill with "decent hours and decent wages, and treat the operatives like human beings with bodies to nourish, minds to develop, and souls to save" (p. 120). But the curse of race soon undoes all the efforts of the Colonel who, despite his high rank in the Confederacy, seems not to have taken race very seriously. Perhaps Chesnutt is attempting some sort of ideological reconciliation by allowing credibility to the myth of the honorable old South, but, whatever may be the truth of that, Chesnutt uses the Colonel's obliquity to inform his readers of the adamant nature of racism. Control of Blacks is a white obsession. The Colonel's inquiries about it and reasonable arguments against it provoke only hostile responses.

The reportage situates Chesnutt's story; its significance is meant to be found in symbolic contrivances. The first is a rebellious Black hero named Bud Johnson whose career repeats Josh Green's in *The Marrow of Tradition* (Boston: Houghton Mifflin, 1901). Bud acts out resistance and is, as a consequence, almost permanently a convict on lease, his labor stolen from him as slaves' had been. Eventually Bud is arrested and lynched for shooting one of the aptly named Fetters family, descendants of a slave trader. Direct assault on racism, it seems, is a wish made attractive by a proud rebel, but futilely self-destructive. Chesnutt's second contrivance presents the Colonel's son Phil reliving his father's boyhood to the extent of receiving a schooling in folktales from the devoted family servant Peter. When both Phil and Peter die as a result of a railroad accident, Colonel French resolves to honor the nostalgia of the plantation tradition by burying the two together in his family plot. Bitter irony enters. The historical South, the real South as opposed to the mythic one, Chesnutt is saying, cannot tolerate enactment of its own self-justifying imagery. Peter's coffin is disinterred and left on French's piazza with a note Chesnutt composes to show his contempt for Southern civilization: "Niggers by there selves, white peepul by there selves, and them that lives in our town must bide by our rules. By order of CUMMITY" (p. 281).

Certainly there seems to be some satire latent in Chesnutt's portrayal of the Colonel, but the manifest form is intended to be tragic. As the Colonel's determination to reclaim the South wavers before events, he states the dream he had for a

> regenerated South, filled with thriving industries, and thronged with prosperous and happy people, where every man, having enough for his needs, was willing that every other man should have the same; where law and order should prevail unquestioned, and where every man could enter, through the golden gate of hope, the field of opportunity, where lay the prizes of life, which all might have an equal chance to win or lose. (p. 280)

In the context of the novel the Colonel's dream appears as an extreme departure from conditions as they are described, but after all it only states the American dream in the nineteenth century reformer's version,

especially in the oratorical language, with its desire for a modern e-
conomy in which prosperity would be the basis and possibility for
justice and fairness. But the South in 1905 was not going to abandon
its racial obsession. The South would get about the business of being
like the North but without regard for social justice. Frustration of
the Colonel's dream indicates how torn was Chesnutt between a hope
of change and an appraisal of possibility. He might share with reform-
ers a vision of an American promised land, but he could not complete
their romance. Nor does he conclude this novel with the outrage he
might be expected to announce if he were only reporting fact, or the
anger that would be natural political expression. Chesnutt was not
to publish fiction again in the remaining twenty-seven years of his
life, at least partly because he could not find a way to resolve the
conflicting imperatives of history and literary vision; yet, he makes
a valiant attempt in *The Colonel's Dream* to give a lift of hope to the
resigned ending of his tragedy. The Colonel reburies his son and the
faithful Peter in New York, and "sometimes, at night, a ray of light
from the uplifted torch of the Statue of Liberty, the gift of a free
people to a free people, falls athwart the white stone which marks
his resting place — fit prophecy and omen of the day when the sun
of liberty shall shine alike upon all men" (p. 290).

Invoking democratic icons, however, will not do to change the grim
picture Chesnutt has given. Tragedy requires some acknowledgment
of the spirit evident in the protagonist's struggle in order to recon-
cile us to conditions which are shown to be inalterable. In the nadir
of American race relations at the turn of the century, conditions
were horrible, but potentially changeable because they were imposed
by people, not God or nature. Chesnutt can locate the promise of
change only in a secularized deity which resolves — that is, completes —
the plot of the novel, but he leaves unexplored the issue the book
was meant to deal with: historical possibility for Afro-Americans.
The alternate endings in outrage or anger might have suggested resolve and will to struggle, but it seems as though Chesnutt could not
lift his despair, and the conventions of plot offered him a way to conclude without the necessity to engage his subject. In *The Colonel's
Dream* literature and history are irreconcilable in a text that could

not be made whole because the author could find Afro-American possibility in neither the one nor the other.

The training in life and science that W. E. B. Du Bois had received by the time he published *The Souls of Black Folk* in 1903, two years before the appearance of *The Colonel's Dream,* had given him a comprehensive way of studying the conditions of the Black South, and in the essays he wrote about the Black Belt he gave his attention to the historical origins of the agricultural system, its present organization, and the life led daily by the people whom he portrayed as inhabitants of an internal colony. Dominated by corporate landholdings, part of an economy too hegemonic to be affected by individual croppers, and excluded by segregation from access to the political and industrial life of the nation, Southern Blacks were in the position of Africans and West Indians in the face of imperial power, but they were begrudgingly called Americans.

The same setting provided Du Bois the basis for his first work of fiction. *The Quest of the Silver Fleece* (Chicago: A. C. McClurg, 1911) resembles Chesnutt's *The Colonel's Dream* in its concern with the establishment of a modern economy based upon racial justice. In a manner characteristic of its author, though, this romance of cotton differs both in scope and in its close attention to Black labor. Whereas Chesnutt alludes to the connection between Northern and Southern economic interests, Du Bois writes on cotton with the world-wide perspective Frank Norris devised for the wheat trade. He introduces as major characters the Taylor family, Northern financiers, and the Cresswells, Southern landholders, blending their tales in romantic entanglements. Also unlike Chesnutt, Du Bois chooses to make many of his characters directly involved in agriculture and by this means avoids the reformist detachment of Colonel French, while introducing as major figures in the narrative representatives of the Black population whose participation in production is essential both to reform of the South and to portrayal of the Afro-American place in the regional economy.

Du Bois claims that there is "no fact or picture have I consciously set down aught the counterpart of which I have not seen or known." This must be true in one sense. One cannot fault the representation of the economics of cotton or the experiences he reports at the Negro school which is the central setting of the novel. Similarly, accounts of debt peonage, legal manipulations to rob farmers of their crops, shoddy political deals in Washington, D.C., and the exacerbation of racism in the textile mills that have fled the Northeast to create a "New South" — these function as instances of the tactics of exposure usually associated with critical realism. At the same time, Du Bois creates characters such as Blessed Alwyn and Zora more typical of hope than realism and advances his story through frustrations of affection, villainy, and heroism — actions befitting the intensified motivations of romance. There is even climactic reversal, an atonement, as the landholder Cresswell leaves money and property to the school where Black farmers will come to know themselves as participants in the panoramic cotton trade.

The apparent contradictions of realistic documentary revelation and romance plotting do not destroy the coherence of *The Quest of the Silver Fleece*. On the contrary, the mix of exposé and romance provides the terms for a successful narrative — the one grounding the story in plausible reality, the other loosing the promise of transcendence into a possible history. The vision of a producers' cooperative requires no more change of heart than Colonel Cresswell's, and even that would not be necessary if another means of gaining land were possible. Besides the premise of possession of land, provided for by the romance plot device, what is a necessity is the collective association of Blacks in resolution to enter the agricultural system and to resist racism. That is utopian in the best sense because it calls upon the dialectic which relates appropriation of the physical world to achievement of subjective consciousness. The vision of socioeconomic change persuades precisely because it is founded upon the known possibilities of collective enterprise.

Modern taste becomes impatient with Du Bois' Victorian literary language, but, to the extent that it draws attention to itself and resists being read as a transparent medium, it denominates *The Quest of the Silver Fleece* as a product of literary conception. The vehicle for documentary content such as information about exploitation of farmers and betrayal of Black interests in politics — the deliberately "literary" language — is also the manner designated by protocol for rendering romance. The historical detail can be corroborated from many other sources; still, the possible weight of evidence cannot overwhelm the author's story and reduce the characters to fated objects. The force of historical events is great, but the desire to transcend immediate historical conditions is also strong, Du Bois' writing asserts. The contention of contradictory forces — first, in Du Bois' mind, and, then, in the representations of his text — promises that through struggle consciousness can be transformed. The figures of the novel may, like their author, find their way to becoming conscious subjects in history.

IV.

Du Bois' romance was unusual for its time, not only because it did not betray a lack of confidence in the possibility of counterplotting, but also because many writers before the 1920s made no attempt at all to counterplot history. Instead, they tried to assimilate prevailing patterns from the general culture to the story of Afro-America, because in their stance toward the post-slavery experience they thought they saw the possibility for Blacks to achieve a place in history by exemplary fulfillment of prescriptions in popular success stories. For these writers, America as it was popularly described by "self-made" men was unquestionably their home, laissez faire business and democracy the source of their social outlook; the secularized pilgrimage to perfection which serves as the template of autobiographical writing in bourgeois America provided their plot.

From the prospect of the secular pilgrimage to perfection of character it seems natural to view a career as self-actualizing, a perspective that seems to promise to lead toward conscious participation in history. Accounts of the success attendant to the will to rise intend to be inspirational, offering readers confirmation of the values of a culture that praises individualism and is confident that good works earn their just reward. The concrete testimonial urges readers to go and do likewise. Predictably Afro-American literature has a high quotient of autobiographies of the self-help variety, accounts of the achievements, modest and grand, of people who overcame racial restrictions. No one, perhaps, can raise questions about undoubted achievement, but one can examine the literary pattern it is given in an effort to generalize a model of the workings of individuals in history. Ready to hand as a convenient text for the examination is a 1919 novel modeled on biography, Herman Dreer's *The Immediate Jewel of His Soul*,[14] composed to present a "new" Negro whose resistance to Klan terror and independence of white or Black institutional authority modifies accomodationist strategy and seems to lift the weight of despair on the eve of the Negro Renaissance.

The hero of Dreer's novel, William Smith, is just that, a hero. Upon graduation from high school his friends give a celebration party where a banner is hung reading: A MAN IN WHOM THERE IS NO GUILE! WILLIAM SMITH – A KNIGHT WITHOUT FEAR AND WITHOUT REPROACH. The community hopes are not misplaced, for Smith becomes both a lawyer and teacher as well as a reforming preacher. One of his sermons, given at length in the text, shows the motives and values of such a man. It is hardly about religion at all in the conventional sense. Instead, it espouses the highest ideals of the religion of Americanism: self-help, accumulation, brotherhood. It also espouses practical political reform by proportional representation and social reform by a program of desegregation, including abolition of laws prohibiting interracial marriage. Smith's progressivism is too fiery for established institutions. He must leave his church and later his school, both ejections making clear that Black conservatism is as much an enemy of improvement as white supremacy. Expelled from organized institutions, Smith is free to embark on the experiment of creating institutions in his own individualist image.

Smith intends to sublimate racial prejudice into hostility against individuals "'who willfully neglect to make the best of opportunities and who expect to reap tho they have not sown. . .'" (p. 145). The transformation of mores will take place through the management and example of Denmark Vesey Estate, his agricultural cooperative, where Smith, dressed in military attire, charismatically directs operations. He sits in court, as it were, dispensing guidance and advice to farmers on rentals, crops, and so forth. Under his tutelage workers receive all they produce, except for a small amount Smith retains in payment for his counsel.

The book is anything but dramatic. Characters are wooden exemplars of their condition, and most of the text is consumed by Dreer's presentation of populist values in the form of orations by Smith. Still, it seeks to produce a dramatic conception of the resolution of racial oppression in a confrontation between Smith and white supremacists. Many whites object to calling William Smith Mister, or are envious of his achievements. Often when the discontented try to arouse opposition to Smith, wise whites describe his contributions to the community and, in direct commentary on the topical slanders then abroad in the land because the the film *Birth of a Nation,* recount the services of other Blacks to the United States. By this means the wish of intellectuals and authors like Dreer is confirmed as justifiable; whites of good will can be reasonable about race, if they are provided the facts. Nevertheless, there are also whites of ill will, most notably members of the KKK, which initiates a physical confrontation with Smith and his supporters. But Smith is ready with an organized armed defense, a just and gratifying development of the novel's rhetoric. All is saved, as it has been clear from the start it would be, when a lawyer appeals to the national pride of the mob, calls for law and order, and leads the assembled in the Pledge of Allegiance to the American flag. Preparedness is the best course of action, but the force of arms, so long as it is available, will not be necessary when the religion of nationalism is strong.

Since Benjamin Banneker wrote to Thomas Jefferson admonishing him to observe that Blacks had been excluded from the application of his philosophical dicta in the Declaration of Independence, Afro-American authors have regularly pointed to the democratic principles derived from eighteenth century philosophy as their own. Often they have pointed with the ironic observation that the practices of the country have been far from ideal, but still it is America's democracy they wish. *The Immediate Jewel of His Soul* shows not the least trace of irony, however, in its invocation of Americanism. In the place of complexity and the recognition of contradiction provided by irony, Dreer's novel uses the simplicities of melodrama and the cartoon of a wish to represent history.

In the period before 1920 and the emergence of the latter-day "New Negro" Herman Dreer's fiction had counterparts in such works as *Hope's Highway* (New York: Neale, 1917), a bourgois novel written by Sarah Lee Fleming; *"The Problem", A Military Novel* (Rochester: Henry Conolly, 1915), a book by F. Grant Gilmore that places its exemplary character among the soldiers of the 9th Cavalry; and several other fictions, not to mention the nonfictional autobiographies discussed in Rebecca Chalmers Barton's *Witnesses for Freedom* (New York: Harper, 1948). Though obscure today, these writers had in their time an audience possibly as eager for their books as for those by Chesnutt, Griggs, Du Bois, or James Weldon Johnson. The mediocre quality of their writing makes them less interesting than their famous contemporaries, but they retain importance for literary history because of the conceptions in their texts. *The Immediate Jewel of His Soul* and the similar works are the equivalent in fiction of *Up From Slavery* and the writings of the early school of Afro-American historians insofar as their motive can be epitomized by George Washington Williams' preface to his *History of the Negro Race in America*:

> I became convinced that a history of the Colored people in America was required, because of the ample historically trustworthy material at hand, because the Colored people themselves have been the most vexatious problem in North America from the time of its discovery down to the present day; because that in every attempt upon the life of the nation, whether by forces from without or from within, the Colored people had always displayed a matchless patriotism and an incomparable heroism in the cause of the Americans; and because such a history would give the world more correct ideas of the Colored people, and incite the latter to greater efforts in the struggle of citizenship and manhood. . . .[15]

As Williams indicates, the text of exemplary careers aims to arouse

Black readers to redouble their efforts to enter the dominant American culture, even if full participation as citizens before the law must be postponed; and for white readers the stark allegory in a tale of striving is meant to inspire willingness to accommodate worthy ambition. It would be impossible to say that another strategy would have worked better in the conditions of uncertainty before 1920. Recommendations for the past is not the purpose of literary historical inquiry. It is very much to the point of literary history, though, to say that the practical inadequacy of the strategy of relying on reasonable persuasion and the invocation of Americanism evident in the systematic repression that continued despite all moral appeal also had a conceptual inadquacy when the strategy was translated into literature.

The linear chronology and unadorned prose of such novels as Dreer's proclaim their intent to reflect an orderly external world. The laws of cause and effect presumed to govern that world seem to require no embellishment, because they are, as a famous American political document puts it, self-evident. Objectively considered, the circumstances of life in America, even for Blacks, should progressively improve. For that reason, and for the reason that past is past and the present is always yielding to the future, the sequence of fictionalized events can be appropriately straightforward. Moreover, writers like Dreer could have observed that the genre of the novel descends through stories of individuals equipped with personal merit. The ideology of the society giving rise to the novel expresses little overt interest in collective social formations; consequently, the characteristic stories of the society represent social class or ethnicity as neither help nor hindrance to the achievement of acceptance and status in general society.

Racism, however, contradicts this ideology and its literary expression, rendering the suppositions of the characteristic story false. Even though its pattern may have exceptional application in some *one* person's life, the story of a rise by individual merit cannot serve a representative purpose for Afro-Americans who, as a group, are deliberately excluded from the application of consensual democratic values. Racism is directed against persons without regard to their merit, because of their membership in a group from which an individual, or fictional persons, cannot disaffiliate.

Encountering the content of their fictions in historical experience, Afro-American authors have called upon frames of reference that are themselves historical products of literary and cultural tradition to explain or plot the significance of the past and project the future. Ordinarily the frames are taken to be objective; that is, they are used as sources of knowledge about the real relationships among events rather than as hypotheses about those relationships. Consequently, it may happen that, although the writer's search is for possibility, the search is short-circuited by the fact that the available history enters a text pre-formed. Genres and types of plot are examples of these prefabricated ways of knowing, as is the received idea that a literary text might be objective in the sense that it will reflect exterior reality.

The genre of the novel is a social formation. To accept it is to accept its latent ideological content. Characteristically ideology conceals its hypothetical nature and assumes the appearance of generalized declaration, so in the novel the bourgeois values of individualism become presuppositions with the appearance of probability certified by repetition in hundreds of stories. Struggling to form fiction reflecting the historical world, the writer can be misled into relying on many of these presuppositions, because he or she cannot find satisfactory plots for Black experience in a style of writing without a means to treat the contradictions of racism. Delany and Du Bois found the romance a congenial form, because its symbolic nature removes the tale from the restrictive style of the realistic novel; and Bontemps and Chesnutt explored tragedy, because it has a place for the defeats that defy rationalism. Yet the tenuousness of resolution in at least two of the works these writers produced suggests that the problematic relationship between literature and history cannot be solved entirely by emplotting. Authentically complete fiction is partly a selection of significant events, partly a function of plot, but it requires as well an outlook or episteme that can appropriate to literature the contradictions of history as it is lived beyond the page.

In the effort to understand the historical world, the writer attempts to re-enact, a process that would be futile if events themselves had to be reproduced. But the events of the past were events of thought as well as material occurrences.[16] In the past the events were subjects of consciousness, and they can be recovered in the substance of their interior quality as thought in the present — in much the same way we rethink the events that we believe account for the shape of our personal being. The problem of the distinction between mental and material reality that engenders the fallacy of assuming history consists of a single, completed sequence of related events dissolves with the recognition, achieved by some modern writers, that the two realities are a unity whose tracks may be followed through the relations of culture. The effort to re-experience history by recovering its thought content distinguishes *Black Thunder* and such a recent classic as John A. Williams' *The Man Who Cried I Am* (Boston: Little Brown, 1967). By use of the devices of the *roman à clef* — incompletely disguised characters and allusion — Williams evokes for readers the authenticity that must be attributed to a text prepared by an author who participated in the events. If credibility by virtue of firsthand knowledge were the only means to engage an audience, however, the novel would not differ significantly from documentary. But Williams, and other writers of what can be regarded as the fiction of popular history — including such works as Margaret Walker's *Jubilee* (Boston: Houghton Mifflin, 1966) and Ernest J. Gaines' *The Autobiography of Miss Jane Pittman* (New York: Dial Press, 1971) — extend the range of story by extrapolation of the possible from Afro-American cultural experience, so that pesonae become typifications of Afro-American character, fictional incident an enactment of collective outlook.

Even that is not enough, though, to particularize the modern writers' adaptation of Afro-American history to literature, for, of course, extrapolation is also at work in the frustrated texts of *Blake* and *The Colonel's Dream*. There is a qualitative difference evident when Williams posits the King Alfred Plan in *The Man Who Cried I Am*, or punctuates the story of the corporate hero of *Captain Blackman* (Garden City, New York: Doubleday, 1972) with devices called "cadences" and concludes that novel with the fantasy of Afro-American victory in the racial struggle accomplished by the use of "passing," not to escape Blackness as conventional mulatto stories would have it, but rather to subvert the white establishment. By these frankly literary inventions Williams' imagined history gives specificity and concreteness to generalized themes of Afro-American consciousness. Dispensing with the manner of realism and the practice of verisimilitude that insists upon reference of the text to an external reality, he gives creation of narrative priority over replication of objective experience, establishing that it is the business of the text to make history in *its* image.

V.

Literature becomes new as writers assume the power to transform their frames of reference; discovery of greater possibilities in the engagement of history by literature begins with awareness that the frames of reference are products of consciousness. The sensitivity and literary confidence involved in that awareness might be illustrated by many writers in addition to John A. Williams, but even more important than listing the authors who have been liberated from the sense of history as fate, though I don't hesitate to do that, is some literary historical speculation about the tendency toward a variety of surrealism in Afro-American writing that eventually led to the subjectively self-reflexive texts that overthrew the tyranny of objective history. Consider the episode in Langston Hughes' *I Wonder as I Wander* in which Hughes records the ridiculous necessity to walk down the railroad track in Savannah to satisfy the white policeman who had failed to prevent him from entering the white waiting room of the train station to buy a New York *Times* but was sure to keep him from using the white door to exit.[17] Recall the foolish interview the young Richard Wright has with a prospective employer who asks him if he steals, as though he could satisfactorily answer, whatever he said.[18] These experiences provoke the authors' disdain, bewilderment, and laughter at the mind-twisting caste system. If one learns the rules, there appears to be order in social relations, but one cannot successfully learn these rules, let alone live by them, because a moment's reflection as a human being reveals their entirely arbitrary nature. Caste rules are consummate examples of bad faith; the world they posit, fundamentally absurd. Hughes and Wright are heirs to a long tradition of recorded instances, many of them in the slave narratives, of the absurdity inherent in the condition of living Black in America. The rhetorical demands of slave narratives may have channeled them into objective narrative patterns, but the consciousness of narrators emerges within the topical rhetoric. A classic representation occurs in Solomon Northup's *Twelve Years a Slave*.[19] Born free and kidnapped for sale into bondage, Northup describes his experience as an assault upon his reason. He knows that he is free, but the terror of the slave dealers forces him to deny his precarious status, accept a false name, and become an accessory to his own enslavement. He is made the agent of his own attempted dehumanization, so that his time in slavery becomes a period of contest between intended objectification and his own corrective subjectivity.

On one occasion Tibeats, the most ruthless of his several masters, plans to hang him for resisting a beating, but is prevented from doing so at the last minute by Chapin, a sympathetic white, who sends a message asking the man from whom Tibeats purchased Northup to intervene. Here is the scene. Northup stands in the strong sun where he has been bound by Tibeats. His death has been prevented, but he remains bound, while all day his savior Chapin paces in uneasiness. "Why," Northup asks,

> he did not relieve me — why he suffered me to remain in agony the whole weary day, I never knew. It was not for want of sympathy, I am certain. Perhaps he wished Ford [the previous owner] to see the rope about my neck, and the brutal manner in which I had been bound; perhaps his interference with another's property in which he had no legal interest might have been a trespass, which would have subjected him to the penalty of the law. Why Tibeats was all day absent was another mystery I never could divine. (p. 187)

Whatever the motives of the whites, they are eventually irrelevant to the fact that Northup must live the moral paralysis of slavery without the chance of satisfactory explanation. Irony alone can express the result of Northup's effort to make sense of an inexplicable incident within the larger frame of slavery's absurdity: "During the whole long day I came not to the conclusion even once, that the southern slave, fed, clothed, whipped and protected by his master, is happier than the free colored citizen of the North" (p. 188).

Even at the conclusion of his narrative when Northup has been declared legally free and judged to have been unjustly treated, order based upon reasonable expectation is out of place. In a brief exchange between Northup and a Mr. Epps, who had once owned him, Epps says he is surprised that Northup is free. "'Now you dammed nigger. . . . why did you not tell me that when I bought you?'" "'Master Epps,'" Northup replies, in a tone he describes as "somewhat different" from the one in which he had customarily addressed Epps, "'you did not take the trouble to ask me; besides, I told one of my owners — the man that kidnapped me — that I was free, and was whipped almost to death for it'" (pp. 238-239). The grimness of Northup's punch line capsulizes the absurd historical institution of slavery, in which arbitrary force rules in a way that the reasonable mind cannot conceive.

Northup's remark also relates his narrative to the folktales which developed for slaves a frame of reference that, through the use of tricks of language and masked motives gained for them some control of their condition. Development of similar tactics in written literature has become the project of recent Afro-American literature, as authors have sought to replace the frames of literary genres generated by white culture with a manner of writing that expresses the subjective feel of experience in a reality that, despite rational suppositions to the contrary, may actually be the way it seems. The deliberate effort to reconstruct the structures for understanding Black experience this way in literature may be said to begin with Richard Wright's story "The Man Who Lived Underground."[20]

Wright's deliberations on form are evident by comparison of revisions he made in typescript with the published versions of the story.

In the typescript a nameless protagonist is arrested, accused of murder and robbery, and badgered by the district attorney until he signs a confession. In a section reminiscent of *Native Son* he is taken to the scene of his alleged crime. This visit is then followed by scenes of the police returning the accused to his home, where his wife is in child labor and then taking him to the maternity hospital from which he escapes into the underground world that becomes the exclusive setting of the published story. Throughout these early episodes, Wright originally included detail of the character's wonderings at his situation and his physical sensations. The detail is particularly full in the description of the confrontations with the district attorney and the flight from the hospital.

The first stage of Wright's revision consisted of cutting the numerous passages that relate sensation and mental pondering. This would be equivalent to focusing attention on action by removing the pondering of motives in Northup's account of the day he spent bound in the Louisiana sun, or cutting the sort of material basic to the representation of Bigger Thomas' psychology in *Native Son*. Removal of the psychological references and descriptions in "The Man Who Lived Underground" eliminates the detached viewpoint of the third-person narrator, along with externally derived explanations of events. The result is projection of an interior state of mind onto exterior events. There is no intermediate point of reference, so a mental sense of absurdity is expressionistically converted into actuality.

Eventually his discovered purpose led Wright to eliminate all the expository introduction (about fifty-eight pages in typescript), leaving readers with no objective information about the character's status, work, or personal relationships when they first read of him hiding in a vestibule while preparing to enter a manhole and begin his underground wanderings in search of meaning. The typicality of the protagonist becomes a matter of consciousness shared with readers, rather than specifications of detail from the realm of categorical reason. In abandoning the assumption that there is a fixed, objective world superior to the consciousness of character — or author — Wright establishes in its place the premise of surreal fiction, in which reality is deliberately appropriated to mental conceptions.

Wright's accomplishment by the revision of "The Man Who Lived Underground" is not singular. Rather its importance lies in demonstrating the possibility for any writer to recode the structures of fiction. The awareness of absurdism latent in the phrasing of the fugitive slave narrators, which is the common property of the Afro-American literary tradition, can be centered in a literary tale, so Wright's example shows, in which the world takes on the form of the Black consciousness experiencing it. With another step, writers become aware that the act of reconstructing fiction can be their subject, their historical interpretation. The way has been opened in literature to master history.

The self-aware text, embodying consciousness within form, arrives with *Invisible Man* (New York: Random House, 1952), a novel that fuses the collective experience of Afro-American history with the process of exploring its subjective transformations. Ellison solves the problem of over-reliance on the presumed objectivity of events that frustrated the plots of his predecessors by having his narrator announce that the representative experiences to be related in the narrative exist as linguistic structures of interpretation, an epistemological stance that erases the distinction between exterior and interior reality and asserts that the reality of *Invisible Man* — as a fiction and as a historical hypothesis — must be met on the level of mind. In one sense there is nothing remarkable about this, because there is no other way but through the mind for a reader to take in a text's reality, no matter how documentary or referential it may be. But, as Ellison's narrator says, "The mind must never lose sight of the chaos against which . . . pattern was conceived."

Like the metahistorian, Ellison's narrator, and of course Ellison himself, sees the events of historical or personal experience as elements for a story that must be constructed by the writer-speaker. The events do not in themselves exist as a story awaiting discovery. They are present in tradition, record, and culture, available for the creative imagination that will highlight and arrange them into plots and modes of expression conceived by writers in the particularity of their language.

The idea that literature can be history-making is widely shared among recent Afro-American authors, so it is appropriate to conclude this discussion by listing a few such writers whose narrative experiments are informed by the understanding that fiction creates its own subject. The self-reflexive linkage of Amiri Baraka's *Tales*,[21] the surreal images of Harlem appearing in Chester Himes' stories of Coffin Ed and Grave Digger,[22] the transformations of utopia in William Melvin Kelley's *A Different Drummer* (Garden City, New York: Doubleday, 1962), William Demby's play with self-consciousness in *The Catacombs* (New York: Pantheon, 1965), Clarnece Major's insistence that "characters and events are happening for the first time" in *Reflex and Bone Structure* (New York: Fiction Collective, 1975), Ishmael Reed's Neo-Hoodoo subversion of "normal" epistemology[23] — each of these, and other examples too, represents an undisguised literary project undertaken with frank acknowledgment of its own subjectivity. Each insists that we attend to it as an act of writing, a making of reality. And, granting all the variety evident in the different experiments, each, in the process of dismantling the structure of genre, confronts the tentative and ambiguous nature of known and written history. Thus do creatures of history enter upon a career as its conscious subject.

NOTES

1.   The phrase "creatures of history" comes so obviously to mind that it needs no specific citation, but for application of it in discussion of some Afro-American writers see Alfred Kazin, *Bright Book of Life: American Novelists and Storytellers from Hemingway to Mailer* (Boston: Little Brown, 1973).

2.   "Black Fiction: History and Myth," *Studies in American Fiction*, 5 (1977), 125.

3.   "History, Fiction, and the Ground Between: The Uses of the Documentary Mode in Black Literature," *PMLA*, 95 (1980), 392-393.

4.   The assertion appears in a summation of radical criticism of historical realism by Lionel Gossman, "History and Literature: Reproduction of Signification," in *The Writing of History: Literary Form and Historical Understanding*, ed. Robert H. Canary and Henry Kozicki (Madison: University of Wisconsin Press, 1978), p. 29.

5.   "The Historical Text as Literary Artifact," in *The Writing of History*, p. 43.

6.   *The Journey Back: Issues in Black Literature and Criticism* (Chicago: University of Chicago Press, 1980), pp. 136-137.

7.   (New York: Dodd Mead, 1937), p. 15.

8.   *Structure and Society in Literary History: Studies in the History and Theory of Historical Criticism* (Charlottesville: University of Virginia Press, 1976), p. 11.

9.   (New York: Viking Press, 1941), p. 147.

10.   Twenty-six chapters of *Blake, or, the Huts of America. A Tale of the Mississippi Valley, the Southern United States and Cuba* were published serially in the *Anglo-African Magazine* during the first half of 1859, and the whole — approximately eighty chapters — appeared serially in *The Weekly Anglo-African* between November 26, 1861, and late May, 1862. Six chapters have not been recovered, but what is extant has been reprinted by Beacon Press (Boston, 1970). Citations in the text are from that edition.

11.   (New York: Macmillan, 1936). Bontemps' account of his preparation for writing *Black Thunder* is contained in the introduction to the Beacon Press reprint (Boston, 1968). Citations in the text are from that edition.

12.   For discussion of the legend and history see T. W. Higginson, "Gabriel's Defeat," *Atlantic,* 10 (September, 1862), 337ff.

13.   (New York: Doubleday Page, 1905). Citations in the text are from the Gregg reprint (Upper Saddle River, New Jersey, 1968).

14.   (St. Louis: Argus Publishing Company, 1919). Citations in the text are from the McGrath reprint (College Park, Maryland, 1969).

15.   (New York: Putnam, 1883), p. v.

16.   Discussion of thought as history occurs in R. G. Collingwood, *The Idea of History* (Oxford: Clarendon Press, 1946), p. 215. For a useful discussion of Collingwood's position, other historians' ideas of history, and their application to literature, see Mark A. Weinstein, "The Creative Imagination in Fiction and History," *Genre,* 9 (Summer, 1976), 263-277.

17.   The Hughes anecdote appears on p. 53 of the Hill and Wang reprint (New York, 1964).

18.   The Wright anecdote appears on p. 176 of the Harper reprint of *Black Boy* (New York, 1966).

19.   Originally published in 1853. Citations are from the reprint edited by Sue Eakin and Joseph Logsdon (Baton Rouge: Louisiana State University Press, 1968).

20.   The story was published in an abbreviated form in *Accent,* 2 (Spring, 1942), 170-176. In a longer version, but one still shorter than the original typescript, it was published in Edwin Seaver, ed., *Cross-Section 1944* (New York: McClelland, 1945), pp. 58-102. This last version appears in *Eight Men* (Cleveland: World, 1961). The typescript bearing evidence of revision is held by the Princeton University Library.

21.   Published under the name LeRoi Jones (New York: Grove Press, 1967).

22.   These police detective characters appear in a cycle of nine novels beginning with *For Love of Imabelle* (New York: Gold Medal, 1959) and concluding with *Blind Man with a Pistol* (New York: Morrow, 1969). All but the last were published first in French translations in Paris. For a discussion and bibliography, see John M. Reilly, "Chester Himes' Harlem Tough Guys," *Journal of Popular Culture,* 9 (1976), 935-946.

23.   The "Neo-Hoodoo Manifesto" appears in *Confrontation,* 1 (1971). Its application appears in *Mumbo Jumbo* (Garden City, New York: Doubleday, 1972), *The Last Days of Louisiana Red* (New York: Random House, 1974), *Flight to Canada* (New York: Random House, 1976), and other works.

Call and Response: Intertextuality in Two Autobiographical Works
by
Richard Wright and Maya Angelou

by

Keneth Kinnamon

In his provocative account of Afro-American literary criticism from
the 1940s to the present, Houston A. Baker, Jr., traces three stages
of development: integrationism, the "Black Aesthetic," and the "Reconstruction of Instruction." As his major representative of the first
stage, "the dominant critical perspective on Afro-American literature
during the late 1950s and early 1960s," Baker makes a strange choice
— Richard Wright, in the 1957 version of "The Literature of the Negro
in the United States." According to Baker, Wright, sanguine because
of the Supreme Court school desegregation decision of 1954, believed

that the leveling of racial barriers in American society would lead to
a homogenous American literature in which minority writers would
be absorbed into the mainstream of cultural expression. Even the
verbal and musical folk forms of the black masses would eventually
disappear with the inevitable triumph of democratic pluralism in
the social order.[1] Actually, Wright's essay is not basically an optimistic
statement of integrationist poetics. It is, rather, a document in the
proletarian-protest stage of Afro-American literature and literary
criticism that dominated the Thirties and Forties, constituting the
stage immediately preceding Baker's first stage.[2] The proletarian-
protest stage anticipates elements of all three of Baker's stages. Like
the integrationist stage it postulates a fundmental unity of human
experience transcending racial and national (but not economic)
boundaries. Its commitment to an engaged literature is as fierce as
that of the Black Aestheticians. And in "Blueprint for Negro Writing,"[3] at least, it advocates a sophisticated modern literary sensibility,
as does the Stepto-Gates school. What it does not do is examine the
special perspective of black women writers, a failing shared by the
following three stages. This deficiency seems particularly conspicuous
now that good women writers are so abundant and female critics are
beginning to assess their achievement in relation to the total Afro-
American literary tradition.

Despite its unfortunate effort at social disengagement, to my mind
the most illuminating effort to provide a theoretical framework for
the interpretation of Afro-American literature is Robert B. Stepto's
From Behind the Veil: A Study of Afro-American Narrative (Urbana:
University of Illinois Press, 1979). In this seminal work Stepto argues
that the central myth of black culture in America is "the quest for
freedom and literacy." Shaped by the historical circumstances of
slavery and enforced illiteracy, this myth exists in the culture prior
to any literary expression of it. Once this "pregeneric myth" is consciously articulated, it begins to take generic shape, especially as autobiography or fiction. The resulting narrative texts interact with each
other in complex ways that constitute a specifically Afro-American
literary tradition and history. In his book Stepto explores this intertextual tradition, dividing it into what he designates "The Call" and

"The Response." In "The Call," he treats four slave narratives (by Bibb, Northup, Douglass, and Brown), *Up From Slavery,* and *The Souls of Black Folk.* To this call he discusses the twentieth century response of *The Autobiography of an Ex-Coloured Man, Black Boy,* and *Invisible Man.* All would agree that, of these nine works, those by Douglass, Washington, Du Bois, Johnson, Wright, and Ellison are classics of Afro-American literature, but notice that all of these authors are not only men, but race men, spokesmen, political activists. By way of complementing Stepto's somewhat narrow if sharp focus, I propose here to examine some intertextual elements in *Black Boy* and *I Know Why the Caged Bird Sings* to ascertain how gender may affect genre in these two autobiographical quests for freedom and literacy and, in Angelou's case, community as well.

In many ways these two accounts of mainly Southern childhoods are strikingly similar. Both narratives cover a period of fourteen years from earliest childhood memories to late adolescence: 1913 to 1927 (age four to eighteen) in Wright's case, 1931 to 1945 (age three to seventeen) in Angelou's case. Both Wright and Marguerite Johnson (Angelou's given name) are products of broken homes, children passed back and forth among parents and other relatives. Both have unpleasant confrontations with their fathers' mistresses. Both spend part of their childhoods in urban ghettoes (Memphis and St. Louis) as well as Southern small towns. Both suffer physical mistreatment by relatives. Both are humiliated by white employers. Lethal white violence comes close to both while they are living in Arkansas. Each child is subjected by a domineering grandmother to rigorous religious indoctrination, but each maintains a skeptical independence of spirit. From the trauma or tedium of their surroundings, both turn to reading as an escape. Both excel in school, Wright graduating as valedictorian from the eighth grade of Smith-Robinson School in Jackson, Mississippi, and Johnson as salutatorian of Lafayette County Training School in Stamps, Arkansas, fifteen years later.

In addition to these general similarities, some highly specific resemblances suggest more than mere coincidence or common cultural background. In *Black Boy* Wright recalls an incident in Memphis involving a preacher invited to Sunday dinner, the main course being "a huge platter of golden-brown fried chicken." Before the boy can finish his soup the preacher is picking out "choice pieces": "My growing hate of the preacher finally became more important than God or religion and I could no longer contain myself. I leaped up from the table, knowing that I should be ashamed of what I was doing, but unable to stop, and screamed, running blindly from the room. 'That preacher's going to eat *all* the chicken!' I bawled."[4] The gluttonous preacher's counterpart in *I Know Why the Caged Bird Sings* is Reverend Howard Thomas, whose "crime that tipped the scale and made our hate not only just but imperative was his actions at the dinner table. He ate the biggest, brownest and best parts of the chicken at every Sunday meal."[5] Wright's literary imagination was first kindled by the story of Bluebeard. As a child Angelous also learned of Bluebeard. A later common literary interest was Horatio Alger, who nurtured Wright's dreams of opportunities denied in the South. To Marguerite Johnson, however, Alger was a reminder that one of her dreams would be permanently deferred: "I read more than ever, and wished my soul that I had been born a boy. Horatio Alger was the greatest writer in the world. His heroes were always good, always won, and were always boys. I could have developed the first two virtues, but becoming a boy was sure to be difficult, if not impossible" (p. 74). One is tempted to think that Angelou had Wright specifically in mind in this passage, but even if she did not, her text provides an instructive gloss on Wright's, pointing out that sexism as well as racism circumscribes opportunity.

Other parallel passages provide additional intertextual clues to a basic difference in perspective on childhood experiences. One of the numerous relatives with whom young Richard could not get along was Aunt Addie, his teacher in a Seventh-Day Adventist school in Jackson. After a bitter confrontation in which the twelve-year-old boy threatens his aunt with a knife, she finds occasion for revenge:

> I continued at the church school, despite Aunt Addie's never calling upon me to recite or go to the blackboard. Consequently I stopped studying. I spent my time playing

with the boys and found that the only games they knew were brutal ones. Baseball, marbles, boxing, running were tabooed recreations, the Devil's work; instead they played a wildcat game called popping-the-whip, a seemingly innocent diversion whose excitement came only in spurts, but spurts that could hurl one to the edge of death itself. Whenever we were discovered standing idle on the school grounds, Aunt Addie would suggest that we pop-the-whip. It would have been safer for our bodies and saner for our souls had she urged us to shoot craps.

One day at noon Aunt Addie ordered us to pop-the-whip. I had never played the game before and I fell in with good faith. We formed a long line, each boy taking hold of another boy's hand until we were stretched out like a long string of human beads. Although I did not know it, I was on the tip end of the human whip. The leading boy, the handle of the whip, started off at a trot, weaving to the left and to the right, increasing speed until the whip of flesh was curving at breakneck gallop. I clutched the hand of the boy next to me with all the strength I had, sensing that if I did not hold on I would be tossed off. The whip grew taut as human flesh and bone could bear and I felt that my arm was being torn from its socket. Suddenly my breath left me. I was swung in a small, sharp arc. The whip was now being popped and I could hold on no more; the momentum of the whip flung me off my feet into the air, like a bit of leather being flicked off a horsewhip, and I hurtled headlong through space and landed in a ditch. I rolled over, stunned, head bruised and bleeding. Aunt Addie was laughing, the first and only time I ever saw her laugh on God's holy ground. (pp. 96-97)

In Stamps pop-the-whip was considerably less dangerous: "And when he [Maya's brother Bailey] was on the tail of the pop the whip, he would twirl off the end like a top, spinning, falling, laughing, finally stopping just before my heart beat its last, and then he was back in the game, still laughing" (p. 23). Now pop-the-whip is not among the gentlest of childhood activities, but surely it is less potentially deadly than Wright makes it out, surely it is closer to Angelou's exciting but essentially joyous pastime. With his unremittingly bleak view of black community in the South, Wright presents the game as sadistic punishment inflicted by a hateful aunt. In Angelou's corrective it becomes a ritual of ebullient youthful bravado by her "pretty Black brother" who was also her "unshakable God" and her "Kingdom Come" (p. 23).

Another pair of passages shows the same difference. Both Wright's Grandmother Wilson and Johnson's Grandmother Henderson ranked cleanliness close to godliness. On one occasion Wright remembers his grandmother bathing him:

> I went to her, walking sheepishly and nakedly across the floor. She snatched the towel from my hand and began to scrub my ears, my face, my neck.
>
> "Bend over," she ordered.
>
> I stooped and she scrubbed my anus. My mind was in a sort of daze, midway between daydreaming and thinking. Then, before I knew it, words — words whose meaning I did not fully know — had slipped out of my mouth.
>
> "When you get through, kiss back there," I said, the words rolling softly but unpremeditatedly. (p. 36)

Naturally the response to this call is a severe beating. Angelou treats a similar situation with humor:

> "Thou shall not be dirty" and "Thou shall not be impudent" were the two commandments of Grandmother Henderson upon which hung our total salvation.
>
> Each night in the bitterest winter we were forced to wash faces, arms, necks, legs and feet before going to bed. She used to add, with a smirk that unprofane people can't control when venturing into profanity, "and wash as far as possible, then wash possible." (p. 26)

No children like to scrub or be scrubbed, but Wright uses the occasion to dramatize hostility between himself and his family, while Angelou's purpose is to portray cleanliness as a bonding ritual in black culture: "Everyone I knew respected these customary laws, except for the powhitetrash children" (p. 27).

In *Black Boy* the autobiographical persona defines himself *against* his environment, as much against his family and the surrounding black culture as against the overt hostility of white racism. Like the fictional persona Bigger Thomas, the protagonist of *Black Boy* is an archetypal rebel who rejects all social norms. In the opening scene he sets his family's house on fire, eliciting a traumatically severe whipping from his mother. His father "was always a stranger to me, always alien and remote" (p. 9). Young Richard subverts his paternal authority by a disingenuous literalism in the cat-killing episode. At the end of the first chapter he recalls his last meeting with his father in 1940, providing an exaggerated geriatric description complete with toothless mouth, white hair, bent body, glazed eyes, gnarled hands.[6] His father was a brutalized "black peasant," "a creature of the earth" without loyalty, sentiment, tradition, joy, or despair — all in contrast to his son, who lives "on a vastly different plane of reality," who speaks a different language, and who has traveled to "undreamed-of shores of knowing" (pp. 30, 31). Wright's symbolic effort to bury his father corresponds to a persistent attempt to come into his own by opposing or ignoring all members of his family, who consistently try to stifle his articulation of his individuality, to inhibit his quest for freedom. Shouting joyously at the sight of a free-flying bird outside his window, Richard is rebuked in the opening scene by his younger brother with the words "'You better hush.'" His mother immediately steps in to reinforce the message: "'You stop that yelling, you hear?'" (p. 3). These are the first words spoken to Richard in *Black Boy*, but they reverberate in other mouths throughout the work. His brother plays an exceedingly minor role before being sent to Detroit to live with an aunt. His mother is presented more sympathetically than are other members of the family, but even she functions as a harsh disciplinarian striving to suppress her son's dangerous individualism. His grandmother and other relatives join this effort, leading often to violent arguments in which Richard threatens them with knife or razor blade.

Outside the family the boy's relations to other black children are marked by fights on the street and in the schoolyard described with the same hyperbolic violence employed in the pop-the-whip episode. In the classroom he has to struggle against a paralyzing shyness that renders him almost mute and unable to write his own name: "I sat with my ears and neck burning, hearing the pupils whisper about me, hating myself, hating them; I sat still as stone and a storm of emotion surged through me" (p. 67). In describing his contacts with the general black community Wright emphasizes brutalization and degradation, as in his account of saloons in Memphis or in this paragraph on life in West Helena:

> We rented one half of a double corner house in front of which ran a stagnant ditch carrying sewage. The neighborhood swarmed with rats, cats, dogs, fortunetellers, cripples, blind men, whores, salesmen, rent collectors, and children. In front of our flat was a huge roundhouse where locomotives were cleaned and repaired. There was an eternal hissing of steam, the deep grunting of steel engines, and the tolling of bells. Smoke obscured the vision and cinders drifted into the house, into our beds, into our kitchen, into our food; and a tarlike smell was always in the air. (p. 52)

Richard learns about sex voyeuristically by peeping at the whores at work in the other half of the duplex in the Arkansas town, as he had earlier watched the exposed rears of privies in Memphis. When he does manage to establish some degree of rapport with other boys, "the touchstone of fraternity was my feeling toward white people, how much hostility I held toward them, what degrees of value and honor I assigned to race" (p. 68). But as the reader of "Big Boy Leaves Home," *The Long Dream,* or biographies of Wright knows, in *Black Boy* the author minimizes the important role his friendship with peers actually played in his adolescent life. Religion is also rejected, whether the peripheral Seventh-Day Adventism of his grand-mother or the mainstream black Methodism of his mother. So estranged and isolated from the nurturing matrices of black culture, an estrangement as much willed from within as imposed from without, Wright was able to utter this famous indictment:

> (After I had outlived the shocks of childhood, after the habit of reflection had been born in me, I used to mull over the strange absence of real kindness in Negroes, how unstable was our tenderness, how lacking in genuine passion we were, how void of great hope, how timid our joy, how bare our traditions, how hollow our memories, how lacking we were in those intangible sentiments that bind man to man, and how shallow was even our despair. After I had learned other ways of life I used to brood upon the unconscious irony of those who felt that Negroes led so passional an existence! I saw that what had been taken for our emotional strength was our negative confusions, our flights, our fears, our frenzy under pressure.
>
> (Whenever I thought of the essential bleakness of black life in America, I knew that Negroes had never been allowed to catch the full spirit of Western civilization, that they lived somehow in it but not of it. And when I brooded upon the cultural barrenness of black life, I wondered if clean, positive tenderness, love, honor, loyalty, and the capacity to remember were native with man. I asked myself if these human qualities were not fostered, won, struggled and suffered for, preserved in ritual form from one generation to another.) (p. 33)

In part this passage attempts to shame whites by showing them what their racism has wrought, but in a more crucial way it defines Wright's individualistic alienation from all sense of community, that permanent spiritual malaise that is both the key biographical fact and the ideological center of his art.

With Maya Angelou the case is quite otherwise. If she never experienced the physical hunger that characterized much of Wright's childhood, he was not raped at the age of eight. Yet here youthful reponse to rejection and outrage is to embrace community, not to seek alienation. *I Know Why the Caged Bird Sings* is a celebration of black culture, by no means uncritical, but essentially a celebration. Toward her family, young Marguerite is depicted as loving, whether or not her love is merited. She idolizes her slightly older brother Bailey. Her Grandmother Henderson is presented not only as the matrifocal center of her family but as the leader of the black community in Stamps, strong, competent, religious, skilled in her ability to coexist with Jim Crow while maintaining her personal dignity. She is a repository of racial values, and her store is the secular center of her community. Crippled Uncle Willie could have been presented as a Sherwood Anderson grotesque, but Angelou recalls feeling close to him even if he was, like Grandmother Henderson, a stern disciplinarian. Angelou would seem to have every reason to share Wright's bitterness about parental neglect, but she does not. When her father shows up in Stamps she is impressed by his appearance, his proper speech, and his city ways. Her mother beggars description: "To describe my mother would be to write about a hurricane in its perfect power. Or the climbing, falling colors of a rainbow. . . . My mother's beauty literally assailed me" (p. 58). Absorbed in their own separate lives, her parents neglect or reject her repeatedly, but she is more awed by their persons and their personalities than she is resentful. Her maternal family in St. Louis is also impressive in its worldly way, so different in its emphasis on pleasure and politics from the religious rectitude of the paternal family in Stamps.[7] Even Mr. Freeman, her mother's live-in boyfriend who first abuses and then rapes the child, is presented with more compassion than rancor.

Afflicted with guilt after Freeman is killed by her uncles, Marguerite lapses into an almost catatonic silence, providing an excuse to her mother to send her back to Stamps. Southern passivity provides a good therapeutic environment for the child, especially when she is taken under the wing of an elegant, intelligent black woman named Mrs. Bertha Flowers, who treats her to cookies, Dickens, and good advice. Better dressed and better read than anyone else in the community, she nevertheless maintains good relations with all and urges Marguerite not to neglect the wisdom of the folk as she pursues literary interests: "She said that I must always be intolerant of ignorance but understanding of illiteracy. That some people, unable to go to school, were more educated and even more intelligent than college professors. She encouraged me to listen carefully to what country people called mother wit. That in those homely sayings was couched the collective wisdom of generations" (p. 97). In contrast to Wright's grandmother, who banished from her house the schoolteacher Ella for telling the story of Bluebeard to Richard, Grandmother Henderson is quite friendly with "Sister" Flowers, both women secure in their sense of self and their mutual respect.

Angelou also recalls favorably the larger rituals of black community. Religious exercises, whether in a church or in a tent revival meeting, provide a festive atmosphere for Marguerite and Bailey. Racial euphoria pervades the black quarter of Stamps after a Joe Louis victory in a prizefight broadcast on Uncle Willie's radio to a crowd crammed into the store.[8] A summer fish fry, the delicious feeling of terror while listening to ghost stories, the excitement of pre-graduation activities — these are some of the pleasures of growing up black so amply present in *I Know Why the Caged Bird Sings* and so conspicuously absent in *Black Boy*.

A comparison of the graduation exercises in the two works is particularly instructive. Marguerite is showered with affectionate attention and gifts, and not only from her family and immediate circle of friends: "Uncle Willie and Momma [her Grandmother Henderson] had sent away for a Mickey Mouse watch like Bailey's. Louise gave me four embroidered handkerchiefs. (I gave her three crocheted doilies.) Mrs. Sneed, the minister's wife, made me an undershirt to wear for graduation, and nearly every customer gave me a nickel or maybe even a dime with the instruction 'Keep on moving to higher ground,' or some such encouragement" (p. 169). Richard feels more and more isolated as graduation nears: "My loneliness became organic. I felt walled in and I grew irritable. I associated less and less with my classmates" (p. 152). Refusing to use a speech prepared for him by the school principal, he resists peer and family pressure, as well as

the implicit promise of a teaching job, in order to maintain his sense of
individual integrity.   Giving his own speech, he rejects utterly the
communal ceremony implict in the occasion:

> On the night of graduation I was nervous and tense; I
> rose and faced the audience and my speech rolled out.
> When my voice stopped there was some applause. I did
> not care if they liked it or not; I was through. Immediate-
> ly, even before I left the platform, I tried to shunt all
> memory of the event from me. A few of my classmates
> managed to shake my hand as I pushed toward the door,
> seeking the street. Somebody invited me to a party and
> I did not accept. I did not want to see any of them again.
> I walked home, saying to myself: The hell with it! With
> almost seventeen years of baffled living behind me, I faced
> the world in 1925. (p. 156)

The valedictorian of Marguerite's class accepts the help of a teacher in
writing his speech, but before he mounts the podium a white politician
delivers the Washingtonian message that "we were maids and farmers,
handymen and washerwomen, and anything higher that we aspired to
was farcical and presumptuous" (pp. 175-176). But this ritual of
racial humiliation is immediately followed by a ritual of racial survival and solidarity. After giving his speech, the valedictorian im-
provises by singing "Lift Ev'ry Voice and Sing" with renewed meaning, joined by all present, the white man having left. From shame the
collective emotion is transformed by the song of a black poet to pride:
"We were on top again. As always, again. We survived. The depths
had been icy and dark, but now a bright sun spoke to our souls. I was
no longer simply a member of the proud graduating class of 1940;
I was a proud member of the wonderful, beautiful Negro race"
(p. 179). Unlike Wright, Angelou stresses the intimate relation of
the black creator to the black audience. Gathering his material from
the stuff of the black experience, with its suffering and its survival,
James Weldon Johnson transmutes the experience into art, giving
it back to the people to aid them to travel the stony road, to fortify

their spirit by reminding them of their capacity to endure. The episode is a paradigm of Angelou's own artistic endeavor in *I Know Why the Caged Birds Sings.*

It is important to recognize that Angelou's Southern environment is as grievously afflicted by white racism as Wright's. Just as young Richard is tormented by whites, so is Marguerite by her employer Mrs. Cullinan, who calls her out of her name, or by Dentist Lincoln, who owes Grandmother Henderson money but will not treat the child's toothache because "'. . . my policy is I'd rather stick my hand in a dog's mouth than in a nigger's'" (p. 184). White violence comes dangerously close to both Uncle Willie and Bailey. Indeed, the town is quintessentially Southern in its racial attitudes, comparable to Wright's Elaine or West Helena or Jackson: "Stamps, Arkansas, was Chitlin' Switch, Georgia; Hang 'Em High, Alabama; Don't Let the Sun Set on You Here, Nigger, Mississippi; or any other name just as descriptive. People in Stamps used to say that the whites in our town were so prejudiced that a Negro couldn't buy vanilla ice cream. Except on July Fourth. Other days he had to be satisfied with chocolate" (p. 47). It is not that Angelou de-emphasizes the racist assault on Black personality and community; it is just that she shows with respect if not always agreement the defensive and compensatory cultural patterns developed to survive in such an environment. This is Maya Angelou's response in *I Know Why the Caged Bird Sings* to the call of *Black Boy.*

One hesitates to generalize on the basis of a single book by one woman writer, but a quick recall of such writers as Linda Brent, Zora Neale Hurston, Gwendolyn Brooks, Margaret Walker, Paule Marshall, Sonia Sanchez, Toni Morrison, Sherley Anne Williams, Nikki Giovanni, Carolyn M. Rodgers, Ntozake Shange, Alice Walker, Gayl Jones, and numerous others suggests that, more than male writers, women are concerned with such themes as community, sexism (especially sexual exploitation), and relations with family and friends. They seem correspondingly less interested in individual rebellion, alienation, and success against the odds. A theory which can encompass both visions, adding community to the myth of freedom and literacy, accommodating *I Know Why the Caged Bird Sings* as easily as *Black Boy,* may follow the stages delineated by Houston Baker and become the primary contribution of the present decade to Afro-American literary criticism.

NOTES

1. "Generational Shifts and the Recent Criticism of Afro-American Literature," *Black American Literature Forum,* 15 (1981), 3-4.

2. Baker seems unaware that "The Literature of the Negro in the United States" in its first version was a lecture Wright delivered in 1945, closer in time and temper to "Blueprint for Negro Writing" (1937) than to the late Fifties. The concluding pages of the essay in Wright's *White Man, Listen!* (Garden City, New York: Doubleday, 1957), pp. 105-150, mentioning the Supreme Court decision, are an addendum for the benefit of European audiences to the lecture first published as "Littérature noire américaine," *Les Temps Modernes,* No. 35 (August, 1948), pp. 193-220. Baker's treatment of Wright here contains other examples of chronological and interpretative confusion.

3. Richard Wright, "Blueprint for Negro Writing," *New Challenge,* 2 (Fall, 1937), 53-65.

4. *Black Boy* (New York: Harper, 1945), p. 23. Subsequent parenthetical page citations in the text are to this edition.

5. *I Know Why the Caged Bird Sings* (New York: Random House, 1969), pp. 33-34. Subsequent parenthetical page citations in the text are to this edition.

6. The extent of the exaggeration is evident from the photographs Wright took of his father at the time, which reveal an erect, black-haired, rather youthful appearance for a man in his early sixties. See Constance Webb, *Richard Wright: A Biography* (New York: Putnam, 1968), following p. 128, and Michel Fabre, *The Unfinished Quest of Richard Wright* (New York: Morrow, 1973), pp. 19, 205. Wright's "description" of his father actually corresponds much more closely to a photograph of a sharecropper in Wright's *12 Million Black Voices* (New York: Viking, 1941), p. 23.

7. George E. Kent discusses this contrast with his customary acuity in "Maya Angelou's *I Know Why the Caged Bird Sings* and Black Autobiographical Tradition," *Kansas Quarterly,* 7, No. 3 (1975), 72-78.

8. Wright did share the racial pride in Joe Louis. See "Joe Louis Uncovers Dynamite," *New Masses,* 18 (8 October, 1935), 18-19; "High Tide in Harlem," *New Masses,* 28 (5 July 1938), 18-20; *Lawd Today* (New York: Walker, 1963), p. 52; and "King Joe," *New Letters,* 38 (1971), 42-45.

Groundwork for a More Comprehensive Criticism of
Nikki Giovanni

by

Margaret B. McDowell

I.

The nature of Nikki Giovanni's poetry cannot be fully understood
nor its significance in recent literary history be established unless critics
provide more perceptive interpretations and assessments of her work
than they have done in the first fifteen years of her career.[1] Such
informed appraisals are long overdue, and her reputation has suffered
from the neglect of her work by serious critics. Those who would
contribute now to more comprehensive and open-minded judgments of
her work will undoubtedly wish to consider the early contradictory

appraisals of her poetry to ascertain what is genuine in them as a basis for this more comprehensive undertaking. I shall summarize, accordingly, the extreme reactions which Giovanni's poetry evoked primarily during the first five years of her career (1969-1974). And I will speculate on possible explanations for these contradictory responses and mediate among the early conflicting judgments, because they significantly affect her reputation to this day.

It is my general conclusion that much of the writing on Giovanni's poetry has been predicated on the critics' misperceptions, their insistence on half-truths, or their rigid and demanding political and personal convictions. Academic literary critics have been inclined to generalize about Black poetry and have failed to recognize the relationships present between the poetry and Black speech or Black music. They have tended also to discover aesthetic excellence only in poetry of intricate symbolic or intellectual complexity. On the other hand, political reviewers of Giovanni's work have overestimated the necessary function of poetry in the furtherance of Black Cultural Nationalism and Pan-Africanism, and they have underestimated her poetry affirmation of Afro-American culture and her realistic portrayals of individual Afro-Americans and their experience. In writing of her poetry, critics have allowed personal and political attitudes not merely to affect their judgment but to dominate it. For example, they have used, in place of objective criteria, the tenet that poets should subordinate their individual creativity to the rhetorical needs of the political or racial group. They have placed excessive value on consistency in the views expressed from poem to poem and book to book as if the persona of a poem is always the author herself and the experience depicted is autobiographical. They have demanded that the author's personal behavior be approved if her poetry is to be judged favorably. Some reviewers have sought in Giovanni's poetry an ideal for Black womanhood and been disappointed either by the assertiveness, impudence, and strength they found in the poetry or, conversely, by the acknowledgment of emotional vulnerability, disillusionment, and fatigue which can also be found in it. The written response to Giovanni's poetry shows relatively little evidence of the application of objective criteria or of clearly formulated critical postulates. In the total body of criticism on her, no systematic, career-long examination of her techniques, her development, or the shifts in her interests and viewpoint can be found. In the reviews, one finds ardent enthusiasm for "the Princess of Black Poetry" and also cutting and humiliating attacks on both the poet and her poetry, but only a handful of writings reflect an open-minded, sensitive, and careful reading of all her work.

The judgments one infers from the popular response to Nikki Giovanni's poetry may ultimately provide more reliable critical assessment than that gleaned from "professional" sources, because such popular judgments are often made by listeners as well as readers and depend on reactions to the immediate clarity of lines; the impact of tone, rhythm, and language; and the integrity of the realism in Giovanni's depiction of Afro-Americans and their experience. The response at the popular level reflects the views of large numbers of people from a wide variety of backgrounds. However, such judgment comes, in part, from the shared enthusiasm of the crowd and the charismatic personality of the poet as well as from the poetry itself, and while the emphasis on the poetry's orality is important in criticism of Giovanni, the listener cannot fully assess the damage done to a poem by a single flawed line or by an awkward beginning, and he or she is equally likely to overlook the rich ambiguities and ironies found in the best of Giovanni's lyrics.

In the past, Giovanni claimed that the criticism of her work was irrelevant. But her attitude appears to have changed. Recently, she has implied that "harder questions" than those asked last year challenge her work this year. Her statements in recent interviews with Claudia Tate and Arlene Elder[2] may, in themselves, provide guidance for an effective critique of an author's achievement throughout a career — particularly of an author like Giovanni, who is still experimenting with technique, growing as an artist, and broadening her vision.

A consideration of the difficulties which Giovanni experienced in the 1970s in establishing her early reputation and of her own recently expressed views on the criticism she has received to the present time might serve to indicate those aspects of her work which call for

further scrutiny.   Among the subjects that have never had full discussion and that demand considerable systematic and reasonable
criticism are (1) an identification of her goals, (2) a definition of her
techniques, (3) discrimination among her aesthetic successes and
failures, (4) an analysis of the changes in her processes of invention
and of revision, (5) an identification of the objects of her satire and
its purposes, (6) an analysis of her use of folk materials, (7) the com-
pilation of a history of the oral presentations of her poetry (before
various kinds of audiences in stage performances, on records, and on
television), (8) an examination of her status as a writer of books for
children, (9) a determination of the shifts in her interests as related
to the forms that she has used, (10) an exploration of the alleged
inconsistencies in her work, and (11) a sensitive analysis of the flexibility, the ironies, and the ambiguities that add grace and substance
to her poems — particularly those in which she develops "the women
and the men" themes.   Her use of Black music (jazz, blues, spirituals,
folk, and popular), which enriches the patterns to be found in her
poetry, and her recourse to stylized elements in Black conversation are
also important features of her work that contribute to the "orality"
for   which she is famous, and these subjects need further investigation.

Each of Giovanni's successive volumes has been marred by the inclusion of some misbegotten poems or prosaic or sentimental lines
(which usually occur at the beginnings or ends of poems).   These
failures repeatedly have claimed disproportionate attention in reviews, blurred the focus of her critics, and delayed the acknowledgment of her developing stature. Consequently, I would view as a first
priority in the building of a comprehensive criticism of Giovanni
the publication of a collection of her poems, selected with exceeding
care.   Such a volume seems crucial to the serious assessment of her
achievement from 1968 to the present and to a more general awareness of her continued promise as a mature poet. With such an ordered
and trimmed presentation of her work, critics might begin to see her
poetry in its proper place in the history of Afro-American poetry and
in its relation to the work of other American poets of the present
time.   Her critics, acting largely upon personal and political beliefs

and preferences, have delayed such observation of Giovanni's work from the perspective of American literary history. While a chronological presentation of the selected poems could encourage developmental studies of the poet, arguments could be made for arrangement by topic, theme, or form.

If Giovanni is eventually to receive her merited place in the history of American literature, it is time for critics to examine the marked division in the response that her work has elicited (a division that began in 1971 and that widened greatly in 1972 and 1973). In 1972 the audiences for her poetry and its readers were highly enthusiastic; academic critics ignored her; radical Black critics, having praised her a year or two earlier, attacked her, mostly on ideological and personal grounds; and newspaper and magazine reviewers wrote brief generalizations and seemed to be reading each other's reviews rather than her poems. A disinterested consideration of her work as literary art appeared impossible when those who read her work praised it extravagantly, sharply attacked it, disregarded it, or commented on it in general formulas. Nor did it seem possible later in the 1970s for writers to consider her career in its totality in order that they might ascertain her development as a thinker and an artist as each new volume appeared and that they might appraise her achievement for what it had gradually become. On the basis of her first widely-read collection, *Black Feeling/Black Talk/Black Judgement* (1970), critics casually placed her in the context of current Afro-American poetry by classifying her with "the Black revolutionary poets" and by referring to her work as representative of "the new Black poetry of hate." Following the reactions which met *My House* (1972) and later volumes, wherein she includes few political poems, no critic has seriously confronted the whole body of her poetry and its relationship to the developments in Afro-American poetry since 1960, and to modern poetry in general.

II.

Before she gained the attention of the critics and the public with

Black Feeling/Black Talk/Black Judgement, Giovanni had attained
a modicum of distinction as a promising scholar and writer, receiving
honors from universities and grants from funding agencies for the
humanities. She graduated in 1967 from Fisk University (her maternal
grandfather, a Latin teacher, had earlier graduated from Fisk; her
parents, both social workers, had graduated from Knoxville College,
also in Tennessee). At her graduation she received honors in history,
a formative discipline in her life. She has continued to read history
as her recreation, and it has influenced her perspective on many contemporary issues. In 1967 she won a Ford Foundation Fellowship
to study at the University of Pennsylvania; in 1968, a National Foundation of the Arts grant to study at the School of Fine Arts, Columbia
University; and in 1969, a grant from the Harlem Council of the Arts.

   She had also by 1970 grown in political and racial perspicacity and
had gone through several phases of awareness of, and commitment to,
Black causes. From early childhood she knew that her gradfather had
changed teaching jobs and smuggled her grandmother, Louvenia, out
of Georgia to Knoxville, Tennessee, one night, after hiding her under
blankets. Louvenia had, as an "uppity" pioneer member of the
NAACP, offended white people with her outspoken assertion of her
rights. Nikki Giovanni's moving portrayal of Louvenia in *Gemini*
(1970) suggests convincingly the effect of her independent, yet emo-
tionally vulnerable, ancestor upon her. In Cincinnati, where her parents
worked in social services, Giovanni learned as a child about urban
poverty, the difficulties that Blacks face in attaining equal justice,
and the struggles that Blacks undergo for economic survival in a
Northern industrial city. During the times she lived in Knoxville,
Tennessee, she saw, through her grandmother's eyes, the relative
powerlessness of Blacks in confronting the racism of the white population in a smaller Southern town. For example Giovanni in 1967
thought Louvenia had been figuratively "assassinated" by the people
who so wanted "progress" in Knoxville that they re-routed a little-
used road, necessitating the displacement of her grandmother and her
neighbors from the houses in which they had lived most of their lives.
She felt that the elderly people grieved to death in alien surroundings.

In *Gemini* Giovanni tells an anecdote about herself at age four. She threw rocks from the porch roof at enemies who chased her older sister from school. She thought her sister should not fight her own battle: she might "maim" her hands, not be able to take her music lessons, and, as a consequence, the music teacher's family might starve. The story anticipates Giovanni's willingness and energy to enter the fight at hand (as in Black Cultural Nationalist enterprises between 1967 and 1969), but it also suggests that the motivation for her militance lay in helping the Black community rather than in gaining power for herself. In college her political activism intensified. Her ambivalence about the politically moderate family heroes — Martin Luther King, Jr., and Roy Wilkins — led her to found a campus chapter of SNCC during the period of Stokely Carmichael's leadership of that organization. As a graduate student at the University of Pennsylvania and then at Columbia (and simultaneously as a teacher at Queen's College and then at Rutgers University) for about two and a half years before the birth of her son (Thomas Watson Giovanni), she supported the Black activists in the leftist and radical Black Arts, Black Theater, and Black History groups; and she spoke at conferences in Detroit, Newark, Wilmington, and New York during the time that Amiri Baraka, Larry Neal, and Ron Karenga became leaders of Black Cultural Nationalism. Although she has consistently retained her commitment to the Black Aesthetic principles that all genuine Black art explore and affirm the Afro-American experience, she has always been ambivalent and cautious about the expectation that noteworthy Black art be "useful" in promoting the struggle for social and political power — and especially about the mixing of para-military activity with poetry. She has never believed that self-determination for a people negated the need for individual self-determination.

By 1969 she had openly dissociated her work from the demands that prescriptive didacticism was making upon her as an artist. By that time, Baraka and his associates had gained national domination of the Black Liberation Movement through para-military means in the Committee for a Unified New Ark, had violently challenged the supremacy of parallel California groups and their leaders, and, between 1970 and 1974, had fought for the support of major coalitions in the Pan-African organizations. Giovanni retreated from such extreme political action, and, as her dialogue with James Baldwin (1973) and some later poems show, she had begun again to appreciate the effectiveness of Martin Luther King. Only occasionally in the 1970s did she write about Black revolution, and then she addressed in prose issues related to equal justice, as in the cases of Angela Davis and H. Rapp Brown.

Giovanni still sees the need for continuing the Black revolution, but she contends that the revolution started four hundred years ago in America rather than in the 1960s and that one confronts its struggles, and experiences its victories, constantly. In frequent public and printed remarks, she undoubtedly alienated certain younger Black critics in the early 1970s as she dissociated her goals for Afro-American power from the more radical politics of the Black Nationalists and the Pan-African liberation groups. In her interview with Arlene Elder, Giovanni describes Africa as the world's richest continent and oldest civilization but indicates that she does not feel a closer relationship to it than to all of the other places on "this little earth" in which she wishes to travel everywhere freely with her son. She regards her poetry as having been little influenced by African culture, because she is Western by birth and no traditionalist. (Curiously, because she views the Near East as an extension of the African continent, she sees the influence of the Bible upon her poetry as African in origin.) The subject matter of her poems has consistently been Afro-*American*.[3]

Giovanni's willingness to limit her political efforts to Afro-American causes has continued to bring her negative criticism, even today, partly because she so openly calls herself a Black American "chauvinist." Since the feminist movement has increasingly linked American women with those in developing nations, some feminist critics of Giovanni have also seen her focus as self-centered. The evidence that political disapproval of her exclusive focus on Afro-American needs, and not on African needs, *still* affects her literary reputation can be seen in the exclusion of her poems from the fine anthology, *Confirmation: An Anthology of African American Women,* edited by Amiri and Amina Baraka (New York: Quill, 1983). The book includes works by forty-nine practicing women poets, and since Giovanni is frequently considered to be today's most widely-read Black American woman poet, perhaps the most widely-read living Black American poet, period, her absence from this volume is startling. A terse footnote in the prefatory material states that Giovanni's contributions were rejected at press time because she traveled in South Africa in 1982.

III.

The most significant development in Giovanni's career has been her evolution from a strongly committed political consciousness prior to 1969 to a more inclusive consciousness which does not repudiate political concern and commitment, but which regards a revolutionary ethos as only one aspect of the totality of Black experience. Her earlier political associates and favorable reviewers of the late 1960s often regarded her development after 1970 with consternation, as representing a repudiation of her racial roots and of political commitment, without perhaps fully understanding the basis for her widened concerns and interests. Giovanni's shift in interest from revolutionary politics and race as a collective matter towards love and race as they affect personal development and relationships brought strong reviewer reaction. (The shift to less favorable criticism, which is apparent in the reviews of *My House,* is also evident in the late notices of *Gemini,* Giovanni's most widely reviewed book.) The problems involved in studying the relationship between this shift in her poetry and the somewhat delayed shift from favorable to less favorable criticism, as her artistry grew, are complex. And they are further complicated by the fact that, at the very time the negative reviews of her poetry markedly increased, her popularity with readers surged dramatically ahead. Witness the late sales of *Gemini* (1971) and *Black Feeling/ Black Talk/ Black Judgement* (1970), the new sales of *My House* (1972), and the record-breaking sales of two of her early albums of recorded poetry. Her audiences around the country grew markedly in size and enthusiasm in 1972, and feature articles and cover stories on "the Princess of Black Poetry" appeared in over a dozen popular magazines in 1972 and 1973.

Studying the relationships between the positive and negative reviews and between the opinions of reviewers and popular audiences is made more difficult by an anomaly presented by Giovanni's *Black Feeling/ Black Talk/Black Judgement:* two-thirds of the poems in this 1970 volume are brief, introspective lyrics which are political only in the most peripheral sense — that they mention a lover as someone the speaker met at a conference, for instance. The remaining third, poems which are strongly political and often militant, received practically all the attention of reviewers. Critics ignored almost completely the poems that foreshadow nearly all the poetry Giovanni was to write in the next thirteen years. In short, the wave of literary reviews that established Giovanni's national reputation as a poet also established her image as a radical. Yet, by the summer of 1970, when these reviews began to appear, Giovanni had been writing solely non-political, lyric poetry for a year. The label "the poet of the Black revolution" which characterized her in the popular media was already a misnomer in 1970, when it began to be popularly used.

The change in stance had, in fact, appeared by 1969, when Giovanni published an article criticizing the leaders of Black Cultural Nationalism. In it, she also rejected the rigidity and the prescriptiveness of the Black Aesthetic, the proponents of which insisted that committed Black writers like herself could only write about changing the Black situation in America in terms of power. She further charged that Black Arts groups had become exclusive and snobbish, and she attacked the Movement's male activists for demanding the subservience of Black women to the male leaders of the cause. In general, she concluded that she could no longer as an artist subordinate her poetry to the politics of revolution. Entitled "Black Poets, *Poseurs,* and Power," the essay appeared first in the June, 1969, issue of *Black World* (pp. 30-34). The aggressive Black leaders of the revolution must surely have read it, but apparently few of her other readers knew of the essay. Since Giovanni had no popular following prior to 1970, her 1969 essay did not become a widely discussed matter in the literary world.

At least initially, readers also seem to have paid scant attention to the philosophical conclusions that Giovanni had arrived at and had announced in her casually organized and conversational essay when it was reprinted in *Gemini*, a collection of prose pieces, in 1971. Most would have been more interested in her angrily expressed charge that the Black Cultural Nationalists "have made Black women the new Jews." Black readers of *Gemini* would have focused, too, on her reaction to the 1968 electoral campaign in Newark: the Black citizens of Newark, she contends, seemed more fearful of their "liberators" than they did the corrupt white politicians who had oppressed them in the past. That Giovanni had, by 1971, felt *some* repercussions from the publication of her article might account for her remark, in *A Dialogue: James Baldwin and Nikki Giovanni,* that "the young Black critics are, I think just trying to hurt people, and the white critics don't understand."

Ruth Rambo McClain, reviewing Giovanni's 1970 poetry collection *Re:Creation* in the February, 1971, issue of *Black World* (pp. 62-64), is one of the first critics to recognize the change in Giovanni's subject and form. McClain regards the many lyrics in *Re:Creation* as "tight controlled, clean — too clean" and sees in Giovanni not only "a new classical lyrical Nikki, exploring her new feeling," but "an almost declawed tamed panther." *Re:Creation,* a small collection, contains a few poems on revolution, the imprisonment of Blacks, and the hatred of white oppressors (perhaps written prior to having arrived at the conclusions Giovanni presents in "Black Poets, *Poseurs,* and Power"). Most of those who reviewed her two 1970 books of poetry wanted more poems of this sort and referred to them as *sharp, vital, energetic,* or *non-sentimental.* A few more detached critics saw the rhetoric in them as somewhat posed and artificial but did not object on political grounds.

Most of the reviews and essays on Giovanni in 1971 recognized no impending change in her work. For example, A. Russell Brooks, writing on "The Motifs of Dynamic Change in Black Revolutionary Poetry" in the September, 1971, issue of *CLA Journal* (pp. 7-17), includes Giovanni in his list of nine poets "in the forefront" of revolutionary poetry, and he identifies her as "one of the first two or three most popular black poets." Placing his comments on her between those on Don L. Lee (Haki Madhubuti) and LeRoi Jones (Amiri Baraka), he refers to Lee as the most impatient, Giovanni as the most popular, and Jones as "the Dean of Black Revolutionary Artists." However, in a later review of *A Dialogue* (*CLA Journal,* December, 1973, pp. 291-294), Brooks speaks of Giovanni's "marked change in her mode of looking at the world and writing about it" as reflected not only in *My House* but "fairly well indicated" in *Re:Creation* and *Gemini.* In a 1971 article entitled "The Poetry of Three Revolutionists: Don L. Lee, Sonia Sanchez, and Nikki Giovanni" (*CLA Journal,* September, 1971, pp. 25-36), R. Roderick Palmer failed to acknowledge Giovanni's shift in vision, seeing her, among these three figures, as the *true* revolutionary: "the most polemic, the most incendiary; the poet most impatient for change, who . . . advocates open violence." Palmer, like many other readers, failed to recognize the preponderance of the lyric mode in the collections of 1970, the preponderance of poems devoted to self-analysis, love, and the exploration of personal relationships; he mistakenly remarks that she "occasionally lends herself to less explosive themes."

On February 13, 1972, June Jordan, herself a Black poet, reviewed *Gemini* in the New York *Times Book Review* (p. 6) in a generally favorable way. She notes that the paragraphs of Giovanni's prose "slide about and loosely switch tracks" but feels that two essays are "unusual for their serious, held focus and for their clarity." She singles out for special comment the 1969 article "Black Poets, *Poseurs,* and Power" and the last essay in *Gemini,* "Gemini — A Prolonged Autobiographical Statement on Why," which closes with the statement "I really like to think a Black, beautiful, loving world is possible." More directly than had McClain, Jordan remarks on what she also identifies as an impending transition in Giovanni's work — because of the attitudes she sees revealed in these two essays. She agrees with Giovanni that the growing militarism in the Black Arts Movement is deplorable and that the Black community itself is the loser when violent strategies pit Black against Black and leave the real enemies "laughing at the sidelines." She observes that Giovanni, in "Black Poets, *Poseurs,* and Power," was telling the world in 1969 of a change occurring in her poetry and in herself. In speaking of the closing essay in the book, Jordan concludes: "When you compare the poetry [apparently she refers here to the revolutionary poems included in the 1970 volumes] with the ambivalence and wants expressed in this essay, it becomes clear that a transition is taking place inside the artist. . . . She is writing, 'I don't want my son to be a George or a Jonathan Jackson!'" A few months later, the publication of *My House*, without revolutionary poems and with most of its lyrics written after 1969, proved June Jordan's careful and perceptive interpretation of Giovanni's intent to have been accurate.

Two of Giovanni's friends wrote positively of her new emphasis on personal values in 1972. Howard University Press editor Paula Giddings, who provided the preface for Giovanni's *Cotton Candy on a Rainy Day* (1978), in a brief review of *Gemini* in *Black World* (August 1972, pp. 51-52), contends that Giovanni's concern for individual Black self-determination places her in a long standing tradition of Black literature. Ida Lewis, Editor of *Encore*, a magazine for which Giovanni wrote a twice-monthly column beginning in 1975 (as well as many other articles), mentions in her preface to *My House* that Giovanni already "has been reproached for her independent attitudes by her critics. . . . But Nikki Giovanni's greatness is not derived from following leaders, nor has she ever accepted the burden of carrying the revolution. Her struggle is a personal search for individual values. . . . She jealously guards her right to be judged as an individual." These two sets of remarks make it evident that Giovanni had heard that attacks on her work were soon to appear in print. In the preface to *My House*, Lewis quotes Giovanni as saying of such Black critics: "We are the *only* people who will read someone out of the race – the entire nation – because we don't agree with them."

In the same month that Jordan's review appeared, Black critic Peter Bailey published a favorable feature story in *Ebony* (February, 1972, pp. 48-54, 56) on Giovanni's rapidly growing popular reputation, but he ominously suggested, as did Lewis, that the negative reaction from certain Black artists and politicians loomed just ahead for Giovanni and her poetry. Unlike Jordan, Giddings, and Lewis, however, Bailey saw her popular reputation as a partial *cause* for the accelerating attack on her work, whereas Jordan had referred to it as a "guarantee" of the interests of her work: "Like it or not," writes Bailey, "— and some people don't like it — she has become a cultural force to be dealt with. She's a much-anthologized poet and she's a lecturer who commands a vast audience. . . . There are black artists — those in what she called 'the black-power literary establishment' — who are convinced that Nikki's emergence as a 'star' will hinder her development as a *black* poet" (pp. 50, 52).

Since the bulk of Giovanni's Black political associates and fellow artists did not understand the basis for her widened concerns as a poet and saw only her apparent retreat from revolutionary politics, few critics who supported the Black Aesthetic applauded her. Dudley Randall (editor of the Broadside Press), Ida Lewis, Paula Giddings, and probably June Jordan recognized the imperative of the artist to follow her or his own vision if one's imaginative poetry is to flourish. Most others regarded Giovanni's new position as a failure in nerve, even a betrayal. In their reviews they commented disapprovingly about her diminished political and racial commitment in turning to the lyric and away from revolutionary themes, and they judged harshly the poems that dealt with sex, love, and family relationships.

These critics seldom attacked either specific poems or specific lines; they simply opposed Giovanni's new ideological orientation. Repeatedly, they stereotyped her unfavorably — as a woman crying for a lover she could not hold, as a mother abandoned with a baby — frustrated and resentful, longing for the return of her man. While she was insultingly derided for "singing the blues," she was almost as often stereotyped as a frivolous woman, joking, laughing, enjoying herself when serious issues of race and revolution needed to be addressed, and as an overly ambitious and successful woman, who had compromised to accommodate and please everyone in order to gain popularity, wealth, and applause. This second stereotype — the too-happy woman — was labeled the "ego-tripper." ("Ego-Tripping" is the name of one of her most popular poems which she often reads to audiences. It derives from folk origins — the tall-tale, the amusing boaster whose exaggeration increases throughout the story or song and has no bounds as explicit details accumulate into a semblance of invulnerable realism. *Ego-Tripping* is also the name of her 1973 book for young people.)

Those reviewers who promoted the stereotype of Giovanni's crying the blues for a lost love said that her poems were sad and lacking in energy; those promoting the ego-tripper stereotype complained that her poems were irrelevant, frivolous, trivial, and derived from European lyric traditions. Giovanni's son was five when this kind of attack was most blatantly made — certainly not an infant —; in 1969 and 1970 when he *was* an infant and when her revolutionary poetry was occupying reviewers, no such references were made. The image of the woman sitting alone and weeping over a sacrificed future must have seemed strange to the crowds who knew of the strenuous speaking and travel schedule which she maintained in the early '70s. In addition, she was writing the poems published in *The Women and the Men* in 1975, and both preparing her dialogues with Margaret Walker and with James Baldwin for publication in 1973 and 1974, respectively, and producing two books of children's poems, written for her son. During part of this time she also continued to teach at Rutgers University.

In any event, whether critics' animosity arose from their disapproval of independent motherhood, envy of Giovanni's success and popularity, or anger at her political withdrawal from the Black Cultural Nationalist acitivity and failure to support Pan-African groups, the bitterness of their reviews is startling. They are as extreme in their negation as were the crowds which welcomed Giovanni wherever she spoke or read her poetry extreme in their enthusiasm. Hilda-Njoki McElroy prefaces her review of *A Dialogue* in the December, 1973, issue of *Black World* (pp. 51-52, 75-78) by satirizing the book as "Who's Afraid of James Baldwin and Nikki Giovanni: A Comedy for White Audiences," starring N. Giovanni who, as a "super cool, funny woman[,] reveals her vulnerability." McElroy then refers to Giovanni's recent honors as "accolades and awards from the enemy."

Kalamu ya Salaam (Val Ferdinand) launched a still harsher attack upon Giovanni's integrity in an essay which purports to be a late review of *My House* and of her record album *Like a Ripple in the Pond* (*Black World,* July, 1974, pp. 64-70). This critic — who edits the *Black Collegian,* is associated with the Nkombo Press in New Orleans, and writes essays, poetry, and plays — had won the Richard Wright Prize for Criticism in 1970. He was active in the Congress of Afrikan People and the Afrikan Liberation Support Committee, and a few months later published a long report on his assessment of African Liberation Day entitled "Tell No Lies, Claim No Easy Victories" *Black World,* October, 1974, pp. 18-34). He is obviously sympathetic to Baraka's progress in the early 1970s towards dominance in the Pan-African groups as he won strength also for the CFUN (Committee for a Unified New Ark). Given Salaam's political background, it is not surprising that he disapproved of Giovanni's 1969 statement on the Black Cultural Nationalists and her refusal to participate in the African liberation groups. Nevertheless, the sense of shock which he expresses in his review rings false, because he is writing about a change that occurred in her work five years before and should have been clear to everyone two years earlier with the publication of *My House.*

In his essay Salaam centers on a quotation from Baraka which describes the Black actress Ruby Dee in a mournful pose, sitting at a window on a rainy day. (Ruby Dee had, since 1940, played roles in *Agamemnon, King Lear, Boesman and Lena,* and *A Raisin in the Sun* and taken other parts in stage plays, films, and television dramas. Like Giovanni, she had produced poetry readings against a background of jazz and gospel music.) Quoting Baraka, "Ruby Dee weeps at the window . . . lost in her life . . . sentimental bitter frustrated deprived of her fullest light. . . ." Salaam continues, "This describes *Nikki* perfectly." He then contends that Giovanni has moved from revolutionary poetry to sad lyricism in *My House* because she is lamenting a lover who has abandoned her, and she now is, like "a whole lot of Ruby Dees, sitting . . . waiting . . . the footsteps of us brothers come back home." His supposed pity for her suddenly assumes a harsher tone: "Nikki has gone quietly crazy." Referring to her lyric about the experience of being a bridesmaid, he taunts her by saying, "A lot of the seeming insanity and nonsense that Nikki verbalizes . . . must be understood for what it is: Broken dreams. Misses. Efforts that failed. I betcha Nikki wanted to be married. . . ." This fictionalized biography completed, Salaam attacks Giovanni's poetry for its sentimentality, its romanticism, and its being influenced by European tradition ("strictly European literature regurgitated"). He scolds her for turning from the unremitting analysis of "collective oppression" in order to "sing the blues" about personal problems. She should have known that "just love" is not an appropriate theme for poetry, because love is an intensely personal experience between only two individuals and, thus, is counter-revolutionary. He concludes that Giovanni does not have the right to "do whatever . . . she feels like doing" because she is, as a Black, still "in captivity." She should see the limits of her poetry within the message "The revolution is, and must be, for land and self-control. And good government."

IV.

It is my contention that Giovanni's rejection of the pressure to write primarily a didactic, "useful" political poetry was not only a sign of her integrity but an inevitable sign of her development. A truly comprehensive criticism of her work must be willing to recognize both her continuing commitment to the attainment by Black people of power in America and a commitment to personal freedom for herself as a woman and an artist. Critics need not only to see the importance of politics in her life but to perceive also that a commitment to politics, pursued with ideological rigor, inevitably becomes constricting to an artist. That Giovanni still writes political poetry can be understood by attending to the anger which she expresses in each volume at the oppression of Blacks, women, and the elderly; she continually deplores also the violence which oppression spawns. She illustrates the conflict between ideological commitment, exacted by political beliefs, and the demands of the artistic sensibility which tend to find such commitment confining and stultifying. She illustrates in her own work and career the same arc that the poets of the Auden generation in England illustrated: the passing beyond a doctrinal basis for one's poetry to a work responsive to an illuminating of the whole of the individual's experience. Giovanni's case is both complicated and made clearer by her connections with the Black Liberation Movement, which has not yet won all its objectives, particularly her affinities to the work of those closely tied to Marxist-Leninist ideology and Pan-African goals.

Giovanni has been viewed by some of her politically ardent contemporaries in the liberation groups as having deserted the movement with which she was at first visibly associated. Her revolutionary poem in *Black Feeling/Black Talk/Black Judgement* made her into a heroic figure for some Blacks, and the myth of her fiery opposition to tyranny was slow to die — even though she had moved away from Black Cultural Nationalism before most of those who hailed the strenuous and dominant voice in her poems knew that she existed. A more comprehensive criticism would permit critics to consider that Giovanni may have gained rather than lost as a result of the development of a personal idiom and of a more lyrical stance in her post-1970 work. In her response to Peter Bailey's questions early in 1972 about the "reproach" from Black activists that was gathering about her and her work, Giovanni displayed again the defiance and staunch independence captured in the anecdote from *Gemini* which features the four-year-old Nikki holding the fort with stones on her porch roof, ready to fight back against detractors: "I'm not about telling people what they should do. . . . The fight in the world today is the fight to be an individual, the fight to live out your own damn ego in your own damn way. . . . If I allow you to be yourself and you allow me to be myself, then we can come together and build a strong union. . . . I'm an arrogant bitch, culturally speaking" (*Ebony,* February, 1972, pp. 54, 56).

In her poetry Giovanni has chosen to communicate with the common reader, as well as with artists and critics; consequently, she has used graphic images from everyday Afro-American life and stressed the "orality" of her usually short poems, often by assimilating into them the rhythms of Black conversation and the heritage from jazz, blues, and the spirituals — reflecting these origins both in rhythmic patterns and borrowed phrases. She has tended to focus on a single individual, situation, or idea, often with a brief narrative thread present in the poem. Her choice of such simple forms has meant that academic critics might well be less interested in her work than in that of the more complex and intellectualized poets most often associated with modernism, such as T. S. Eliot, Ezra Pound, and W. H. Auden. She avoids the allusions to classical literature and mythology, the relatively obscure symbolism, the involved syntax, the densely-packed idiom, and the elliptical diction often characteristic of such poets. If the verbal and structural forthrightness of Giovanni's poetry in some measure accounts for the paucity of academic criticism of it, this elemental quality accounts also for her popular acclaim by thousands who come to hear her read her work. Like a folksinger, she senses the close relationship of poetry with music, since her poetry, like music, depends on sound and rhythm and is incomplete without oral performance and without an audience. (At times, especially in her children's poetry, she relates her poems to a third such art, dance.)

Throughout the 1970s Giovanni read her poetry and lectured on campuses, at churches, and on radio and television. Paula Giddings reported in the preface to Giovanni's *Cotton Candy on a Rainy Day* (1978) that Giovanni appeared before as many as two hundred audiences a year during the 1970s, commanding substantial speaking fees.[4] Today she continues to make public appearances but on a less strenuous schedule. As a poet of the people, Giovanni renews the tradition of the bard, prophet, or witness who sings or chants to inform the people, to subvert tyranny, and to bring an audience together as a community to celebrate a cause or person or a heritage, or to establish a basis for sympathy and understanding of one another's suffering or problems. For Giovanni's audience participation at a poetry reading can be as much a part of the aesthetic experience as congregational expression may be part of worship experience.

Giovanni's acceptance by the public was strong in 1970 and grew in 1971 with the publication of *Gemini,* and in 1972 and 1973 it greatly increased, in counterpoint to the negative reviews of *My House* during those years. In 1969 the *Amsterdam News,* a Black New York weekly found in 1909, listed her as one of the ten most admired Black women in America. By 1970 and 1971 journalists and television speakers generally referred to her as "the star" or "the Princess of Black Poetry." June Jordan, in reviewing *Gemini,* commented in 1972 that the book's interests were "guaranteed by Miss Giovanni's status as a leading black poet and celebrity," and she referred to Giovanni's "plentiful followers" who claimed her as "*their* poet," so directly did she speak to them (The New York *Times Book Review*, 13 February, 1972, p. 6).

The popular media both reflected her burgeoning popular reputation and strengthened its further growth. Besides the many feature articles on her poetry and personality in major popular magazines, over a dozen in 1972 and 1973 alone, she frequently appeared on late-night television talk shows, and she read her poetry regularly on *Soul*, a one-hour television show of music, dance, drama, and literature for young people (sponsored by the Ford Foundation). In 1970 she established her own company, NikTom Records, Ltd., and then recorded albums on which she read her poetry against a musical background — first, gospel; and later, blues, jazz, rock, and folk. Two early albums were best-sellers, and one received the national AFTRA Award for Best Spoken Album in 1972.

Giovanni says that she speaks for no one but herself, but she actually has become, in her poems, the speaker for many diverse groups and individuals. She has revealed a sincere interest in the people from many backgrounds who come to hear her or who write to her. Though in her early work she made use of a militant rhetoric with images of violence, she deplored — even in her first major volume — the actual violence seemingly endemic to American life. In one of her first poems, "Love Poem: For Real," she mourned the fact that "the sixties have been one long funeral day." In her poetry she is ardently sympathetic to those who have died uselessly and goes on in each new volume to lament the senselessness of the results of prejudice and intolerance, the public tragedy that she makes personal tragedy in her poetry — from the Ku Klux Klan murders of civil rights workers in Philadelphia, Mississippi, through the assassinations of public leaders in the 1960s, to the murders of kidnapped children in Atlanta.

She has attracted feminists with her portrayals of the women in her family and of elderly Black women. They have noted her frequent dedications of poems to women and have been impressed by her courageous assertion that she had her baby in 1969 because she wanted a baby, could *afford* to, and didn't want a husband. The more traditional leadership of the National Council of Negro Women, moreover, has honored her with a life membership, and she has praised their inclusive program of advocacy and membership policy. Young protesters against the draft and Viet Nam involvement crowded her campus lectures, but she also encouraged high school students at assemblies (often Black students) to avoid an alignment with "hippie" groups and to follow a disciplined life — to aim higher, work harder, and demand bigger rewards. After the inmates of the Cook County Jail presented her with a plaque, she boasted that prisoners and students were her best supporters. She relished ceremonies in which mayors from Gary, Indiana, to Dallas, Texas, gave her keys to their cities. With more somber pomp and ceremony, she was in three years (1972-1975) awarded four honorary doctorates.[5]

One example of the acclaim Giovanni received in 1972 and 1973 can be found in an event honoring her which combined the setting of the Kennedy Center for the Performing Arts, a formally attired audience of government dignitaries and other celebrities, a several-month-long publicity promotion in the *Ladies' Home Journal,* and the financial backing of Clairol (a large manufacturer of hair products) with a one-hour television extravaganza which pre-empted network programs. In 1972 Giovanni received one of seven "Highest Achievement Awards" from *Mademoiselle* as "one of the most listened to of the younger poets" (*Madamoiselle,* January, 1972, pp. 66-68). In the more highly publicized *Ladies' Home Journal* "Women of the Year" contest in 1973, she became one of the eight winners (from among eighty nominees on ballots printed in the magazine, which thirty thousand subscribers clipped, marked, signed, and mailed that month). A jury of prestigious women who made the final choices for the list included Shirley Temple Black; Margaret Truman Daniels; Eunice Kennedy Shriver; the presidents of the National Organization for Women, the General Federation of Women's Clubs, the National Council of Negro Women, Women in Communications, and two women's colleges; the dean of a medical college; a recruiter for high-level positions in the Nixon administration; and a woman Brigadier General in the U. S. Air Force. Besides Giovanni, the list itself in-

cluded such famous women as Katharine Graham, publisher of the
Washington *Post*; Shirley Chisholm, recently a Presidential candidate;
and actress Helen Hayes. Other nominees included Coretta King;
Dorothy Day; Judge Shirley Hofstedler; sculptor Louise Nevelson;
historian Barbara Tuchman; authors Joyce Carol Oates, Anne Sexton,
and Pearl Buck; musicians Beverly Sills, Joan Baez, Carly Simon, and
Ethel Waters; athletes Billie Jean King, Chris Evert, and Peggy Fleming;
feminists Bella Abzug, Betty Friedan, Gloria Steinem, and Aileen
Hernandez; former ambassador Patricia Harris; sex researcher Virginia
Masters; Patricia Nixon; Julie Nixon Eisenhower; and Rose Kennedy.
The awards (pendant-pins with three diamonds, specially designed for
the occasion by Tiffany's) were presented by Mamie Eisenhower,
news commentator Barbara Walters, and Senator Margaret Chase
Smith. The ceremony, hosted by actress Rosalind Russell, was viewed
by an estimated television audience of thirty million.

The nomination ballots had identified Giovanni as a "Black consciousness poet," and the award presentation statement cited her as
"a symbol of Black awareness." Although it also described her somewhat patronizingly as a person "rising above her environment to seek
the truth and tell it," readers of her poetry know that its "truth"
derives not from her rising above her environment but from her having
remained so close to it. This mass-media event offers evidence of the
poet's rapid rise to celebrity and provides evidence of the widespread
recognition of her and her poetry. This popular acclaim would seem
to be an affirmation of her decision four years earlier to write on a
wide variety of subjects and to reach as wide a number of people of
differing backgrounds and personal characteristics as possible.

V.

The problems arising from Giovanni's early critical reception linger.
As we move in the direction of providing a more adequate base of
understanding and assessment of her work, it is fortunate that three
good sources of Giovanni's own views on the criticism of poetry
(particularly her own work) have appeared in the last two years: the

verse preface to Giovanni's *Those Who Ride the Night Winds* (1983), the 1983 interview with Claudia Tate in *Black Women Writers at Work,* and the 1982 interview with Arlene Elder.

As I mentioned earlier, negative criticism of Giovanni – often based on personal or political bias rather than sound literary assessment – gains strength by pointing to a particularly poor poem or an unfortunate line. Giovanni's process of revision (or discarding all or part of a poem), therefore, has special relevance in her continued development. As she describes her process of revision to Claudia Tate, she essentially discards an entire poem if it appears to present several problems or a major problem. Otherwise, when she discovers a recalcitrant line or two, she "starts at the top" and rewrites the entire poem – perhaps a dozen times – rather than working on a particular line or phrase. She finds this radical rewriting necessary to insure the poem's unity: "A poem's got to be a single stroke." It is particularly important to understand this characteristic process, established over fifteen years, as one begins to criticize Giovanni's forthcoming works. According to Arlene Elder's introduction to her interview with Giovanni, the poet is about to embark on an experiment with much longer poems (1,200-1,500 lines) after a career of writing short poems. Since one cannot rewrite a long poem a dozen times upon encountering problems in a few lines, Giovanni's revision process may radically change.

One already sees changes of probable significance between Giovanni's most recent book, *Those Who Ride the Night Winds,* and her books of the 1970s. In many of the poems she is using a "lineless" form: the rhythmic effects come from measured groups of words or phrases of fairly regular length separated from each other by ellipses, but appearing otherwise to be prose paragraphs. Except for works before 1970, she has (more than other contemporary Black poets, such as Sonia Sanchez or Haki Madhubuti) avoided such unconventional typographical devices as capitalizing all the words in a line, separating a single syllable between lines (Bl-Ack), or spelling for the sake of puns (hue-man, Spear-o-Agnew, master-bate). She has probably done so, in part, because of the artificiality of these tricks – but more often because she stresses the oral nature of her poetry, and such typography has little effect on the spoken word. One wonders, then, whether she is, in her latest volume, moving away from the emphasis on the oral. She may also be seeking a bridge between the freedom of prose and the more exact structuring of poetry. In this book she also includes a number of poems about individual white people — John Lennon, John F. Kennedy, and Billie Jean King, for example. New critics of Giovanni will need to know her earlier work and the nature of its development to understand and evaluate the changes that appear to be approaching in her career.

From the Tate interview, one learns much that is significant about Giovanni's views on good criticism. She now claims that she does not care whether her critic is black or white, but the individual should understand her work, or try to do so, before writing on it. In her view critics must not permanently "brand" a work so that other critics unconsciously embrace that judgment. They should not expect consistency within an author's canon, since such an expectation denies the fact that an artist may grow and change. In reviewing a book, they should place it in the context of the rest of the author's work. They should not assume that the voice ordering the poem and the experience described in the poem are necessarily autobiographical. They should not aim to injure an author personally by referring to private matters instead of concentrating on the work apart from the author's life. They should not question a writer's integrity because they happen to disagree with the ideas expressed in the work. Giovanni's comments, though offhanded, are pithy: "There would be no point to having me go three-fourths of the way around the world if I couldn't create an inconsistency, if I hadn't *learned* anything." "You're only as good as your last book. . . . God wrote one book. The rest of us are forced to do a little better." "You can't quote the last book as if it were the first."

In her preface to *Those Who Ride the Night Winds,* Giovanni invites her readers to hurry along with her as she flies the uncharted night winds, because she is *changing,* and because — as the Walrus said — the time has come to talk of *many* things. If she still feels distrust of critics, in this preface she suggests a willingness to listen, as in the interviews she suggests a desire to be energized as a poet by "better questions this year than last." In spite of her mixed experience with critics, she does not see herself as their victim, because she knows that she was free to choose a safer occupation than that of writer and did not do so. In the "lineless" poetry she uses in her new book — the first unconventional typography she has used since 1970 — she puns on the "bookmaker" as a professional gambler and her own game of chance as a "maker of books": "Bookmaking is shooting craps . . . with the white boys . . . downtown on the stock exchange . . . is betting a dime you can win . . . And that's as it should be . . . If you wanted to be safe . . . you would have walked into the Post Office . . . or taken a graduate degree in Educational Administration . . . you pick up your pen . . . And take your chances . . ."

Giovanni's critics, who often limit themselves to reviews of her separate books, devote little attention to her development from year to year and provide little specific analysis of the significant aspects of the form and structure of her poetry. No critic has fully discussed the variety of her subjects and her techniques. Beyond this, personal bias and political needs, rather than a commitment to judgments based on sound theoretical postulates, dominate much of the criticism which does exist on her work. Those who have attacked her poetry most severely have failed to understand Giovanni's compulsion to follow her own artistic vision as well as her continued commitment to Afro-American culture. Her great popularity among readers of many ages, classes, races, and economic backgrounds is at variance with the neglect of her work by critics or their tendency to patronize her and her work. Sympathetic and sophisticated studies of her work are a prime necessity if she is to achieve the recognition due her as a literary artist. Such studies, it is hoped, would encourage her to achieve her full potential as a poet and would also attain for her the reputation that the corpus of her work calls for.

NOTES

1. Giovanni has published eight books of "adult" poetry — *Black Feeling/Black Talk* (1968; rpt. Detroit: Broadside Press, 1970), *Black Judgement*

(Detroit: Broadside Press, 1968), *BlackFeeling/Black Talk/Black Judgement* (New York: Morrow, 1970), *Re:Creation* (Detroit: Broadside Press, 1970), *My House* (New York: Morrow, 1972), *The Women and the Men* (New York: Morrow, 1975), *Cotton Candy on a Rainy Day* (New York: Morrow, 1978), and *Those Who Ride the Night Winds* (New York: Morrow, 1983) — and three books of verse for juveniles — *Spin a Soft Black Song* (New York: Hill and Wang, 1971), *Ego-Tripping & Other Poems for Young People* (Westport, Connecticut, and New York: Lawrence Hill, 1973), and *Vacation Time* (New York: Morrow, 1980). Her published prose includes *Gemini: An Extended Autobiographical Statement on My First Twenty-Five Years of Being a Black Poet* (Indianapolis: Bobbs-Merrill, 1971), *A Dialogue: James Baldwin and Nikki Giovanni* (Philadelphia and New York: Lippincott, 1973), and *A Poetic Equation: Conversations between Margaret Walker and Nikki Giovanni* (Washington, D. C.: Howard University Press, 1974). A collection of Giovanni's manuscripts is housed in the Mugar Memorial Library of Boston University.

    2.   "Nikki Giovanni," in *Black Women Writers at Work,* ed. Claudia Tate (New York: Continuum, 1983), pp. 60-78; "A MELUS Interview: Nikki Giovanni," *MELUS*, 9, No. 3 (1982), 61-75.

    3.   Giovanni included a few poems on Africans in *My House,* and she refers to African history and anthropology occasionally in her prose. In a 1972 interview with Gwen Mazer (*Harper's* July, 1972, pp. 50-51), Giovanni mentioned her hope of being able to take her son, who was learning Russian and Chinese at the age of three, to Africa to help him understand his heritage as she had not understood hers as a child. But after another decade and three trips to Africa, she told Claudia Tate that going to Africa to live was not the solution for Black Americans, who would be strangers there, much as they have remained strangers in America. Being an alien, she concludes, is an asset; it makes one equally comfortable with every place on Earth.

    4.   In 1972, Giovanni's standard fee for a university appearance was $2,000.

    5.   From Wilberforce University in Ohio in 1972, from Ripon College in Wisconsin and the University of Maryland—Princess Anne Campus in 1974, and from Smith College in Massachusetts in 1975.

"Dialect Determinism": Ed Bullins' Critique of the Rhetoric
of the Black Power Movement

by

Leslie Sanders

I.

It was Black Power rhetoric that signaled the end of the Civil Rights
Movement. In the earlier movement, the language of the Black Church
predominated, notably the exceptional oratory of the Reverend Martin
Luther King, Jr., in which the language of the Church and that of
American social ideals were brilliantly combined. In King's rhetoric,
the injustice American blacks suffered and the justice they sought
were made vivid; made vivid also was the mode through which their
fight was conducted: confrontation through non-violence combined
with the discipline of Christian charity.

The Black Power Movement explicitly rejected the non-violence of which King spoke, and its rhetoric differed accordingly. Whereas King spoke of the ballot, Malcolm X included bullets as the alternative; whereas King prayed for brotherly love from behind the bars of a Birmingham jail, Malcolm X asked what kind of men stood by while other men murdered their children. Whereas King spoke of Christianity, Malcolm X and others offered the alternative mythology of Islam, particularly its Black Muslim variant; whereas King spoke of the failure of the American Dream, Black Power advocates, influenced by analyses of colonialism, and particularly by the work of the Martinique philosopher/psychiatrist/revolutionary Franz Fanon, spoke of the dialectical relationship of oppressor and oppressed and sought to understand the Afro-American predicament as analogous to that of subject colonial peoples.

Not only the images, logic, and sources of authority of the two rhetorics differed, but also their accents: whereas the rhetoric of the Civil Rights Movement was Southern and familiar to the rural as well as to an urban audience, that of the Black Power Movement was decidedly Northern, strictly urban and often derived its logic and authority from the ethics of the streets where many of its early adherents struggled for survival.

Certainly earlier Afro-American leaders had urged defensive and even offensive violence. Nat Turner explicitly saw himself as an avenging angel; David Walker called for violence in his *Appeal* of 1829; many slaves realized that in identifying themselves with the Chosen People they were also praying for the Divine vengeance of which the Old Testament speaks. During the Red Summer of 1919, Claude McKay wrote:

> If we must die, let it not be like hogs
> Hunted and penned in an inglorious spot,
> While round us bark the mad and hungry dogs,
> Making their mock at our accursed lot.
> If we must die, O let us nobly die,
> So that our precious blood may not be shed
> In vain; then even the monsters we defy

Shall be constrained to honour us though dead!
O kinsmen! we must meet the common foe!
Though far outnumbered let us show us brave.
And for their thousand blows deal one deathblow!
What though before us lies the open grave?
Like men we'll face the murderous, cowardly pack,
Pressed to the wall, dying, but fighting back!

— a poem whites found so alarming that it was read into the Congressional Record as a sign of imminent black insurrection. More than race loyalty motivated the passion with which black America followed the careers of such boxers as Jack Johnson, Joe Louis, and Muhammad Ali. What was new about the Black Power Movement's explicit advocacy of violence was its public quality. Neither was the language veiled nor were the discussions confined to the black community.

While violence was central to the Movement's rhetoric, violence was far from its entirety. In the main, the Black Power Movement sought to redefine black Americans' perceptions of themselves and their relation to the larger American society. While certain advocates were completely literal about the violence they urged, more often than not, those who engaged in the rhetoric of violence proposed an imaginative testing, indulgence, and validating of fantasies that had long lain buried in the collective imagination of American blacks. As Clay says, in Amiri Baraka's landmark play *Dutchman* (1964), "If Bessie Smith had killed some white people she wouldn't have needed that music. She could have talked very straight and plain about the world. No metaphors. . . . Crazy niggers turning their backs on sanity. When all it needs is that simple act. Murder. Just murder! Would make us all sane!"[1]

Although Baraka was among the most disconcertingly literal of the advocates of violence, his work continually explores the relation of word and act, of imagination and reality. He believed then, and does now, but for different reasons, in violent revolution, but the violence he sought to exorcise in much of his poetry, prose, and drama is the internalized violence which deforms and prohibits both self-knowledge and clear judgment of the world.

II.

> I went to see *The Toilet* and *Dutchman,* and when I saw
> *The Toilet* the whole world opened up to me because I
> never knew that I was right by writing *Clara's Ole Man.*
> . . . I didn't really find myself until I saw *Dutchman.*
> That was the great influence on my life. LeRoi has greatly
> influenced many young black artists. . . . he essentially
> created me as a playwright. . . .[2]

By 1969, when Ed Bullins made these remarks to interviewer Marvin X, Bullins was at least as influential as Baraka, at least in the theatre. Playwright-in-residence at the most important black theatre of the period, the New Lafayette Theatre in Harlem, he had also edited the Black Theater issue of *The Drama Review* (Summer, 1968), a volume which immediately became the new Black Theater's manifesto, and in fact the manifesto of the Black Arts Movement. Also in 1968, he won the Vernon Rice Drama Desk Award for an evening of three plays (*Clara's Ole Man, The Electronic Nigger,* and *A Son, Come Home*) produced and directed by Robert Macbeth of the New Lafayette (but staged downtown at the American Place Theater because the New Lafayette had just burned down). In 1969 he edited for Bantam the similarly influential anthology *New Plays from the Black Theater.* More awards and grants followed, including three Obies for Distinguished Playwrighting — in 1971 for *In New England Winter* and *The Fabulous Miss Marie* and in 1975 for *The Taking of Miss Janie.* By 1972 there had been at least fifteen productions of Bullins' plays at an impressive array of New York theatres, and he is now the author of over fifty plays, at least twenty of which have been produced and over forty published.

Bullins' major work of the period in question, however, was written and developed at the New Lafayette Theatre, and almost all of his work has its Harlem audience in mind. Most of Bullins' plays lovingly but unsparingly examine the lives of ordinary ghetto dwellers, their dreams and illusions, and particularly the way they themselves are authors of their own suffering. These plays of the black experience (the term is Bullins') embody the intent of the Black Theater of the period, but they are not typical of it, except in their choice of the ghetto as setting and subject. The plays normally identified as "black theater" were what Bullins called "black revolutionary theater": plays directly about conflict, either with whites or with internalized white culture and its deforming effects on black society.

Bullins wrote in both modes, but his plays differed markedly from those of most of his contemporaries in their attitude toward the rhetoric and mythology of the Black Arts/Black Power Movement of which they were a part. In various ways, and even while using it, Bullins suggested that *rhetoric* was a substitute for action rather than a prelude to it and that it constituted an evasion rather than a revelation of the transformations upon which a healthier society could be predicated.[3] Most of Bullins' "black revolutionary plays" depict the revolutionary scenario in order to test it. He challenges his audience to engage in the fantasies proposed, but then disturbs their fantasies by a voice within the play which comments on the vision in which the play engages.

For example, his early play *Dialect Determinism (or The Rally)* depicts a rally/church service through the eyes of a visitor who, the play suggests, remains unengaged only because it is his "first time." During the rally, Boss Brother harangues his increasingly excited audience with militant but illogical propositions ranging from "I call you Brothers for we have a common experience . . ." to "In brotherhood there is power, and all we want is power . . ." to "So as de most honest people on de face of the earth, we don't have to fool ourselves by sayin' it's some kind of holy crusade . . . if we get our chance finally to kick the hell out of somebody else for a change. . . ."[4] He claims to be a series of messiahs ranging from Hitler to Marx to Martin Luther King, Jr., Lumumba, Castro, and even L. B. J.; he has the ghost of Malcolm X evicted when it appears to challenge him; and he finally urges the crowd to produce a martyr. Not the fools they seem, the members of the crowd turn on him in a frenzy while the visitor and a girl he picks up slip away. "Never seen my people in such high spirits. Well, good night, brother. Good night, sister. Peace by with you," says the doorman as they leave (p. 37).

Dialect Determinism is characteristic Bullins: he wrote it in 1965 while at the same time closely involved with the formation of the Black Panther Party in San Francisco and in the developing of Black House, a cultural center which the Panthers used as a base. While it may be read as an attack on the Panthers (Black House dissolved in 1967 over a quarrel between the political activists and the artists who espoused cultural nationalism), there is no trace of the play's being seen as political treachery, then or later. *Dialect Determinism* is a satire about rhetoric without substance, about the dangers of a mob, about politics as emotional catharsis rather than as a reasoned guide for action. It foreshadows what Bullins was to do even more dramatically in later plays which ask the questions no one else within the Movement was asking, at least in a public forum. And he usually got away with it.

It Bees Dat Way (1970) admits a mixed audience (no more than twenty-five people and most must be white) to a room which is set as a Harlem street corner. The play consists of their being molested by pimps, prostitutes, and pickpockets. Tension erupts among the black characters, and one of them, Corny, advises the whites to leave the room before there is real danger, saying to the others, "Dese here people ain't the ones to get . . . they ain't got nothin' . . .just like you and me . . . they just work for them that made dis mess. . . . The ones to shoot is who what made this mess."[5] As the whites leave the room in twos and threes, Corny preaches to them: "SHOOT THE PRESIDENT . . . HE'S CUTTIN' OFF WELFARE . . . AND SENDIN' YOUR BOY TO VIETNAM. . . . SHOOT YOUR GOVERN-MENT . . . THEY'S THE ONES MAKIN' WAR ON YOU! . . ." (p. 15). As the last of the whites leave, sounds of sirens, crowds, gunfire, and riot erupt.

The impact of the play for a white audience is primarily discomfort-ing. As the black actors are extremely aggressive, it is not likely that the average white audience member would readily make the connection between the revolution he is urged to join and the un-savory behavior of the characters he has just encountered. For black members of the audience, however, the experience the play provides is more complex. If they enjoy the discomfort of the whites in the audience, the violence that builds quickly in the confined space, they are then robbed of completing their fantasies and reminded that what they have just enjoyed is too easy: such victims have little to do with what real revolution is about.

In *Death List* (also 1970),[6] Bullins proposed an image even more terrifying: the play consists simply of a black man cleaning and loading a rifle while calmly reading a list of sixty-eight names of black American leaders who signed an advertisement in The New York *Times* in support of the State of Israel. He punctuates his reading with comments and the refrain: "Enemy of Black People." A black woman joins him, entreating him not to fulfill the mission given him by the "Central Revolutionary Committee." Her arguments are various, but essentially she asks whether the black world of the future for which the revolution is being fought can be predicated on the ruthless violence for which the man is preparing himself. Her final accusation is that he has become the "white-created demon" of which they were warned. Her appeals are to no avail.

Notably, white reviews of the play attended only to its vicious attack on black leaders; little regard was taken of the woman's voice. Certainly the play is brutal: almost anyone, black or white, no matter how militant, would resist the inclusion of at least some of the names on the list. The play in its entirety, however, is far more than a political statement about the racial implications of U. S. support of Israel against the Palestinians.

Projected into a not-distant future in which a well-organized black revolutionary guerrilla army is conducting a consistent and presumably effective war against the United States, the play tests the revolutionary scenario at its most explicit and criticizes it in two ways. The first is a continual concern of Bullins: the fact that so much of Black Power politics was internecine rather than clearly directed at the roots of oppression. The second involves a variant of the question posed by the doctrine of non-violence, the question of whether, even when one acknowledges the necessity of violence in the name of change, violence does not simply beget itself. Bullins' abiding question, then, is whether and in what ways the rhetoric of Black Power is an advance over the ethics of the street, where people turn against each other over the ethics of the street, where people turn against each other and where violence is the tenor of human relations.

Bullins had proposed these questions in a more extended fashion in 1969 when, under the pseudonym Kingsley B. Bass, Jr., "a twenty-four-year-old Blackman killed by Detroit police during the uprising of 1967," he wrote *We Righteous Bombers,*[7] a reworking of *Les Justes,* Camus' meditation on terrorism and the terrorist. To Camus' plot and dialogue Bullins adds a further twist. His terrorists do not know — although in prison Jackson, the man who threw the bomb, discovers — that the Chief of Police is the Grand Duke and the man he has killed was an actor. Moreover, at the end it is suggested that while in prison Jackson chose to take the place of the prisoner who had bargained years off his sentence by becoming the executioner. Not only have the terrorists accomplished nothing, they do not even know if Jackson has remained true to them. In Bullins' play there is a question prior to the philosophical issue raised in *Les Justes* about whether violence can advance the cause of goodness and whether a man can murder with integrity. That prior question is posed as a problem of illusion: Bullins' terrorists do not even know if their target is real. *We Righteous Bombers* did not go unremarked: it was the subject of a heated symposium at the New Lafayette Theatre in which, unexpectedly, Baraka was one of Bullins' strongest defenders.[8] Characteristically, Bullins did not attend and, at least publicly, to this day denies that he wrote the play.

The philosophical issues raised in *Bombers* are not, however, Bullins' main concern. Other issues, apparently of less significance, are actually prior, in Bullins' eyes, to the moral issue of whether a new society can be born of violence. These issues may be characterized by the question: what exactly is the reality that needs be transformed? *Street Sounds: Dialogues with Black Existence* (also 1970) exemplifies his method of inquiry. This play is a series of forty monologues by such characters as "Harlem politician," "lover man," "seduced and abandoned," "black revolutionary artist," "non-ideological nigger," "black student," "wild child," and "Harlem mother." The delineations are brief, witty, and often moving; each exposes in the character not only what he or she thinks, but what he or she conceals from him/herself. The only unremitting portrait is a self-indulgence: the black critic attacks the kinds of plays Bullins writes, accusing him of creating a negative image of the race and of bad art.

In *Street Sounds,* the voices of Black Power, whether concerned with art or with politics, are only several among a multitude, and what emerges from the play is the sense that they describe the black experience no more or less accurately than any of the others. In fact, if anything they evade what must, for Bullins, be confronted first: the tangible, day-to-day experience of pain, failure, aimlessness, being trapped. For example, the "workin' man" says:

> Yeah . . . I've been workin' on this job for years. My whole family does, almost, at least my mother and sisters with me. I'm a foreman now. Make pretty good bread . . . Since we got a union now . . . tryin' to buy me a house . . . if my F.H.A. loan ever comes through. If you had'a seen me fifteen years ago . . . I was a bad nigger . . . I was out of work, bummin' around, no prospects . . . My crime partner, Tootsie, and me were trapped . . . trapped inside of ourselves, inside our surroundings, inside our experience. Yeah, those sound like some good words, you understand? I can rap them some . . . although I can't write them so good . . . Mom got me a job where she worked. And that's where I've been since. Didn't know I could or would work that hard and steady. I still drank and ran around and did other things but I worked. Tootsie didn't work steady but we still ran together. Even pulled an occasional job . . . And I grew fat. Tootsie got hisself killed last year by some broad's husband . . . and now I'm scared to death to stay out late at night because my old lady's threatened to lock me out and not let me in . . . Damn . . . I wonder what the next twenty years is going to be like.[9]

His speech is infinitely more eloquent than that of "the rapper," who intones:

> Brothers, we are slaves. Slaves in this moment of history. Nothing short of that, however we wish to disguise this fact . . .

> And what I am calling for is a slave revolt . . . An honest-
> to-god revolution. The time has come for us to throw off
> the shackles of the slavemasters. The time has come for
> us to rise up as men and rulers of our own destiny. The
> time has come for us to assume our roles on the world
> stage of revolution. . . . (pp. 178-179)

The "workin' man's" eloquence, like that of many of the other characters, lies in its simplicity and concreteness: the facts of the character's daily life make his simple generalizations almost superfluous. The "rapper's" rhetoric concerns ideas so remote from the details of existence that they obfuscate the realities that must be confronted and transformed if any revolution is to succeed. Bullins insists in almost all his work that what is can only be changed by being confronted. The "rapper's" rhetoric obscures this necessity because it invites its audience to evade rather than to transcend those realities.

In several full-length plays, all of which deal with race relations, at least in part, Bullins introduces a black nationalist figure and through these figures continues his critique of the Black Power Movement's rhetoric. The three principal figures are Ernie in *The Pig Pen* (1970), Gafney in *The Fabulous Miss Marie* (1970), and Rick in *The Taking of Miss Janie* (1974). These three characters have in common their rhetoric (their insistence on defining absolutely everything in terms of the black man's struggle for liberation). They all also display arrogance and superiority towards anyone who fails to define the world as they do, and displeasure (in Gafney, amounting to prudishness) over other characters' carryings on. Ernie judges Len for his white wife while lusting after her; Gafney is disgusted by everything that occurs at Marie Horton's Christmas party; Rick attacks Peggy for being a lesbian. Yet, Bullins insists in *The Fabulous Miss Marie,* unless the militant can ally himself with the street nigger, specifically, and more generally can come to a compassionate understanding of all aspects of the black community, his rhetoric will amount to nothing.

In *The Fabulous Miss Marie,* Gafney encounters Art, a character from another Bullins play, *Goin'a Buffalo*. Art is a ruthless con-artist and Gafney is horrified by him. At the end of the play, Art has overstepped his boundaries with Marie, who was using him as shamelessly as he was her, and she throws him out. The following interchange completes Art's dialogue with Gafney:

> **Gafney:** Art, there you are. . . . I see you're still standing around. What are you going to be doing when the revolution comes?
> **Art:** (Softly) Gafney . . . without me you won't have a revolution.
> **Gafney:** Oh, man . . . (Gafney looks at Art, Art feints, then jabs him sharply in the nose).
> **Bill** [the host]: Art . . . damn . . . what's going on here?
> **Gafney:** Oww . . . you shouldn't have done that . . . Don't you know I'm non-violent . . . you stupid, ignorant nigger![10]

Periodically throughout the play, which takes place at Bill and Marie Horton's Christmas party, the tv shows scenes of Civil Rights marchers being beaten on the streets of some Southern town. Wanda, Marie's niece, is their only defender. The older characters, all middle-class, either fear or feign ignorance of or reject what the young people are doing, principally because they see it as threatening the world they have struggled to create for themselves. Art, of course, rejects both the non-violence and the altruism in their behavior. At first Gafney backs Wanda: "Teach sister! . . . Tell 'em where it's at!" (p. 22). As the play progresses, however, Gafney becomes a less and less sympathetic figure as we see that he is critical not only of Art but also of Wanda, whose life is painful and complicated, or Marie and her friends, whose illusions he does not understand. As complex as her struggles have been, Marie Horton is admirable, as tough as Art, as loving as she can be given the sorrows in her life. Wanda's plight is the most desperate, but Gafney does not take her up on her offer of herself, so concerned is he with winning his argument with Art. Thus he leaves Wanda to be exploited by both Bill and her boyfriend Marco. Love between men and women is the principal barometer of social health in Bullins' plays, and in none of them does the cultural nationalist measure well.

The Taking of Miss Janie is Bullins' retrospective on the period of the Black Power Movement and its counterpart in white society. Peggy sums up his analysis succinctly:

> **Peggy:** We all failed. Failed ourselves in that serious time known as the sixties. And by failing ourselves we failed in the test of the times. We had so much going for us . . . so much potential . . . Do you realize it, man? We were the youth of our times . . . And we blew it. Blew it completely. Look where it all ended. Look what happened?
> (They all look out at the audience)
> We just turned out lookin' like a bunch of punks and freaks and fuck-offs.
> **Rick:** It has been said: "That if one doesn't deal with reality, then reality will certainly deal with them"
> **Peggy:** Amen.
> **Rick:** But I am not allowing myself to be held to blame. I am not allowing myself to be other than glorious. History will vindicate me.
> **Peggy:** Hey, man . . . you know, you never left yesterday. You're confused like all of us.[11]

The structure of *The Taking of Miss Janie* is the story of Monty's rape of Miss Janie; the play opens just after the rape and closes with its prelude. In the interim is the story of the Sixties told episodically with breaks for monologues from each of the significant characters, some of whom appear in Bullins' earlier works. Monty, the black poet, meets white Janie in his creative-writing class and means to have her. She insists the relationship remain platonic, and for thirteen years he complies: they are close, helpful to each other, even real friends. In the meantime, Monty marries and leaves Peggy, who later marries a white man, leaves him, and becomes a lesbian. Monty also has an on-going affair with Peggy's best friend Flossie, a good-time woman with little morality but a great deal of honesty. He drifts aimlessly, in and our of school, in and out of writing, but constant in his life is Janie. Janie, meanwhile, sleeps with many men, both black and white, has an abortion with Monty's assistance, and breaks with Lonnie, her long-time white boyfriend, a third-rate jazz player.

The one marriage that endures the Sixties is that of Len and Sharon, characters who first appear in *The Pig Pen.* Black Len is a student of black culture and history and the man responsible for the awakening of many others. Sharon is Jewish, as a young woman had been very spoiled and naive, but, as she appears in *Miss Janie,* is mature, realistic, and tolerant. Len has turned capitalist, still sees himself as the great teacher, and justifies all he does by saying he is an intellectual. Their relationship, though far from shallow, is full of compromise, which Sharon confronts more readily than does Len.

Janie, the symbol and object of Monty's obsessions, is a complex mixture of the calculated and the naive: "I'll be true to Monty. To keep our friendship alive. And perhaps our relationship will mature into the purest of loves one day. An ideal black/white love. Like sweet grapes change with age and care into a distinctive bouquet upon choice, rare wines" (p. 214). But she also admits to Flossie that she knows Monty's abiding interest in her is because "he's got what he wants from you . . . and he wants what he thinks he can get from me" (p. 227). According to Peggy, Monty is selfish and cruel. Certainly his relationship with Janie, although not without feeling, has little to do with love. Finally, Bullins concludes, behind all the talk, the romance with Mao, Fanon, and Voodoo (as Monty hurls at Mort Silberstein in their epic battle at the end of the play), are fantasies of domination. When all was said and done, what Monty really wanted was Miss Janie — and he got her, at a high price to both of them. Self-gratification triumphed over the creativity with which the decade began. Bullins' analysis of the failure of the Sixties summarizes his attitude toward Black Power rhetoric as well.

III.

Bullins does not mean to say, in all this, that what was said was of no value. In the real sense he was then and remains now a black cultural nationalist. Yet he shuns public engagement in politics and, considering his centrality to the Black Arts/Black Power Movement, made remarkably few statements which relied on the Movement's rhetoric. He sees his task as an artist as, simply, to extend people's vision of what is: Rick's cliché about reality dealing with those who fail to deal with it is also Bullins speaking. He believes people must confront first the realms in which they are the authors of their own unfreedom: their difficulty with love, with manhood, with the panaceas of drugs, crime, sex and violence, and romantic notions of machismo. Unless and until these abiding problems are confronted, political rhetoric, for Bullins, is meaningless, the violence Black Power proposed no more than the violence on any street corner in Harlem — and equally misdirected.

His work implies not only a comment on the rhetoric of Black Power but also on the rhetoric of the Civil Rights Movement. The non-violence King proposed is equally distant from the basic experiences of the people of whom Bullins speaks. Getting beaten up makes as little sense to him as does self-indulgent aggression. He understands fully the complexity of racial oppression, and in other plays deals with it acutely. However, that oppression is only a given in the lives of his characters, never a focus. In his major work, his eye never swerves from the self, from the black community as he sees its actual existence. The black political leader who is emblem of his beliefs is Malcolm X, but in *The Pig Pen,* in which the death of Malcolm figures, only the poet Ray and a white man, Mackman, truly mourn his passing.

Like Malcolm, Bullin's vision is urban, secular, and of the streets. It is there he finds home truths, and these are the abiding ones. Anything that deflects from dealing with them must be examined with care. Finally, Bullins queries the connection between the generalized analysis Black Power rhetoric proposed and the daily personal pain and complexity of individual existence. In suggesting that the former provided an evasion rather than a helpful understanding of the latter, he does not mean to negate the former's validity, only to test it and show where it is wanting. Bullins' mode of establishing the vision Black Power rhetoric proposed is contained rather in the phrase with which he prefaces most of his lists of characters: "The characters in this play are Black." He then proceeds to explore their world.

NOTES

1. In *Dutchman and The Slave* (New York: Morrow, 1964), p. 35.

2. Ed Bullins, "Black Theater" (an interview by Marvin X), *Negro Digest,* 18 (April, 1969), 16.

3. Not always: his *The Gentleman Caller* (1969), an absurdist piece in which a black maid presides over the destruction of her white employers, the Manns, and his "A Short Play for a Small Theatre," in which a black actor shoots every white in the audience, are more in Baraka's style of "poster art" or manichaean morality play. *The Gentleman Caller* is in *A Black Quartet* (New York: NAL, 1970); "A Short Play . . ." is in *The Theme Is Blackness: The Corner and Other Plays* (New York: Morrow, 1973).

4. In *The Theme Is Blackness,* pp. 22, 24.

5. In *Four Dynamite Plays* (New York: Morrow, 1971), p. 15.

6. In *Four Dynamite Plays.*

7. In *New Plays from the Black Theater,* ed. Ed Bullins (New York: Bantam, 1969).

8. A transcript of the symposium was published in the New Lafayette Theatre's journal *Black Theatre,* No. 4 (April, 1970), pp. 16-25. Whereas most of the participants attacked Bullins and the play for raising questions that were not resolved, at least not in a way that strengthened the audience's revolutionary purpose, Baraka defended Bullins, saying that there was a need for what he characterized as "poster art," which made unequivocal revolutionary statements, and also a need for plays like *Bombers,* which raised difficult and complex issues that did not meet with easy resolution. Both Baraka and Larry Neal also argued that a mark of the play's success was the very furor it caused, the strong response it elicited.

9. In *The Theme Is Blackness,* p. 160.

10. In *The New Lafayette Theatre Presents,* ed. Ed Bullins (Garden City, New York: Anchor, 1974), p. 65.

11. In *Famous American Plays of the 1970s,* ed. Ted Hoffman (New York: Dell, 1981), p. 230.

The Umbra Poets' Workshop, 1962–1965:
Some Socio-Literary Puzzles

by

Michel Oren

Umbra was a group of young black poets that held weekly meetings
in New York's Lower East Side from the summer of 1962 to late 1963;
it published two issues of a poetry journal with the same name. Some
of its members — Tom Dent, Calvin Hernton, David Henderson, Ishmael
Reed, Askia Muhammad Touré, Joe Johnson, Lorenzo Thomas, Norman Pritchard — have since become well-known in the literary world.
Umbra was an early salient of the Black Arts Movement, and it seems
to have split rather violently over its members' differing understandings
of what actions a cultural nationalist stance entailed. The recounting
of this apparently simple narrative gets so caught up in problems and

difficulties that one can come to feel that these obstacles may themselves be the real story. If Umbra was to some extent a microcosm of the artistic, social, and political context in which it occurred, these problems may be seen as the fissures or boundaries that delimit and define that context. This perception will become clearer in the process of looking at some of the problems.

☐ Ten different Umbra members have been interviewed in the course of this study, and their accounts present major conflicts, rather like the film *Rashomon,* where it seems impossible to establish a definitive version of what really happened.[1] This is particularly true for the split, where there is disagreement on whether Norman Pritchard was really kidnapped (and whether at knife- or gunpoint) and forced to surrender the Umbra bankbook, how each of the three journal editors voted at each stage about publishing a crucial Ray Durem poem, and whether the cause of the split was the incipient nationalism of some members or their class backgrounds or jealousy at Hernton's predominance over the group and the attention some members' work received at the expense of the group as a whole.

☐ The very presentation of these conflicting accounts risks reopening old wounds. At a national black writers' conference at Howard University in 1978, Tom Dent and Askia M. Touré, from what had been opposing Umbra factions, jointly called for an end to the continuing gossip and divisiveness surrounding "one of the literary legends of the century, that of the Umbra fight." Touré recalls: "Here we were now into middle age and with all the problems besetting black people and black culture and black literature, and here guys and women were feuding about something that happened twenty-something years ago. So both Tom and I called for an end to this nonsense because we have serious work to do in Afro-American literature and the whole status of black writers in this country." This is work I certainly wish to support. My reasons for presenting this material are a respect for the positions of both sides, which were argued with great seriousness and integrity; a conviction of the historical importance of the episode, which will justify even such a tentative presentation as this one; a desire to acknowledge in print the kindness of ten Umbra members who spent in some cases considerable time with me; a hope that such understanding of the episode as this account provides will spare the next generation of black poets the necessity of re-enacting it in the same painful form; and a feeling that better appreciating the complexity of the issues the participants faced and dealt with at an e-motional ignition point may heighten a sense of common involvement in an important historical moment among them.

This study of a group of black poets who lived and worked on the Lower East Side has been put together by one who is neither black nor a poet and who was not even living in the country at the time in question. This distance from the material, whatever its advantages, may give some tentativeness to its conclusions. However, two Umbra poets who have attempted histories of the group, David Henderson and Joe Johnson, have evidently not completed them; Johnson says that after twenty years he is "still too close to the material." Hopefully, the near future will see more definitive accounts published by the poets themselves.

This study was prepared as part of a larger work investigating the extent to which the leadership of the American artistic/political avant-garde had, in the '60s and the '70s, passed to groups of blacks, women, and regional poets and other artists — those who seem to have been relegated to the "margins" by American mainstream culture. Such groups then — and their critics later — attempted to navigate some turbulent eddies of competing beliefs and conflicting theories. My own course in this study has been to try to steer between a methodology that considers art and life as a continuum, and one which reads the Umbra narrative or narratives as a literary text which refuses closure and whose gaps should be read symtomatically.[2] These gaps, ruptures, fissures, or boundaries are of three sorts: the obstacles to understanding that arise from the conflicting narratives of the members, the watershed of the Umbra split and the minor divisions of its predecessor organizations, and the problematically disruptive behavior of one of the seemingly least important Umbra members, an attempted symptomatic reading of which ends this study.

☐   It would help to understand the evolution of Umbra — where it came from and where it was heading — if we were able to break it down into phases, and at the same time to reconstruct the dialectic of inputs, splits, recapitulations, and reformulations in the groups and movements, artistic and political, that prepared the ground for Umbra and reaped its harvest. Situating Umbra in its geographical context might also be useful.

One can identify a "pre-Umbra phase" from perhaps 1957 (when the poet Raymond Patterson held a reading with Calvin Hernton in the former's Lower East Side apartment) to the summer of 1962. In 1960 Patterson organized a series of six poetry readings at the Market Place Gallery in Harlem. These included Lloyd Addison and the work of Calvin Hernton (read by another poet, since Hernton was no longer in New York), and they were attended by Tom Dent and Rolland Snellings (later Askia Muhammad Touré).[3] At this time, the Dutch anthologists Rosey Pool and Paul Breman were in the States collecting the work of black poets for their books which were to appear in 1962. Patterson put them in touch with Addison, Hernton, Oliver Pitcher, and James W. Thompson in Detroit. Pitcher (born 1923), Patterson (born 1929), and Addison (born 1931) were older than most Umbra writers; they were to make brief but important appearances at the Umbra workshop, where their work offered a variety of models for the younger poets. Hernton and Dent (both born 1932) were, except for Art Berger, the oldest of the Umbra regulars. Thompson (born 1936) joined Umbra later.

Tom Dent was, from 1959 on, living and working in Harlem for the New York *Age,* a black weekly, and then for the NAACP Legal Defense Fund. In his search for other young disaffected black poets, he met Addison and Patterson at the Harlem readings. He began spending more and more time on the Lower East Side, and moved there in January, 1962.

In a second phase, Hernton returned to New York, and Dent found Hernton and his young protegé David Henderson and then sent out a call to all young black writers in the area to meet at his house. Thus began a series of Friday night workshops remarkable for the intensity of their critical spirit and enthusiasm. ("The criticism was never harsh — but grown men broke down in tears," Brenda Walcott reports.) The name "Umbra" was taken from a poem read by Addison. The group began to take on an identity. They decided to produce a poetry journal and named Dent editor and Hernton and Henderson associate editors, and these editors actually put out one issue, in early 1963.

The year and three months in which the workshop met regularly and intensely should be divided between this second and what might be considered the group's third phase, marked by the adherence to the group of Reed, Pritchard, Thomas, and others, and also by the appearance of certain tensions which were to prove disruptive. During this phase the workshop poets began to hold public readings as a group.[4] From Richard Wright's time there had been single black writers who had held the public eye as representative of "the black writer" and who had succeeded each other, but the group rejected this sort of tokenism and began to read eight or ten at a time.

A fourth phase would cover the period of the split in the group, from November, 1963, to the early months of 1964. The journal editors had previously agreed to include in the second issue a poem by Ray Durem (not a group member) derogatory to President Kennedy and to his children; but after Kennedy's assassination they felt the poem to be in bad taste and, after some disagreement among themselves, decided to withhold it. A faction including Ishmael Reed, Rolland Snellings (Askia M. Touré), Albert Haynes, and the Patterson brothers, Charles ("Charmy") and William, who were considered the strongest cultural nationalists in the group, vehemently protested this decision. A fistfight erupted, and then this faction abortively tried to take control of the journal by inducing the treasurer, Norman Pritchard — the manner in which this happened is not clear — to give them the Umbra bankbook and then go with them either to the NAACP Legal Defense Fund or the bank, where the money was kept. Meetings ceased. Dent went into hiding, according to one account, and knowing the printer's would be watched, had the galleys moved surreptitiously to another printing house. After several months Dent announced a big gumbo party (he is from New Orleans) which the opposition did not attend and at which he distributed the second issue — without the offending Durem poem.

A fifth phase would include most of 1964 and early 1965. Attempts to mediate the split came to nothing. There were wrangles about money and about what would become of the magazine. Ideological positions as well as individual stances became more clearly defined. In March, 1965, at a poetry reading in Le Metro coffeehouse, Dent was assaulted by an armed guard; Reed, despite his belonging to the opposition, went to Dent's defense. The incident, which both Dent and Reed ascribe to Mafia attempts to take over the readings and use them as a front for undercover operations, apparently brought to an end all Lower East Side readings and precipitated the dispersal of the entire scene, black and white.[5] In this same month, Amiri Baraka led what had been the Umbra opposition faction into Harlem, where they opened the Black Arts Repertory Theater/School (BART/S). In April, Dent disengaged himself from the Lower East Side scene and returned to New Orleans to work with the Free Southern Theater. He left the preparations for a third issue of the magazine in the hands of James Thompson, the new editor. David Henderson restarted the readings in another place and kept them going for another three months as the "Bowery Poets Co-op."

Two taped interviews, neither completely satisfactory, had already been conducted by Dent and other Umbra members with Ralph Ellison. In a sixth, "post-Umbra" phase, the new editors — Thompson, Steve Cannon, and Lennox Raphael — did a third session with Ellison. The edited text of these sessions was intended for the third *Umbra* issue, which encountered continual delays. Dent, back in New York from November, 1965, to March, 1966, realized that not only would the group not reassemble but that its members were spreading out all over the country. Although the third issue was already in type, he took the editorship away from Thompson and gave it to Henderson, who Dent felt had a better chance of staying in touch with the members. The Ellison interview was published in 1967 by *Harper's Magazine*.[6] The next year Henderson put out a third issue in the form of an "Umbra Anthology, 1967-1968." In 1970 he put out "*umbra/blackworks*" in tabloid form, and in 1974 from the West Coast he produced a final "Latin/Soul" issue of *Umbra*.

Umbra did not go through these phases in a vacuum. In the background were the developing Civil Rights Movement in the South, its more skeptical and nationalistic counterpart represented by Malcolm X in the North, the Harlem riots of 1964, and the efflorescence of the Black Arts Movement itself, which is thought to have peaked around 1970. These larger currents found expression in several group efforts that preceded Umbra: The Organization of Young Men, founded by LeRoi Jones in 1961 on the Lower East Side; its successor, with which it merged, the On Guard for Freedom Committee, founded by Calvin Hicks, which was primarily a Lower East Side group but which maintained an office on 125th Street in Harlem; two Monroe defense committees, one backed by the Communist Party, according to Harold Cruse, the other Trotskyist (in Monroe, North Carolina, Robert F. Williams, an ex-Marine, had led the local black community in an armed defense of its civil rights against the Ku Klux Klan and was wanted by the FBI for "kidnapping"). Poets belonged to these groups, which were primarily political, just as Julian Bond, Andrew Young, and Robert Brookins Gore, associated with civil rights policies, visited Umbra, which was primarily a group given to reading and criticizing poetry; no rigid line seemed to exist between politics and poetry. There were also groups purely devoted to poetry which were precedents for Umbra and which gave some of its members a taste for group endeavor in the arts, such as the one, led by Robert Hayden, in which Calvin Hernton participated while a student at Fisk at Nashville, or the one made up mostly of garment workers led by the Belgian unionist leather worker Henri Percikow, from which Henderson brought Lorenzo Thomas to Umbra and from which these two in turn brought Art Berger, an "old Lefty" who was white and almost twenty years older than anyone else in the group. There were also groups or movements that followed from Umbra, such as the Black Arts Repertory Theater/School in Harlem, the multicultural groupings of writers organized by Ishmael Reed on the West Coast, and activities connected with such enterprises as the Free Southern Theater and the Congo Square Writers' Workshop (Dent), Radio KPFA in San Francisco (Henderson), the Black Arts Center in Houston and the poets-in-the-schools program (Thomas), and the Neighborhood Arts Center in Atlanta (Touré), in which poets exercized and transmitted a tradition of group activity that had been acquired in Umbra. Most of these groups can be categorized according to the mix of political ideologies they represented; Thomas has traced the influence of three such ideologies during this period — that of NAACP political activism, that of radical Left (usually Communist Party) activism, and that of the Booker T. Washington/Garveyite tradition of black self-reliance and self-sufficiency (see Figure 1). Thomas also notes the continuing influence of the Harlem Renaissance, through Harold Jackman, who encouraged Raymond Patterson to do his 1960 series of Harlem readings and who put him in touch with the anthologist Rosey Pool, and especially through Langston Hughes, with whom the Umbra editors formed a personal relationship and whose *Ask Your Mama — Twelve Moods for Jazz* (1961) served as an important model for the group. Hughes should be considered among the poets, black and white, whose work was influential in Umbra, together with Ree Dragonette, for example, whose work was important in Hernton's individual development.[7]

The kind of historical consciousness which Thomas' diagram represents is a product of the Umbra workshop, which used to discuss "the need not to consider ourselves sprung from Zeus' head, to see the connection between what we were doing and what black people had done before," according to Brenda Walcott. Such thinking led Johnson to suggest to Dent the Ellison interview, in order to establish "if not an ideological continuity then a chronological one, so that you could see the evolution and divergence in black cultural styles"; if this linkage had been established more quickly, he believes, it might have stabilized the group and prevented its dissolution. Outside of Umbra, Harold Cruse was another person concerned in establishing such linkages. During the BART/S period he often discussed with Touré and Larry Neal "the whole question of the historical discontinuity of the estrangement between generations. I think that Harold saw himself as a living link between the generations," Touré reports.

Umbra met on the Lower East Side, but the more politically-minded young black poets of this period also seem to have felt an ambivalent attraction to Harlem and responsibility for the black masses there, and they oscillated between the two areas. Although Dent was probably the only member of On Guard who lived in Harlem, the organization maintained an office there, and the militant wing of

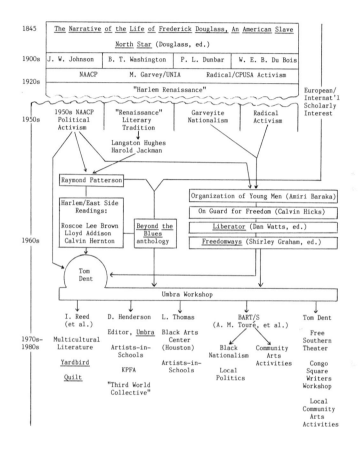

Figure 1
"A 140-Year-Old-Tradition"
(copyright © 1984, Lorenzo Thomas)

Umbra later went to Harlem with LeRoi Jones to found the Black Arts Repertory Theater/School. A group of older black writers, the Harlem Writers' Guild led by John Oliver Killens, met in Harlem, but the black bourgeois mainstream there would, in Dent's words, have seen the Umbra poets as "too wild, militant, and experimental." They were more at home in the Lower East Side scene and shared its Bohemian disaffection for American culture.

The Lower East Side or East Village was an area of dilapidated tenements and cheap rentals, where, according to Brenda Walcott, Poles, Ukrainians, Italians, Jews, blacks, and Hispanics "lived together in sort of a shaky truce" and where tolerance existed for the Hare Krishna, the Karista free love society, racially mixed couples, artists, and black poets who wrote according to very unacademic standards; that is, the general freedom of the neighborhood made itself felt in the Umbra poets' life styles and in their poems. From 1960 to 1965 the "LES" was also locus of a "ferment" in American letters that revolved around series of coffeehouse poetry readings, just as in the '50s and early '60s the single 10th Street block between Third and Fourth Avenues had been home to seven co-op art galleries plus the Club, and hangout of the Abstract Expressionists.

Perhaps the complex relations — or lack of them, in certain cases — among all these poets and artists, black and white, might be better understood through being schematized. A sociological tool called "network analysis" describes the flow of information, ideas, goods, money, power, support, and the like that circulate most profusely through such a scene or ferment. In the arts, such networks "tend to create 'against' some established principles or images. It is the sense of embattlement that leads to common bonding," Kadushin notes.[8] "Density" refers to the proportion of people in a group or network who interact with each other. Groups such as Umbra would be the cores of greatest density in the networks out of which they had coalesced, and also the most oppositional nodes; that is, the whole scene might be inset in the larger society as a sort of oppositional subculture while groups would turn some of their opposition on the very network or subculture that had in a sense generated them. Opposition would be, after all, a kind of relation, but there might also be areas in this network in which the relation or flow was interrupted and black or white poets or artists did not enjoy hanging out with one another. Such interruptions could be bridged, as for example by the New York School poets, who had the reputation of preferring the company of painters to that of other poets or by certain Umbra poets such as Lorenzo Thomas, who published in *C* Magazine and who had prior links to the poets of Ted Berrigan's group, itself affiliated with the New York School.

Within Umbra, one could diagram nodules of energy in which certain individuals had particularly close relations, whether temperamental, stylistic, ideological, or sexual; but because, in practice, distinctions among these types of relationships tended to blur, one might better understand a poet's ideology through appraising his temperament. In a more extended study, Joe Johnson has suggested, the Umbra women could supply particularly valuable information of this type. Even in a preliminary way, one can see that Reed was closer to Snellings and to Hernton than to Dent, while Jane Mackenzie (Poindexter) was closest to both Dent and Reed among the men and to Walcott among the women. The three editors were close; Henderson had been brought by Hernton into the group and was the latter's protegé. Such alliances both cemented the group and potentially pulled it apart.

One could also, if only to document the diversity of backgrounds in Umbra, diagram the geographical and cultural regions from which its members came — North and South, city and country, Afro-American and Afro-Caribbean. Dent was from New Orleans and Hernton from Chattanooga; Reed had been born in Chattanooga but had grown up in Buffalo, New York; the Patterson brothers had been born in North Carolina but had grown up in Harlem. Henderson, Johnson, and Pritchard had all been born in New York. Haynes, Thomas, and Lennox Raphael had Afro-Caribbean backgrounds.

☐   The Lower East Side context leads to another problem: Umbra can most fully be understood in the context of black cultural history — it is not really comprehensivle without that context — but Umbra also is a key element in the Lower East Side literary ferment of the early '60s, which has itself become a significant episode in American literary history. Moreover, Umbra is, with certain modifications, a late member in a series of avant-garde groups that began with the Impressionists and Symbolists in nineteenth century Europe and which have been responsible for revolutionizing the forms of Western art. They have all been characterized by an oppositional stance, a fusion of art and politics that originates in a common utopian impulse, the use of manifestoes and little magazines, and the introduction of innovative work. In the case of Umbra there are also inner and outer audiences, respectively black and white, and the opposition is directed primarily against the outer one — that is the group's major difference from the European form of avant-garde.

To consider Umbra in the contexts of the Lower East Side scene and the avant-garde is to risk losing sight of the group's historical specificity and uniqueness, yet to refuse to do so is to risk denying Umbra its historical importance.

Umbra's oppositional stance comes from a cultural nationalism intensified by events at a national political level. Should its story be told from a nationalist viewpoint or from a stance of presumed objectivity? Any movement of cultural nationalism, whether it involves Basques, Quebecois, Kurds, or American blacks, has "progressive" as well as reactionary aspects, and even non-members of these groups will recognize the building up of self-respect (what Larry Neal refers to as "the consolidation of personality") as one of the more liberatory and progressive ones. A literary history based on truth should probably not ignore the truth of the uses to which that history will be put.

Such considerations complicate even further the problem of assigning the origins of certain stylistic innovations in Umbra either to jazz or the close interrelation of the arts in traditional African society on the one hand, or to the impulse to synaesthesia and *Gesamtkunstwerk* of European modernism on the other. A case in point involves a pre-1965 poem of Norman Pritchard's, about which Lorenzo Thomas writes:

> Another member of the Umbra group, N. H. Pritchard, investigated the African underpinnings of "Black English"

before most of us even understood the significance of the term. Pritchard's early experiments, which were to lead to a "transrealism" that resembles concrete poetry, resulted in poems written in tampered English in which the combination of sounds approximated vocal styles and tones of African languages. Pritchard's poem "Aswelay" is a fine example of the experiment.[9]

Given the presence in the group of the Pan-Africanist Rolland Snellings (later Touré) and the idea that Pritchard allowed himself to be kidnapped, according to one report, out of sympathy with his kidnappers' views, this conclusion appears entirely reasonable, although difficult to prove. In the absence of a statement of intention from Pritchard, can we discount the possible influence of Langston Hughes' repetitive jazz poetry, as in *Ask Your Mama,* or contemporary sound poetry from Europe or South America? Thomas himself has said elsewhere that Pritchard "at that period was dealing in a mixture of Langston Hughes, Beckett and Joyce that also approximated African language." An assessment of Pritchard's work in 1967 reported, "At large are the influences of the early imagist work of Ezra Pound between 1912-1917, along with the early Japanese HaiKai Poets, Matsu Basho (1644-1694) and Yosa Buson (1716-1783). In the balances of language we have the folksiness of Paul Laurence Dunbar (1872-1906) and Geoffrey Chaucer (1343-1400) and the later works of romanticist Samuel Coleridge (1722-1834) and again Ezra Pound in The Cantos."[10] Such eclecticism makes it difficult to separate out influences at work in a single poem.

"Umbra did not represent the style of black writing and black thought that became encrusted and almost formularized, with a few writers like Don L. Lee and LeRoi Jones establishing the stylistic mold in the late '60s," Dent remarks. But to what degree did Umbra continue the innovative tradition in black writing? Ellison had described the shift in styles in his *Invisible Man* from Naturalist to Expressionist to Surrealist, and had suggested that Realism was not appropriate to certain unbelievable, improbable aspects of black life in this county. In the same way Baraka has pointed to a rejection of the writers of his generation:

> We thought that Naturalism was a musty, non-adventurous
> kind of pursuit, a kind of academic status-quoism. A lot of
> us . . . like I was always interested in Surrealism and Ex-
> pressionism, and I think the reason was to really try to get
> below the surface of things. . . . The Civil Rights Move-
> ment, it's the same thing essentially, trying to get below the
> surface of things, trying to get below the norm, the every-
> day, the status quo, which was finally unacceptable, just
> unacceptable. All those various things, the Organization
> of Young Men or On Guard or Umbra, were all attempts
> to go past the given, go past what's supposed to be ac-
> cepted and acceptable.[11]

In this typically avant-garde stance, the breaking of syntax and the
disruption of oppressive social conditions spring from the same impulse and seem part of the same enterprise. From such a stance certain
contemporary innovative black prose writing may, perhaps, be derived — such as that of Reed, Hernton, Clarence Major (published
in *Umbra*), William Demby (interviewed by Johnson), William Melvin
Kelley, Charles Wright, and Carlene Hatcher Polite. The Umbra poets
interviewed Ellison, and it is tempting to draw the line of descent
from him through Umbra to the writers just mentioned, especially
since Eugene Redmond affirms that "*Umbra* had a particular interest
in linking the post-Beat movement with the (often ill-termed) avant-
garde."[12]   The militant and utopian fusion of art and politics that
characterizes avant-garde groups would, thus, be complemented by
the avant-garde characteristic having to do with fostering an innovative
style.

   Yet Reed, for one, insists that his style is not innovative:

> I consider myself a classical Afro-American writer. I work
> out of the Afro-American cultural tradition, out of folk-
> lore, and my work probably has more in common with
> black folk art, the visual . . . which emphasizes fantasy,
> humor, and satire. . . . The distortion of my characters
> also originates from African tradition, if you look at the

> sculpture. . . . I wouldn't call myself an avant-garde writer.
> . . . [*Mumbo Jumbo* is] not experimental writing. . . . It
> looks different but that's because people don't know our
> tradition.   There're certain things that are jumbled up,
> certain disparate things that you would normally associate,
> which go together in that book but you know Afro-Amer-
> icans have been making quilts for years. Even in Scott Jop-
> lin you get a mixture of European parlor music and rag-
> time.

Dent too suggests that the innovative aspects of a black avant-garde
may lie outside usual Western expectation. It happens that the novel
is not an African form and in contemporary Africa is written principally by those whose education has been Western. The development
for Afro-Americans of innovative forms developed from traditional
African culture is of concern to writers such as Dent:

> There is a marvelous tradition of storytelling, but if we
> follow that tradition the type of written stories we may end
> up telling may be sixty-page stories with a great deal of
> poetry in them, and if we could invent a way to do it,
> music also. . . . To really attack fiction in terms of what
> we know from our culture, we would have to figure out
> new ways to do what is consistent with what is old and
> essentially non-literary. . . . Considering what black writers
> could or will contribute to the national literary avant-garde
> would involve . . . not just discussing being black or talking
> about it, but depicting black reality in such a way that it
> has an integrity in black culture itself. This is an ongoing
> struggle, but writers like Edward Kamau Brathwaite of
> Jamaica and some of the African writers are actually de-
> veloping revolutions in style. Armah is into a new kind of
> novel very different from the novels he wrote when he was
> teaching at Harvard: *2000 Seasons* is very different from
> his first novel, *The Beautyful Ones Are Not Yet Born*.
> The poet and playwright Okot p'Btek of Uganda in his

> *Song of Lawino* is trying to render traditional culture,
> music, and rituals in a way that probably wouldn't be
> accepted in European theater but works in Africa. I think
> of the black literary avant-garde in that sense.

This aesthetic is not proposed by Umbra but is in a sense an offshoot
of it, since Umbra did raise issues of cultural nationalism and did give
Dent a taste for group experiences such as the Free Southern Theater
and the Congo Square Writers Workshop, where he developed this
aesthetic

☐ Avant-garde groups have traditionally participated in a scenario
in which marginals take over the center for however brief a time before
cooption sets in. Artists are marginal to centers of power in Western
societies, the more so if they happen also to be blacks, women, or of
provincial origin ("regional artists"). Are groups of black or women
artists able to bond or unite themselves along different lines from the
usual white male groups? The writings of Touré and Neal in the '60s
suggested that black artists might be able to avail themselves of African
or Afro-American traditions of community solidarity for such purposes.
Neal urged that

> the Western tendency to force the artist into a state of iso-
> lation and alienation must be resisted. It is unhealthy,
> and finally leads to decadence — a sickness of the soul
> that paralyzes and prevents the artist from perceiving
> the essential humanity of his people. The Black writer
> must not get hung-up in cracker dialogues about indi-
> viduality. It has no social meaning to Black people who,
> while upholding collective values, have never been op-
> pressive toward creative individuality.[13]

Collective traditions, while they might potentially constrain individuals,
might also be a valuable resource against the sort of splintering that
overtook On Guard and Umbra. To what extent they were operative
in this scene would need to be determined by research beyond the
scope of this paper.

A related question has to do with the roles played in such a "marginal" group by individuals themselves marginal to the group by virtue of being white or women or both. Umbra had two important white members, Art Berger and Nora Hicks. What was their role in such a group? Berger speaks of "something in my personality. . . . I always find myself on the other side. I found myself a white with to some degree a black consciousness, with a black sensibility." He was a lone male in the feminist movement and was for years a "male camp follower" in a women's coffee house. Then he went to California and, though unable to speak Spanish, found himself able to relate to Chicanos, "even with the *cholos,* that's the Chicano street people, the gangs, got them interested in seeing that the graffiti that they were doing was a creative act." When he worked as a school consultant among Chinese-Americans, "there was something that enabled me to evoke or elicit from the Chinese kids what Anglos couldn't do. . . . After a while I was able to turn that quality around and do it with anybody that was not of my group but the other." "Maybe," observes Berger, "my role in Umbra was that I was the token whitey. Some of them didn't know what to do with me because they got caught in this love/hate ambivalence. They liked me, especially Charlie Patterson — he liked me a lot and yet he hated me. So that may have been a necessary role — to force them to be able to see that you can relate to whitey. . . ."

As for Nora Hicks, according to Dent, she "deserves a novel." At the time Umbra started she was the wife of Calvin Hicks, founder of On Guard, whom she had met through Communist Party youth activities. "Nora had a strong black identification," remarks Dent.

> Never in my life have I met anybody who was not black who identified so strongly with blacks and who wanted so deeply to be black and eventually convinced herself that she really was black though she looked perfectly Caucasian and who was knowledgeable about blacks. . . . Despite the fact that there was an extreme fantasy at the very core of her existence, it was so serious and so intense and backed up by intellectual ability that she was able to make friends

with blacks. It wasn't like we were tolerating Nora. We were all very close to Nora. So that when Nora and Calvin broke up and Calvin began to go with Brenda [Walcott] and he and Brenda finally married, we did not cut our relationship or our friendship to Nora. In fact Nora and Brenda were close friends. . . .

Nora Hicks was a journalist who organized fund-raising events and parties, and kept group records. Her apartment was a hangout or "cultural center" for the group, and she played a supportive role as "housemother"; the poets "came and cried on her shoulder."[14] In fact, she and the other Umbra women seem to have been one force that held the goup together. Nora's friend Ann Guilfoyle and Mary Anne Raphael (married to poet Lennox Raphael) were white, yet the issue of voting rights and influence on policy of white wives and girlfriends seems never to have come up in Umbra as it had in On Guard. Walcott and Jane Mackenzie (now Poindexter) were black; the latter worked for the black editor Charles Harris at Doubleday and played an important but little recognized role in bringing Hernton and perhaps Reed to the attention of a larger public ("she is a pivotal figure in mainstreaming these guys," says Johnson). But in general the women were there "to serve or observe. It was a very macho group," Walcott recalls. She was respected for her outspoken political opinions, but never had the courage to read her poems to the group. "The women had a common problem — they didn't take themselves seriously enough to write about it."

"On one end Umbra was a literary group, but on a deeper level it was really a social grouping, sort of like a commune in which all those people who were really searching could interact and find some level of communication with kindred spirits that wasn't phony or superficial," Dent recalls.

Nora and Jane became friends and Jane and Brenda were close friends and still are, lifelong friends. And I look at that kind of friendship and tie as more than what you could explain through normal interactions in American

life. I mean it was really an attempt to bridge the loneliness, the dispossession that all of us felt in America. And
so we were seeking a kind of intensity and a level of
seriousness in our relationships from each other that was
most uncommon. That really is the secret of the whole
Umbra bind.

Besides women and whites, one might also classify as "marginal"
to this group of black male poets the small number of visual artists
— Tom Feelings and Joe Overstreet — and musicians — primarily
Archie Shepp — who attended the workshop. Feelings, who had
worked with Dent on the New York *Age,* had been invited to Umbra
together with Rolland Snellings (a painter who turned to poetry with
Umbra's encouragement) to prepare a cover for the first issue (Feelings' design was used). Shepp, with literary interests, had had a couple
of plays produced. But the workshop had musical interests too, since
the Five Spot jazz club was located nearby and members had an opportunity to hear John Coltrane, Thelonious Monk, Charlie Mingus,
and Eric Dolphy play there. Dent explains, "We saw those new musicians as representing a kind of strength and poetry of the black experience which we strongly identified with. So in everybody's poems
— David, Calvin, Askia, myself, Joe Johnson — there are references
to the new music, [and] some of us wrote poems dedicated to specific
musicians. . . ."

☐   How Umbra split and what the causes and implications of this
event were are all problematical issues. But before considering the
split directly, it might be instructive to recall that Umbra was one in a
sequence of groups that constantly merged and split, and to briefly
mention its immedaite predecessors, the Organization of Young Men
and the On Guard for Freedom Committee, both of which were
started in 1961.
    LeRoi Jones (Baraka) started the Organization of Young Men down-
town as an outgrowth of political interests awakened by his 1960
trip to Cuba. He recalls: "We weren't certain just what we wanted to
do. It was more like a confirmation of rising consciousness. We issued
at least one statement, but the sense of it was that we knew it was time

to go on the offensive in the civil rights movement. We did not feel part of that movement. We talked vaguely about going 'uptown' to work. But what work we did not really understand."[15] Besides Jones, this group's more active members included Walter Bowe, historian Harold Cruse, poets A. B. Spellman and Joe Johnson, musician Archie Shepp, photographer Alvin Simon, and cinematographer Leroy McLucas; the last four were to become associated with Umbra. All were black, and Baraka recalls that most had white wives or lovers. The group made "fierce political statements," but its actions were limited to leafleting Newburgh, New York, to protest the way the mayor was distributing welfare. Cruse read aloud parts of what was to become his book, *The Crisis of the Negro Intellectual,* and the group made abortive plans to bring it out as a pamphlet. The Organization of Young Men did not prosper. Dent, who was not a member, thinks this was because "that group pretty much gravitated around LeRoi Jones. He had a habit of moving from one type of interest to another each year or so, and when he moved on and his interests went elsewhere, I think the group just fell apart." However, Johnson recalls that Jones did not dominate this group, which had several members with "firm political ideology": "One of the reasons for the dissolution of the Organization of Young Men is that there's a strong Marxist-Leninist line to it, and Jones can't completely buy that." Finally it was saved from splitting by being merged with On Guard.

Calvin Hicks founded On Guard for Freedom, and its original members seem to have included Walter and Nan Bowe, Bobb and Virginia (Hughes) Hamilton, Tom Dent (who had worked together with Hicks on the New York *Age*), Brenda Walcott, Sarah Wright, and Rosa Guy; the last two provided a link with the Harlem Writers' Guild. On Guard's politics seem to have been predominantly cultural nationalist and Pan-Africanist rather than Marxist, although it was also strongly pro-Cuba and had several Cuban members. On February 15, 1961, Hicks and other On Guard members were violently expelled from the Security Council chamber at the United Nations, into which, with members of other black nationalist groups, they had forced their way to protest UN policies in the Congo and the murder of Patrice Lumumba.[16]

Originally On Guard had met downtown, but after its merger with OYM, Jones and certain others began to press for a Harlem connection — although Dent was perhaps the only member actually living in Harlem — and Hicks rented an office on 125th Street. The group now consisted of both men and women, including a number of white women married to or living with black men. However, reports Baraka, in On Guard "it was an unwritten rule that our wives, lovers, &c., weren't to go uptown with us. The exception to this was Hicks' wife, who was explained as "an Egyptian,' though to the untrained or spontaneous eye, she looked extremely white." Perhaps this was an attempted solution to the split that occurred in On Guard around an issue which Dent has formulated as follows:

> The split developed over the issue of how much of a role whites, and it was basically white women, would play in an organization primarily concerned with black nationalism in the Afro-American struggle. Some people felt that they should have a supporting role, a minor role. But those people who were married to whites or deeply involved with white women felt that they couldn't go for that, that the whites had to have as much voting rights and say in the whole policy of the organization as anybody else.

Another cause for the On Guard split, according to Dent, was a tension between those who were content to be writers or artists and those impatient for political action — one of the splits that later became apparent in Umbra. But Baraka denies this: "Everybody in there wanted to be an activist. . . . A lot of the activists in it were artists, but it wasn't conceived as any kind of artistic organization." For him, a secondary cause of the split was the uptown-downtown tension: "I don't think the organization could stand the contradiction between people living downtown who really wanted to work in Harlem." And he finds some cause for the split in Calvin Hicks' personal problems.[19]

However, before On Guard could disintegrate entirely, it was overtaken by the aftermath of events in Monroe, North Carolina, and in particular by the struggle to prevent the extradition of Mae Mallory back to that state for trial. A Monroe Defense Committee was formed, and Hicks became executive secretary. An unsuccessful bid by the Socialist Workers Party to supplant Communist Party influence in that committee led to the formation of a second, Trotskyist committee, the Committee to Aid the Monroe Defense. When the smoke had cleared from the battle between these two committees, On Guard had disappeared. Cruse sums up acidly:

> The story of the On Guard group and the two Monroe Defense Committees is a graphic lesson in the frustrating politics of interrracialism. It was compounded and confounded by the melange of incipient nationalism in the North, armed self-defense in the South, and integrationism plus leftwing political and propagandistic intervention. As a practical and expedient way out of the confusion, Calvin Hicks was able to substitute Williams' movement for the Harlem program his On Guard group was able to create for itself. But all it amounted to in the end was just another Northern protest that swiftly petered out.[18]

Umbra was an attempt by certain writers to rebuild the cultural functions of On Guard. Jones (Baraka) did not follow these writers into Umbra because his career was by then advanced to the point at which he did not need Umbra. But the extent to which the split in Umbra recapitulated the breakups of its predecessor groups and the extent to which it introduced new elements may now be more clearly seen.

Let us look more closely at the famous Umbra split. According to Reed,

> In 1963 *Umbra* was irreparably split over a poem written by Ray Durem. Two of the three editors argued that the poem — which was critical of President Kennedy — was in bad taste, in light of the Kennedy assassination.

> Several dissidents held that since the poem had been ac-
> cepted for publication before the President's murder, and
> since any poem acceptable for *Umbra* was presumably
> above any particular historical event, the poem should
> have been printed. They accused the two editors of timid-
> ity, and a very bitter and intense struggle took place whose
> repercussions were felt throughout the sixties.[19]

Hernton amends this published account of Reed's by explaining that
it refers to a second stage of editorial negotiation about this poem.
In a first stage, before the assassination, the votes of Dent and Henderson had apparently prevailed over that of Hernton, who was offended
by what he considered "a very slanderous 'dirty dozen' type of poem"
about the Kennedy children. After another day or two, Kennedy had
been shot and Hernton called a meeting to reconsider the poem's
inclusion. Dent, feeling "trapped in the Durem poem," telephoned
Durem to ask advice in this situation, but the controversial poet had
just died. "That forced me into even more of a trap," Dent recalls.
Finally, he voted not to print the poem, with the results that Reed
describes.

Touré, a dissident, recalls that "my particular faction felt the poem
was precise, concise and to the point." Durem's very fair skin color
does not impede the Garveyite Touré from calling him "an outstanding
poet," although, in Henderson's view, "if Ray Durem had been a
black poet we would have published the poem. Ray Durem was a
white poet who wrote in the black style. And I didn't feel that we
had any great commitment to his work because we were committed
to black authors." Is it true then that Henderson twice voted for
the Durem poem, especially since the dissident William Patterson soon
started a fist fight with Henderson over the latter's position? Hernton
considered Durem "a marginal man, torn between black and white,
the kind of warring on either side of the veil that Du Bois described.
But he was definitely a very, very angry person and vitriolic against
racism in his writing."

When the fact that the editors had reversed themselves became
known, a great controversy erupted in the group, especially among
those members whose cultural nationalist sentiments fueled what

Touré calls their "young fiery zealousness." The group were all "at an ignition point in terms of excitability," recalls Joe Johnson. "It was a very inflammatory time." What turned out to be the last meeting of the Umbra workshop took place in Snellings' (Touré's) house in a room dominated by his big wall map of Africa, and the fact that Henderson and William Patterson, in Art Berger's words, "had grown up together and been old street boys together in Harlem" did not prevent their coming to blows. Berger and his wife left quickly then — or perhaps they had already been asked to leave — and the three editors followed shortly. The dissidents then seized the treasurer, Pritchard, who had custody of the Umbra bankbook. Touré reports, "We seized Norman and refused to let him leave because we felt that if we could not be heard democratically then doggone it the journal would not come out. We were certainly firebrands. . . . We held Norman as hostage, drove with him to Brooklyn to his parents' home and secured the bankbook and sat on it in order to prevent *Umbra* from coming out." One version is that Pritchard went at knife- or gun-point. Dent was disappointed that Pritchard came out again and surrendered the bankbook instead of staying inside his house once he got there, but Dent very shortly got "Charmy" Patterson and Reed to return it to him. Reed, supposedly one of the abductors, recalls returning the bankbook but denies the abduction: "I hear Tom Dent and Rolland Snellings (Askia Muhammad Touré) recently . . . appeared on a panel where they denied that such a thing happened. Norman Pritchard was supposed to have been kidnapped. I can't imagine anyone kidnapping Norman Pritchard. He's a large fellow, capable of taking care of himself." Dent denies that there was any knife or gun. He doubts that there could have been much more than $25 in the account (Johnson thinks $200), since Umbra raised all its publication money through small benefit parties (Archie Shepp played without a fee) at the "Advance" Communist youth club. However, Henri Percikow may have given Umbra $750, half the treasury of his group of worker-poets, under pressure from its Umbra members who resented the "dogmatic and heavy-handed" aesthetic he tried to impose on black writers; they had helped raise this money, they said on leaving the group, and wanted some of it.

The Umbra split was overdetermined in the sense that it had enough causes to have wrecked several such groups. Some members have said that its atmosphere was so volatile and intense that Umbra could not possibly have lasted much longer. "There was a great deal of passion floating around the room," recalls Wascott. "The political climate and the turbulence of the world at that point were so great that it would have been very difficult for a group like that to survive," adds Jane Poindexter. "If it weren't the issue of Ray Durem's poem, then it would have been another issue a month later or two months later." Umbra was a literary workshop, but it was also a support group for young artists joined in their alienation from their home backgrounds, from Harlem literary traditions, and from mainstream American culture. Dent and Johnson, respectively, explain.

> None of us — not Rolland, not Ish, not David, not Cal, not me — could go back home, ever again. Nor have any of us been able to . . . I mean go back into the world of your parents and have them understand really what you're doing or why, the rationale of your whole life style, and your purpose in life to the extent that you have one. And I think we each knew that when we reached the Lower East Side, and that's why we needed each other, because we needed that mutual support that came from severing ourselves . . . from the limitations and the expectations and the restrictions of our backgrounds.

> The people in Umbra were more or less refugees, displaced, in the sense of the exiles who went to Europe during the '20s, both black and white, or the black American expatriates. I think we were more or less expatriates here, within our country. We were maybe outside of established, traditional black schools of writing.

At different points the various members would have outgrown the urgency of this mutual need. The recognition that the group, and especially outside readings, afforded would have hastened this process for its more precocious members.

For those less talented or less advanced in their careers, the attention given certain Umbra members who were invited to read and publish fostered jealousies that also came to have a disruptive effect on the group. The three editors and Reed attracted a disproportionate amount of outside attention, some members felt.

> "Why David, why not me, why didn't they come and ask me? Why David or why Calvin or why Tom or why Ish, why not me?" Even if they didn't say it, you could see it when they would come back to the group meeting, especially if the newspapermen would write you up . . . or if a new publication was coming out on the Lower East Side. . . . And if the editor would call you up and say, "I've heard you read a poem somewhere and I would like to publish that poem — can I have it?" . . . So when *Streets* comes out, there's Franz Fanon, LeRoi Jones, Jean-Paul Sartre, and Calvin Hernton. Well, I didn't do it. Some guy just called me. What am I supposed to say — can I go back and ask Umbra if I can submit a poem to y'all? . . . I eventually got a contract, quite luckily, with Doubleday to do a book. Well, that also made me stand out in Umbra like a sore thumb for certain people. . . . When I got a cover story published in *Negro Digest,* that caused nervousness, agitation in the group.

Here Hernton recollects some of his triumphs and annoyances in Umbra. Together with Dent the oldest in the group (except for Berger), Hernton in Umbra times had already a Master's degree in sociology and a published volume of poetry. His dominance in the group had evidently become so strong that Dent cites the resentment it occasioned as the principal cause of the Umbra break-up. Henderson, ten years younger than Hernton, was his protegé and was resented because of the "favoritism" Hernton showed him.

Like most statements about Umbra, Dent's about Hernton's dominance meets qualification and even contradiction from other group members. Thomas, for example, remarks that at the very point that

you might say Calvin was most dominant artistically, he certainly was
not most dominant personally.

> In those days Calvin would show up at readings in Ray
> Charles wraparound sunglasses, long sort of Ellis Island
> black overcoat, and basketball sneakers. He would proceed
> to stand up in front of the room — he'd never take his
> coat off — pull his poems in a rumpled roll out of his
> pocket and proceed to blow everybody's mind when he
> read the stuff. . . . I don't know what kind of dominance
> he was exerting because he was for six months at least very
> much acting the role of the mad poet.

This role did not prevent Hernton from promoting himself; in fact,
the role was itself a kind of promotion. It also seems to be true that
Hernton had what Dent calls "a mad side and a sober side, with no
middle ground. When he was in his mad side, I wouldn't even talk
to him." Berger affirms that at that time "he walked a very tight
edge, psychically," while Jane Poindexter agrees that "he was intimidat-
ing, but I think that was just his own craziness that we found intimidat-
ing more than anything else. Calvin, I know now . . . was not a person
to be feared. He is basically a very gentle human being who does not
thrive at all on dissension or ugliness or bitterness."

Resentment over the promotion of individual poets also touched
Art Berger, who as an older poet had connections that allowed him to
act as an impressario; Berger had also managed to get a collection of
Umbra poems published, with his introduction, in the July, 1963,
Mainstream.[20] Touré recalls:

> Sometimes it seems as though Art would tend to promote
> one group of Umbra, like he would set up readings with
> Calvin, David, and Ishmael and . . . well, no, let's see, Tom,
> Calvin, and David, and I think once or twice Ishmael got
> in there. And some of the rest of us would hear about it
> and that bothered us because we felt that Umbra was one

family, one collective, and it seemed like one group was being sort of pushed a little bit. But certainly in terms of the article in *Mainstream,* he was very fair and he showed at that time all sides of Umbra.

The range of such personal resentments tends to merge at one extreme with those generated by the rising tide of cultural nationalism within the group. Brenda Walcott says that the Umbra split took place between Marxists like herself and nationalists. Whether or not this is true, it may be helpful to look briefly at the tide before considering what it bore. Who were the nationalists and what did they want? "The dissidents," according to Reed, "were promoting a form of 'cultural nationalism.' They included Askia Muhammad Touré, Charles and William Patterson, and Albert E. Haynes, Jr., who all moved to the Harlem community shortly after the split, where they aided Ameer Baraka in conceptualizing the Black Art Repertory Theater and School."[21] Reed has left himself out of this subgroup, for which he was the spokesman and principal strategist, probably because by 1970, when he wrote this, his position, which some considered conservative, had also become vehemently anti-nationalist. Insofar as Umbra constituted a support group for expatriates, these people seem to have replaced its support with that of their own nationalist subgroup and then that of the BART/S.

It may be that the nationalists did not know what they wanted except for their impulse to work itself out, to define itself. This is Joe Johnson's notion.

Nationalism as an ideology at that point for many members of the group was very ill-defined. . . . The act of definition of what nationalism was led to the breaking up of the group. Within the context of the workshop, many people who went on to espouse stridently nationalist views were able to define what nationalism was. . . . Umbra itself was essentially a sort of nationalist movement, not in the terms expressed by Karenga, Baraka, or Huey Newton, but in the sense of expressing a certain consciousness using

materials, using subject matter, and trying to explore
certain techniques in poetry that are consciously and
definitely from Afro-American experience.

Thomas affirms that the Umbra project was one of "trying to give
voice to the Afro-American experience in real terms, everyday terms
that relate to ordinary people. . . . How do you get the everyday life
of black people into literature and art and understood and appreciated
as what it is for its own beauty?" That was the original Umbra program, one that could accommodate a variety of cultural statements
and even the presence of a few whites particularly interested in black
culture. But the nationalist impulse was to press beyond that into a
kind of activism that found expression either in cathartic poetry or
in the streets and media. In this sense the split occurred between

those who wanted more to do with action and those who
felt that writing itself was enough. Not only in Umbra
but in the entire black literary movement, there were
people who literally were trying to find ways to make
poems, if you can do that, become bullets. Baraka talked
about that, and a lot of his work can be analyzed that way.
He wants you to leave his plays and put down his poems
feeling moved, changed, angry — if you are white, mad
and insulted; if you are black, to somehow feel that it is not
just literature but really a kind of social action. . . . I feel
that my options and Calvin's options pretty much had to
do with wanting to express whatever feelings we had,
through art and through honing that and developing that.
That is what split On Guard — the people who wanted to
really be writers or some kind of artist, and those people
who wanted to be activists. To some extent the same
pressures existed within Umbra.

In these remarks of Dent's, "activist" seems to mean "nationalist,"
whereas in the Organization of Young Men the term had had a more
Marxist orientation. These views on the nationalist wing come from

the faction around the editors, which opposed that wing (Dent himself became more nationalistic during his Free Southern Theater days). In Hernton's view,

> Umbra was not a politically activist group as such, and activism was becoming the thing during this period. Everybody who was anybody at a certain point during the '60s was some kind of activist, hell-raiser politically, Marxist or Garveyite or black revolutionary. And we had put on affairs, we were interested in cultural aspects, we did a lot of readings, our work made certain political statements, but as individuals we did not become leaders and activists and go on TV or lead marches. And certain of the people who initiated the split in Umbra wanted this kind of thing or at least yearned for it, wanted some kind of action, action-action, and accused Umbra of backsliding, and this motivated them to try to take it over.

Snellings actually went South for a while to work with a friend in SNCC. "He wanted to be a poet laureate. He needed to be close to some action," Dent believes. The position of the nationalist wing, says Johnson, was not that of Black Power but was just "pointlessly aggressive in the sense that it wasn't defined in terms of ideology, just in terms of 'I'm blacker than you are.'" They began to take the other Umbra members to task for hanging out or sleeping with white people or for using in their poems long or difficult words, which they said were "white folks' words." In this sense, the split perhaps reflects a division in educational levels within the group, since some of those who took this position had barely finished high school and had had nothing published. But perhaps this educational division itself reflects class differences: so Pritchard's kidnapping was "more or less a class attack because he'd come from a very wealthy family, and those people who kidnapped him at knife- or gunpoint to retrieve the Umbra bankbooks were people who weren't members of the middle class, whose social attitudes were quite different from Pritchard's upbringing, and who weren't opposed to pushing their points through heated arguments or fights." This very suggestive thesis of Johnson, that class differences caused the Umbra split, must be qualified, because although Dent and Pritchard were in background upper-middle-class, Hernton and Henderson, for example, came from a working-class background; and only Pritchard, who was living with his parents, had upper-middle-class means. "We were finding a way to put our backgrounds behind us. Later we would have to reintegrate them to do creative work," says Dent. He also points out that violence is not specific to working-class people: much of it has come from young people who, rebelling against wealthy backgrounds, have used violence to prove their radical credentials.

There was a feeling in the nationalist faction that the white members were somehow trying to take over the group. In 1983 it was still vivid in Reed's memory that "there was also a split between the liberals and the blacks . . . Jewish liberals, I guess. . . . They had a great deal of power. They had considerable influence over the magazine, Art Berger and some of the others. . . . They were printing the magazine and we felt that we could put the magazine out." However, Dent and Hernton (respectively) are quick to defend Berger:

> Art Berger was our one white member — a beautiful person who sent us a formal request that if we waived the black rule he would be honored to join. And we voted thusly and he came in and he wrote the first article about the group in *Mainstream.*

> What Art Berger did was contribute a lot of his printing skill and make certain connections with the printing houses, with paper, with set-up men. He had nothing to do whatever about policy or selecting stuff to go into the magazine, or the philosophy of the magazine or the group. He was in many ways a servant who contributed what we wanted and what was beneficial to everybody.

A further reason not directly connected with nationalism has been offered as a reason for the dissolution of Umbra. Walcott remembers

Dent as "a well-organized, hard-working young man" who was not only a writer but an administrator — a combination hard to find. Johnson suggests that the structure he provided for the group disintegrated when he left New York:

> I view Umbra as a phenomenon held together essentially by Tom Dent, who was at that point ideologically clear about what he wanted. . . . You have to see a sustained effort on the part of Tom to work out his particular relationship with folk culture, with literature and his literary values. He is an individual who can because of his character in many ways encourage and facilitate interaction between people of different outlooks. His training allowed him to get things done and to do them well in terms of deadlines and editorial responsibility. . . . Emotionally and ideologically he provided a situation which was quite temporary for people to, in many cases, act out their madness.

Johnson explains that any "high" art has a folk base: "To understand it, to be able to manipulate it so well that it becomes part of you, is to give you a certain undeniable strength in exercising and confronting your art." Dent, endeavoring to place himself within black culture, was able "through the strength of his persistent self-questioning . . . to create or organize an atmosphere where that kind of exploration was possible" for others as well as himself. He "comes from a long line of educators," and that "energy, missionary zeal that he's probably indoctrinated with . . . had a positive transference to the formation of organizations and social situations where learning could take place." Dent evidently became fed up with the wrangling over what would become of the magazine and put his energies into the Free Southern Theater instead. Although the solution was a creative one for Dent personally, Johnson believes, it was disruptive and ultimately fatal to Umbra. Dent agrees that he could have continued the magazine, "but that would have been different from the communal thing." The Umbra poets had become "lines that intersect at one point and keep on going."

Two poets, Touré and Thomas, have seen a parallel to the split over Durem's poem in Malcolm X's famous remark, made at the same moment, that Kennedy's assassination was "the chickens coming home to roost" in terms of the violence America had exported to Vietnam and the Third World; this remark was the occasion for Malcolm's silencing and eventual expulsion from the Nation of Islam.[22] The comparison with the martyred nationalist leader, of course, lends stature to the Umbra nationalists. But what real balance sheet can be drawn up for the two factions, as well as for individual and group life within Umbra? In most cases, group and individual interests do not really conflict: avant-garde groups have historically served as springboards to launch waves of young male artists on their careers; once that has been accomplished, the groups have often been abandoned. Where there is conflict, it should be seen in terms of possible infringements of an implicit contract made between a group of individuals, rather than in terms of a dogmatic nationalist ideology demanding conformity. Either faction might accuse the other of violating such a contract — some of the nationalists might argue that individual readings by the editors did nothing to promote group interests; the editors might contend that the nationalists' attempt to move toward a black aesthetic changed the understanding on which Umbra had been founded.

In retrospect, the Umbra split has all the inevitability of a wave about to break: some will let the wave carry them, and others will try to hold on to shore. The apparent fatality of this event is not one that attaches to most historical movements and — apart from the pain, dislocation, and loss of support that the event caused the participants — can be witnessed with a degree of assent. It is fortunate that there was a Black Arts Movement, just as it is fortunate that there were some black poets who questioned the Movement's excesses. Even these excesses (a phenomenon that occurred at the Movement's margins) have positive aspects for, as Johnson says about the Patterson brothers, "they force people to find out ideologically who they are. They project certain thoughts, feelings, non-ideologies that tell us who we really are. . . . They're part of human behavior, and we have to include ourselves in that." Margins or boundaries define a territory. Umbra itself may be seen as a marginal or privileged time, a rupture in the flow of individualistic, everyday activities related to what Victor Turner, in his studies of both Ndembu rituals in Zambia and some rituals in this country, calls "liminal" or transitional periods; they are characterized by *communitas,* in which the hierarchical distinctions of everyday life are dissolved and for a moment egalitarianism prevails.[23]

Around 1964 Johnson described to a fascinated LeRoi Jones the current dynamics among Umbra members; the next year, the whole nationalist faction except Reed went with Jones to Harlem to start the Black Arts Repertory Theater/School.[24] In the meantime this faction had lived with Reed on East 5th Street where, as Reed recalls, "I was paying the rent an awfully long time because I was a socialist and believed that when other people got jobs they'd chip in, but that never happened." Reed complained to him daily, Hernton recalls: "Ish would work, he would find a job and these guys came and laid about in his house and yet wanted to tell him how to live. And when he was away working they were there rumbling through his stuff and finding these poems he was writing, and when he came back they would sit around with air in their jaws and wouldn't talk to him and when it would finally come out, they had seen this big word or some Greek reference and accused him of using the white man's language and references." From this experience are drawn two characters who appear in nearly all Reed's novels — they "have a pretense at being nationalists, they seldom have a job, they are like moochers, they go around and feed off of other people and the first chance they get, they rip the person off." When they called his Jewish girlfriend a "Zionist agent," Reed moved out and the others then took up residence with Baraka. However, Reed says that he rarely saw Hernton during the East 5th Street period. Further, Reed says that Al Haynes never moved into that house — he "disappeared"; yet he seems to have gone with the others up to Harlem.

Even at the time of the split, Reed is supposed to have switched alliances several times. Touré complains that he later veered round to take "right wing" and "nonprogressive" positions, although in Reed's latest books "his position on blacks and Third World people and women seems much improved." What explains such zigzaging?

Johnson, who has worked with Reed in two publishing ventures since Umbra, ascribes it to the latter's mercurial and feisty personality: "Certain patterns emerge. He has to have a fight. . . . He was a very disruptive influence. Ideologically Umbra was the appropriate place for him." Hernton believes that "Ish is for the winning group and if he thinks you're going to win he'll be on your side. When he thinks you're going to lose he leaves you and switches to the other side quickly." He went along with the nationalists because "he was for power and he was for the way he thought they were going to win. But when he saw they were losing. . . ." Berger concedes that Reed can be "opportunistic" but finds him often gamely taking the loser's side: "Ishmael wove in and out of different positions and he was always in polemics with whatever the prevailing position was, so therefore he ultimately came into conflict with the separatists." Jane Poindexter, Reed's ex-girlfriend from Umbra days, asserts, "I would not characterize Ishmael as a nationalist or as a socialist. Ishmael believes in mumbo jumbo essentially. I don't think he has any thought-out, coherent political analysis. He probably has a moral and ethical one but not a political one. . . . I don't think he's incapable of taking [an ideological or political position] or having one, but I think he's very capable of renouncing it the next month." Reed himself says, "I was never really part of the New York group. I was always considered a Buffalo, someone who was from the sticks, from the provinces and who didn't know how to button his blazer and didn't have all the apparatus of the genteel and civilized person." Perhaps this quality of being an outsider accounts for some of Reed's mobility.

There is in Hernton's and Johnson's comments a tendency to dismiss some nationalist activity of this time as "pathological." The "Foreword" to Umbra no.1 had insisted that "UMBRA will not be a propagandistic, psychopathic or ideological axe-grinder," Hernton's phrase, in which Johnson hears

> certain fears that are being expressed, which will probably eventually be acted out in a very ideological, maybe psychopathic way. But I think that when you look at the movements of the '60s, there's a certain tint of psycho-

pathology that runs through them, a certain fear. You'll probably see it in groups like the Weathermen, probably see it in underground movements that were to emerge maybe five or eight years after Umbra was formed. There was a tremendous fear of where and what American society was going to do, with them or us, whether blacks or American leftists. . . .

Hernton himself finds that

movements or groups . . . tend to draw persons into their ranks for all kinds of reasons, and one reason is that the people are mad. We expected that in Umbra. You would have people there who would be somewhat mad, fringe people, hangers on with all kinds of pathological psychiatric problems. Now if these people can be sort of rehabilitated . . . but if they can't, and during the '60s a lot of stuff . . .was involved in the mentality, in the psychology, or in the psychiatry of some of the nationalists at that time.

Who is referred to here? Reed very soon did an about-face and took an anti-nationalist stance. Snellings (Touré) was generally respected, first as a painter and then as poet and, during this period, columnist for the *Liberator*. Touré stoutly defends Haynes from such accusations:

Al Haynes was a black activist and freedom fighter. He's from a solid Afro-Caribbean working-class family. He was a college graduate and a school teacher and was very active at Tufts University directing its cultural center and helping to develop Black Studies there. He currently works in Florida at a People's acupuncture clinic, where he applies Third World acupuncture techniques together with psychotherapy in the Afro-American community. Al Haynes was never connected with anything psychopathic.[25]

That leaves the Patterson brothers, Charles ("Charmy") and William. They both caused considerable trouble at the Black Arts, and the latter had a nervous breakdown and was hospitalized not long after that period. There is a tendency to make this pair representative of the cultural nationalist wing of Umbra.

In the section of his *Autobiography* dealing with the BART/S, Amiri Baraka (Jones) devotes considerable space to the Pattersons, whom he partly fictionalizes under the names "Shammy and Tong Hackensack."

> What began to be obvious to me before too long was that Shammy was volatile and unpredictable, but he had a basic respect for me as a writer. . . . His brother had a deep malady, probably some kind of advanced paranoia. What was predictable about him was the negativity he carried with him, no, *wore,* like a wet suit.

> Shammy had a love-hate relationship going with me. He envied me, I think, the celebrity of the well-known writer, and liked, I think, being associated with me. But at the same time he did not like to be in my shadow and secretly he thought he could write as well as I. His brother Tong hated me, because Shammy emulated me in many ways, even down to mannerisms and the way we dressed. So not only would they fight, I had to struggle with Tong because of his craziness, often directed at me. I also had to stop the wild-acting Shammy from getting jumped on by any number of Black Arts regulars and Harlem citizens who wanted to kick his ass. Finally, there were more people wanting to kick the two Hackensack brothers' asses than you could kill with a submachine gun without a lot of extra clips. They were a major problem at the Arts.

> . . . Shammy would work. And he would do most of what we agreed on, though he might come up with some improvisation or alternative reading of it that would be

puzzling. He wrote plays of some real value and was ready
to direct them and find actors and do the work necessary
for us to get an audience. Tong did nothing. He would sit
in his office with a small court that quickly developed. . . .
What they did was mostly criticize and undermine whatever went down in the Arts. They opposed most programs
if only by doing nothing.[26]

Baraka tells several amusing anecdotes about the Hackensacks' disruptive behavior. Apparently they were "nutty" individuals. Another
view (Johnson's) is that they were lumpenproletarians, which if true
would make their malady social rather than individual. It would also
fit Johnson's class analysis of the Umbra split. There is a tradition
descending from Marx which equates lumpens with Bohemians and
views both of them pejoratively: they are a kind of rootless riff-raff
that have broken with their social class and are too demoralized and
self-destructive to be organized for political effect; often they are
hangers-on of the art world. From a Marxist point-of-view, it would be
a far more serious indictment of the BART/S as a cultural nationalist
movement to say that it had attracted lumpens than to say that it had
become a refuge for a couple of nuts; the second might just be an un-
lucky accident, while the first might show either an inherent flaw or
improper orientation in an organization that aspired to serve a working-class community. That is the reason that Baraka, who has been
criticized from a political point of view on account of his own pre-
1965 Bohemian period, and who in his *Autobiography* shows himself
sensitive to such criticism, is eager to clear the Pattersons from the
stigma of being lumpens:

I don't think they were lumpen. They were basically working-class black youths who had some psychological problems. I don't think those psychological problems necessarily
changed their class base. A lumpen is somebody who's
destroyed by capitalism — a prostitute or junkie or something like that. . . . I think they were kind of nutty when I
met them. I don't think they got nutty in the struggle.

> They might have got nuttier. . . . You can be sick in the
> working class and still be in that class. Lumpen is another
> class altogether, a small class and, as Mao says, a dangerous
> class.[27]

Baraka suggests that lumpens can be broken from the petty bourgeois
as well as from the proletariat. His associate at the BART/S, Askia
M. Touré, agrees that the Pattersons were not lumpens: "Lumpen
are pimps, dope pushers, prostitutes, gangsters." However, he does
not dissociate Charmy from Baraka's Bohemianism.

It seems that at a certain point confrontations took place within
the BART/S between Touré, Larry Neal, Harold Cruse, Bobb Hamilton,
and William Patterson on one side and Baraka and Charmy Patterson
on the other. Touré recalls,

> We had some differences with Baraka around the whole
> question of the Black Arts Theater really reflecting the
> Harlem community or whether it would just reflect Baraka
> and his Bohemian friends from the Village. The grass roots
> community forces, the black activists and other people
> were legitimately putting pressure on myself and Larry
> Neal. They were raising the question, What's going on
> here? This is a black community, we have our traditions
> — is this going to be a truly black cultural thing or just the
> Village moved uptown? And so we led a struggle to make
> Baraka aware of his responsibilities vis à vis the Harlem
> community, and in that conflict William Patterson sided
> with us against his brother Charles.

Later Baraka had trouble with Charmy, and after Baraka left Harlem,
Charmy was one of the group who confronted Larry Neal and shot
him in the leg. Touré continues:

> Patterson had gotten involved with some very adventuristic
> elements who tended to be anarchistic — I would say more
> anarchistic than lumpen. Some were offshoots from the

Nation of Islam. There was one particular character by the
name of Johnnie Moore who had a very negative effect on
Charles Patterson's development. Later on Charles was
influenced to the point that they began to get a number
of guys together and engaged in a lot of activities which
helped to disrupt the movement in Harlem. I'm not at
all sure that this was accidental. They may have been
tools for other interests. I know there were forces which
not only shot Larry Neal but drove me out of Harlem,
attempted a move on my life and if it had not been for
some of Malcolm X's bodyguards, I may have been killed.
. . . Remember, Larry Neal and I were dynamic members
of the staff of *Liberator* magazine, which was doing a lot
of things to upset the status quo in this country. . . . Some
of the same forces who disrupted the Black Movement,
the Panthers, in later days may have been at work here
and may have used people like Johnnie Moore and Charles
Patterson to disrupt the Black Arts Movement.

Anarchist theory has always legitimized Bohemians and lumpens by
celebrating the revolutionary potential generated by their very rootlessness. Of course it is also possible that rootless people might be
more easily manipulable. But it seems, in Touré's account, that Baraka
(perhaps because of his Bohemian background) assisted in Charmy's
legitimization:

In the time that I have known him, no one has dominated
Baraka. If people were with Baraka it was because Baraka
wanted them with him. . . . We have to keep in mind that
Baraka considered Charles Patterson to be one of his
lieutenants and that he felt that Charles was reflective
of a lot of the black people's anger and passion and that's
why he kept Charles around.

"Charmy was really responsible for running Baraka out of Harlem,"
Dent notes, adding that an "unnecessary regality" and a tendency to

surround himself with sycophants seemed to hinder the latter from investigating more closely Umbra's experience with Charmy. "He should have learned from our mistake."

The subject of Charles Patterson and what he represented both in Umbra and in BART/S becomes more complex the more it is pursued. Jane Poindexter's impression of the Pattersons' activity at Umbra meetings is negative:

> So far as I'm concerned the Patterson brothers were crazy. I think they were hoods. Charmy couldn't write a poem if his life depended on it. And the other brother didn't even have any pretensions as to being a poet. . . . The Pattersons were bums. And a lot of bums popped up in the '60s and were given credibility because of their political rhetoric. I have no respect for the Pattersons. I have no sympathy for the Pattersons, I'm sorry. They were hoods. They were little penny-ante thugs.

She never saw either Charmy Patterson or Al Haynes as nationalists; the latter was "a very sweet guy" who was not "the most astute person in the world." She does not think of Snellings as a nationalist either during the Umbra period, although a poem such as "Cry Freedom" in the May, 1963, *Liberator* shows this recollection to be mistaken.

Art Berger says that Charmy was also known as Tshombe, as in the name of the Katangan leader of the '60s accused of selling out to Western interests. Charmy became friends with Art Berger and his family and came over to his house a number of times, Berger says. He considered some of Charmy's writing and his behavior in some respects to be psychotic. "It's amazing that he did not commit homicide. He was very prone to violence." He also considered Charmy to be a good playwright. "He really had a very strong ability to verbalize in speech and in writing, and he really comes out of the old tradition. He could rap, he could snap, and he incorporated that in his main love, which was black theater."

In 1979 Berger, who now teaches poetry therapy, invited Hernton to address a conference of the New England Council of Creative Therapies. Berger recalls that his theme was to show how, for the black poets, the poetry experience was not just purely an esthetic experience but a therapeutic one for themselves. Calvin said that by the time he himself went to live in Ronald Laing's house [Kingsley Hall], he was either going to commit suicide or homicide. A lot of them were very disturbed . . . the whole climate of the Civil Rights Movement and the conflicts and tension and frustrations . . . they manifested their disturbances in different ways. [An example is] the violent writing of Charles Patterson, beautiful, a great writer, brilliant, very graphic, but some of the one-act plays that he wrote were things like he wanted to do — just go down the street with a machine gun and shoot up whitey. . . . A couple of those plays were produced in their black theater in Harlem, but in a certain sense that kind of writing was therapeutic because if he hadn't written it he might have gone out and done it.[28]

This recalls Paul Goodman's thesis that all avant-garde writing is therapeutic for the writer, whose objective is only secondarily *épater les bourgeois*; primarily it is to expel those false and hypocritical social values ("introjects," Goodman calls them) which he or she assimilated in childhood, and whose purgation constitutes a form of therapy. In this case the social values would be the "double-consciousness" that W. E. B. Du Bois first noted in 1903, and whose destruction Larry Neal, in his Afterword to *Black Fire,* the 1968 anthology which included Charles Patterson's one-act play "Black Ice," singled out as the most important goal of the Black Arts Movement: "Most contemporary black writing of the last few years, the literature of the young, has been aimed at the destruction of the double-consciousness. It has been aimed at consolidating the African-American personality."[29]

There was a period, according to Berger, when Charmy was "really extremely sick, very dangerous"; although he tried to restrain himself, he would start fights when whites tried to get admitted to Black Arts performances in the East Village. "Maybe he was entitled to that

anger, even if the anger was sick." In his kind of anger and his attitude, Berger finds Charmy to have been a younger Ray Durem.

He also finds Charmy not to have been a lumpen but "a street
person — and there's a difference. A street person gets caught up in
the street as a kind of counter culture. There's a struggle to survive
and some of the street people are lumpens, others work, others hustle,
others steal, some are artists." Charmy was not a lumpen because he
put energy into his writing and produced it; he was not a hanger-on
of the art world who merely gave himself the label of "writer." Berger
further objects to the use of "lumpen" here because "I find the term
'lumpen' a put-down. A lumpen will sell himself to any side. So therefore I can't see Charlie Patterson as a lumpen." This point should be
considered in the light of Touré's remarks cited above. Charmy managed to keep writing by having a succession of white girlfriends support
him; apparently he did not work for pay. Berger considers Charmy
a kind of anarchist or nihilist — apart from his writing, he "would not
really subject himself to discipline." When last spotted by Baraka,
"Shammy" was an international drug dealer.

Of course, Marx's conflation of Bohemians and lumpens and his
denunciation (in *The Eighteenth Brumaire*) of them both should
be revised to meet today's conditions. What particularly offends
Marx about such people is the absence of the grandeur and heroic
qualities associated with the 1789 Revolution, the slipperiness that
permits them to skip from class to class, or out of class boundaries
altogether. Today such behavior may be approximated to the sly,
trickster-like resistance of the American slaves or the guerrilla tactics
of liberation armies.[30] As for the others on Marx's list, the discharged
soldier may have refused to fight in Vietnam, and the jailbird been
a political prisoner victimized because of race. The porter and knife-
grinder are hard workers, while a romantic air clings to the tricksters
and mountebanks, who also seem akin to artists. As for the *literati* . . .

Perhaps the only ones who can accurately be called "lumpens" today
are, as Berger suggests, certain "street people," and of these the younger ones may be counted instead as a reserve labor force whose alternat-
ing experience of work and exclusion from it is thought to give them
some revolutionary potential. Only those street people over thirty

who have been consistently unemployed and on welfare, who have no consciousness of contradictions in society because they have never been involved in production, may today be considered true lumpens. Yet the discussion is worthwhile because it raises questions about whether the role of people such as Charmy Patterson should be considered central or accidental in artistic/political ferments such as the Black Arts Movement, and whether they can have any constructive effect in furthering the goals of such movements.

Finally these larger questions absorb figures such as Charmy, who seem to sink back into the shadows of the questions' apparent undecidability, together with the Umbra split and all the problems raised by a symtomatic reading of the narrative of events leading to and following from it. And what are the conflicting versions of this narrative after all but attempts to reconstruct Umbra as it might have been, or even should have been? After the split, as David Henderson says,

> . . . all the poets continued to work in concert with each other, but with much more caution because aware of the bizarre ending. Most people made up after the split and regretted the split but felt that at some point it had been necessary. . . . It was just a little incident really as it turns out in terms of time, and people continued to work together down to this day. And perhaps it's better to have these kind of things be penumbra rather than umbra, a little more shadowy than real black, real hard black — more, you know, lighter, lighter.

Here one of the gaps or fissures that opened during the '60s yawns again to swallow back its issue. Boundaries should indeed be erased when they become obstacles to the passage of new life, and old wounds healed, although this one has been slow to do so. Before it achieves total closure and recedes into the maw of history, we might want to recall that margins are fertile and productive places; from them avant-garde groups such as Umbra make incursions, however short-lived, on the "centers" of culture, which are never the same again. Picaresque or trickster-like figures such as Charmy have also traditionally been associated with margins or boundaries — those boundaries separating realms which ultimately resolve into those of life and death.[31] Tricksters mediate these realms; their mobility, their rootlessness, allows them to cross the boundary and go either way — toward a kind of empowerment brought about by their spurts of energy, or toward barren anomie and alienation. Tom Dent, having read a rough draft of this article, would not like to see Charmy blamed or held solely responsible for disrupting Umbra and BART/S:

> With Charmy, he never reached a level, artistically, where he was on top of his game. He was like a stuck needle [in a record]. His personal devils, whatever they were, were always at him, and he was on the verge of some kind of disintegration. He may have disintegrated by now. . . . The last time I saw him was at an Afro-American writers' conference at Howard. He said he'd been in Europe. He just looked lost, very lost, looked like a shadow of himself. He was very athletic-looking, kind of slight, and despite the image of violence which a lot of people had associated with him, he was very mild-mannered and very soft-spoken. I could hardly believe it was him.

Against such casualties are the forty books estimated to have been produced by authors associated with Umbra, authors who are some of the most productive in Afro-American literature today. They seem still to draw much strength and support from memories and associations of their Umbra days. Here Jane Poindexter reviews her memories of them:

> I think they were very special people. . . . There was nobody, there was no mother, there was no father who would say, "God, my son wants to be a poet — isn't that wonderful." They showed, all of them, tremendous courage, particularly as black males, to say, "This is what we're going to do." And I respect them enormously for that

decision. Whenever one goes against the tide, it makes
for a kind of craziness. It has to because you have to have
a belief in your ability that isn't shared by any other
person that you know and love. And they found each
other and that's not easy. How many of them were there
out there? They had to really look for each other. And
they supported each other for as long as they could. . . .
It's much easier now because of them for some little
black kid to say, "Hey, I write poetry," or "I'm going to
write a short story," and to write it the way he wants
to write it and the way he feels it and the way he knows
it to be true. . . . That was Umbra's contribution. Black
artists owe them a debt that they made a difference.

NOTES

1.   I am grateful to Art Berger, Tom Dent, David Henderson, Calvin C.
Hernton, Joe Johnson, Jane Poindexter, Ishmael Reed, Lorenzo Thomas, Askia
Muhammad Touré, and Brenda Walcott for finding time for these interviews,
which were held between 1978 and 1984. Raymond R. Patterson was kind
enough to supply information about his work building up poets' networks in
the pre-Umbra period. My special thanks go to Tom Dent, Joe Johnson, and
Lorenzo Thomas for discussing Umbra with me repeatedly and for reading a
rough draft of this article, and to the latter additionally for his unpublished
'Bibliography of the Umbra Workshop.'" I also wish to acknowledge the support
of two Organized Research Grants from the University of Houston-Downtown.
2.   The first methodology might have affinities with that of Houston
A. Baker, Jr., in "Generational Shifts and the Recent Criticism of Afro-American Literature," *Black American Literature Forum*, 15 (1981), 3-21; the second
might be closer to that of Henry-Louis Gates in "Preface to Blackness: Text
and Pretext," *Afro-American Literature: The Reconstruction of Instuction*,
ed. Dexter Fisher and Robert B. Stepto (New York: Modern Language Association, 1979), pp. 44-69, and in "The 'Blackness of Blackness': A Critique of the
Sign and the Signifying Monkey," *Critical Inquiry*, 9 (1983), 685-723.
3.   Patterson had attended meetings of the Harlem Writers' Guild, and
Guild member Sarah Wright was one of the readers in his series.
4.   Johnson says he recalls an Umbra group reading at St. Mark's Church
at an earlier period. Both Johnson and Reed claim to have brought Pritchard
into the group.

5.   Johnson questions whether the Mafia was involved. Berger says, "It was almost as if some kind of lumpen element was trying to provoke the black poets, and the owner of the Metro was not very cooperative in getting rid of that element."

6.   *Harper's Magazine,* March 1967, pp. 76ff.

7.   Dragonette was another person interested in communal activity: she was at the center of a group of poets known as the "Calliope Workshop" and was later active in establishing Westbeth, a cooperative apartment residence for artists.

8.   Charles Kadushin, "Networks and Circles in the Production of Culture," in *The Production of Culture,* ed. Richard A. Peterson (Beverly Hills, California: Sage, 1976), pp. 107-122. The literary scene is described — although not to the satisfaction of some Umbra poets — in Allen De Loach's *The East Side Scene: American Poetry, 1960-1965* (Garden City, New York: Anchor/Doubleday, 1972), pp. 1-21. For a description of the gallery scene, see *Tenth Street Days: The Co-ops of the 50's,* ed. Joellen Bard (New York: Education, Art & Service, Inc., 1977), and *Womanart,* 2, no. 3 (1978), 15, 27.

9.   Lorenzo Thomas, "The Shadow World: New York's Umbra Workshop & Origins of the Black Arts Movement," *Callaloo,* No. 4 (1978), pp. 54-55.

10.   W. Francis Lucas, "Norman H. Pritchard, poet," *Liberator,* 7, No. 6 (1967), 13. Another version of "Aswelay" is in N. H. Pritchard, *The Matrix, Poems: 1960-1970* (Garden City, New York: Doubleday, 1970), pp. 14-16.

11.   Ellison's remark is in "The Art of Fiction VIII: Ralph Ellison" (an interview with Alfred Chester and Vilma Howard), *Paris Review,* No. 8 (1955), pp. 66-67; the Baraka quote is from my 21 June, 1984, interview with him in Houston.

12.   "Stridency and the Sword: Literary and Cultural Emphasis in Afro-American Magazines," *Tri-Quarterly,* No, 43 (1978), p. 558.

13.   Lawrence P. Neal, "The Black Writer's Role," *Liberator,* 6, No. 6 (1966), 9.

14.   The words and phrases in quotes are Art Berger's. In later years Nora Hicks is said to have changed her first name to "Amara" and to have taken a doctorate in Afro-American Studies at the University of California/Santa Cruz.

15.   Amiri Baraka, *The Autobiography of LeRoi Jones/Amiri Baraka* (New York: Freundlich, 1983), p. 168.

16.   New York *Times,* 16 February, 1961, pp. 1, 10, 11. An article, "Negro Extremist Groups Step Up Nationalist Drive," in the New York *Times,* 1 March, 1961, pp. 1, 25, mentions On Guard.

17.   Interview with Baraka, 21 June, 1984.

18.   Harold Cruse, *The Crisis of the Negro Intellectual* (New York: William Morrow, 1967), p. 370.

19.   "Introduction," in *19 Necromancers From Now,* ed. Ishmael Reed (Garden City, New York: Doubleday, 1970), n.p.

20. *Mainstream,* 16, No. 7 (1963), 3-14. Berger claims that the jealous intervention of Herbert Aptheker on the *Mainstream* editorial board forced him to cut the historical parts of his introduction, and that the Umbra poems would not have been printed had he not agreed to do so: Aptheker "wanted to have the market cornered in the Left on any kind of scholarship about anything black."

21. "Introduction," in *19 Necromancers From Now,* n. p.

22. *The Autobiography of Malcolm X* (New York: Grove, 1965), p. 301. I am grateful to William Simon for raising the points discussed in the rest of this paragraph and in the next one.

23. Victor W. Turner, *The Ritual Process: Structure and Anti-Structure* (Chicago: Aldine, 1969), and "Liminal to Liminoid, in Play, Flow, and Ritual: An Essay in Comparative Symbology," *Rice University Studies,* 60, No. 3 (1974).

24. In June, 1984, Baraka said, "It became clear to me that Umbra was a prototype of the Black Arts."

25. Berger insists that Haynes is middle-class.

26. *The Autobiography of LeRoi Jones/Amiri Baraka,* pp. 205-207.

22. The criticism referred to above is to be found in Werner Sollors, *Amiri Baraka/LeRoi Jones: The Quest for a "Populist Modernism"* (New York: Columbia University Press, 1978). An instance of Baraka's sensitivity to such criticism can be found on p. 207 of his *Autobiography.* Baraka's opinion, cited here, is from the 21 June, 1984, interview.

28. After leaving the U. S. with Joe Berke, with whom he subsequently wrote *The Cannabis Experience,* Hernton spent nine months with the R. D. Laing community in London. As for Charmy being known as Tshombe, Johnson affirms this and Thomas denies it.

29. Paul Goodman, "Advance-Guard Writing in America: 1900-1950," in *The Idea of the Modern in Literature and the Arts,* ed. Irving Howe (New York: Horizon, 1967), pp. 124-143; W. E. Burghardt Du Bois, *The Souls of Black Folk* (1903; rpt. Greenwich, Connecticut: Fawcett, 1961), pp. 16-17; Larry Neal, "An Afterword: And Shine Swam On," in *Black Fire,* ed. LeRoi Jones and Larry Neal (New York: William Morrow, 1968), p. 647.

30. Marx's denunciation of Bohemians in *The Eighteenth Brumaire of Louis Bonaparte* may be found in *The Marx-Engels Reader,* ed. Robert C. Tucker (New York: W. W. Norton, 1972), p. 479. For trickster-like resistance, see Lawrence W. Levine, *Black Culture and Black Consciousness* (New York: Oxford University Press, 1977).

31. Compare Claude Lévi-Strauss, *Structural Anthropology* (New York: Basic Books, 1969), p. 229, and *Mythologiques: l'Homme nu* (Paris: Plon, 1971), p. 621.

Black Theater in the Sixties*

by

Amiri Baraka

The importance of black theater in the '60s goes far beyond its existence as a group of theatrical performances. In essence, it was another form of the Black Liberation Movement during that period, reflecting the Movement's focus, vitality, and meaning.

For every period of social upheaval there is usually a corresponding artistic movement. In effect artists register the movement of the people. It is the social movement, the peoples' movement that is principal. The backward art for art's sake people (really just supporters of the status quo in society) persist in thinking that it is art basically which shapes life rather than life shaping art. Quite the contrary, it is the peoples' movement, their struggle that moves the artists, and the most sensitive of these artists then attempt to capture the real meanings, the vital essence of the life of the majority itself.

Another important idea is that, in most periods of social upheaval, drama is put forward as a leading art form simply because it is the most ambitious of the art forms (except for film) since the theater actually proposes to show us people in the act of life. It is drama then that can most realistically express the social/human motion, collectively or particularly.

The literary movement that accompanied the black convention movement in the 1830s was literally part of the continuing anti-slavery struggle that culminated in the Civil War. The slave narratives, the first real genre of African-American writing to appear, not only signaled the beginning of African-American writing during the same period, a native American writing by black people, but also a full-fledged assault on the hated institution of slavery.

The functional literature created by the free blacks of the North was part of the same social eruption; the *Appeal* of David Walker as well as Garnett's, Douglass's, and Langston's speeches and manifestoes form a central part of this literature. Similarly, Frederick Douglass's *Narrative* as well as the slave narratives by writers like Moses Roper, Henry Bibb, the Crafts, Linda Brent, William Wells Brown, H. "Box" Brown, Jacob Stroyer, James W. C. Pennington, and scores of others were not only an assault on slavery but a literary movement as well. And this writing ranks among the most interesting writing done by Americans in the 19th century. Certainly, as Bruce Franklin points out in his book *The Victim as Artist and Criminal*, it is simple racism to speak of 19th century American literature and not make reference to the slave narratives. In fact Frederick Douglass is one of the finest writers the U. S. has produced!

In the 1920s, the Harlem Renaissance, that initial 20th century flowering of black art which signaled the emergence of a Northern, urban intelligentsia, reflected also the movement of the black masses from farm to factory, from countryside to city, the migration to the North. It also reflected the fact of intensifying struggle by black people for democracy during this same period, after the brutal, repressive period of 1876 to 1915, in which the Reconstruction was destroyed, the civil rights bills passed as a result of the Civil War were ruled unconstitutional, and "separate but equal" became the law of the land — completely overturning the democracy won in the War and by the 13th, 14th, and 15th Amendments. By 1905 blacks could not vote anywhere in the South, and the highest example of "white art" from Hollywood was the 1915 film *Birth of a Nation,* which justifies the destruction of the Reconstruction and is in essence a Ku Klux Klan recruitment film.

The period which followed saw the rise of an intensified social resistance to this long period of repression. The Niagara Movement, NAACP, and Urban League all came into being in those early years of the 20th century, a result of various class forces at work in response to the growing restiveness and aggressiveness of the black masses. And then came Marcus Garvey's UNIA, the largest and most influential black mass organization, as well as the African Blood Brotherhood, and by the '30s there was a growing black presence in the Communist Party, U. S. A.

This period was defined by the fierceness of black (indeed mass working-class) resistance. And the energy and vision of the period provided the social and political and even ideological base for what was called the Harlem Renaissance.

Langston Hughes, Claude McKay, Zora Neale Hurston, Jean Toomer, Wallace Thurman — all were literary expressors of a whole social epoch. Hughes, among the most sensitive, shows in the development of his verse an earlier "Black Is Beautiful," "African Consciousness" period as well as a later, more sharply defined internationalist and anti-imperialist period in almost exact reflection of the heaviest (social) spirit of his times.

It was a renaissance of black mass movement, and so the literature and art that expressed the entire human dimension most deeply likewise spoke of, and was itself, renaissance. Langston Hughes' 1935 play, *Mulatto,* with its symbolic and literal theme of Afro-American rebellion, was the most famous and one of the longest running works of the time.

The '60s were classic in terms of the proposition I have been making.

The period itself was one high point of black social and political re-surgence after the repression of the Eisenhower, mummified, Mc-Carthyite, Cold War, Korean War '50s. In the '50s the leading in-tellectuals of the black nation were attacked: Hughes, before the Un-american Activities Committee; Du Bois, accused of being the agent of a foreign power and driven into partial exile; Wright, hounded, con-fused, and into permanent exile; and Paul Robeson, struggling to the end, Red-baited, white-balled, and taken away and sentenced to virtual house arrest.

When *Brown v. the Board of Education* proposed the end of "separate but equal," which had been the law of the land since 1897, American Apartheid, it demonstrated a change in the period and announced the expansion and intensification of the Civil Rights Move-ment.

In the arts, the '50s also were a period of reaction and aggressive backwardness. Not only were the leading progressive artists and in-tellectuals in the black national movement attacked, but academics embraced the oppressive formalism of the so-called *New Criticism,* by whose tenets art could only be understood *removed* from its social and political contexts; i.e., separated from real life. This movement reflected in literature the rightist/McCarthyite trend in society. And like that political reaction, it aimed to drag art away from the majority. (It's no coincidence that the chief formulators of this New Criticism called themselves *Southern Agrarians* because they upheld the old feudal slavery society. Allen Tate called his critical collection *Reaction-ary Essays,* and indeed they were.)

One notorious trend was to openly attack Afro-American writers for "focusing too much on black life." The non-black or anonymous Negro writer became a proposed vogue, mostly for the white bourgeois literary world. Black literature has generally been ignored, hidden by the white racist, monopoly capitalist rulers' literary establishment. When the treatment of black literature has been unavoidable, the writing has been casually, or on occasion intensely, "analyzed" as *inferior,* mainly because any true description of the U.S. from black eyes cannot be complimentary. Black literature cannot be *useful,* much less beautiful, to the white establishment, which seeks merely to legitimize the present social system.

Both Ralph Ellison and James Baldwin came to public notice during this period upholding formalism and condemning the best part of Richard Wright, his critical realism. Although Baldwin later renounced such formalism and disconnection of art from social reality, not only with his own work but with his plunge into the Civil Rights Movement, Ellison has maintained his formalist, New Critic-like stance, to the detriment of us all.

The '60s was a distinct response to these stances and the overall "non-black," bourgeois, "integrated" context. As the Civil Rights Movement deepened, it seemed to many of us that Lorraine Hansberry's *A Raisin in the Sun* (1959) was the perfect theatrical form of that Movement. Although many of its practical solutions had real meaning only to the black petty bourgeoisie, in the main it spoke to the democratic strivings of the black majority. Along with Hughes' *Mulatto,* it remains one of the longest running black plays on Broadway.

By 1964, the early aspects of the Civil Rights Movement, led openly by the black middle class, the best example of which was Dr. Martin Luther King, had already drawn to a close.

The Montgomery Bus Boycott of '57, which ushered in the leadership of Dr. King and the petty bourgeois Southern clerical leadership of the Southern Christian Leadership Conference, by 1960 had been muscled slightly to the left by the student sit-in movement, which led to SNCC and CORE's freedom rides. A more militant period was upon us.

The very principles of King's non-violence and passive resistance were being questioned by the early '60s. Malcolm X and the Nation of Islam had risen in the public consciousness and had begun to influence the Black Liberation Movement. By 1963, the Birmingham bombing and resultant counterattacks by the black masses in the streets of that city made the March on Washington not only a huge democratic protest rally, but the actual culmination of the non-violent, Dr. King-led Movement.

In rapid succession, Medgar Evers' murder in Mississippi and the assassination of John Kennedy took the mood of Birmingham to its fullest expression and significance. Non-violence was not a universal principle of the Black Liberation Movement anymore!

Malcolm X's pronouncement, early in '64, of black rebellions to come projected him, after his ejection from the Nation of Islam as a rival political force, squarely into the leadership position of the Black Liberation Movement.

In almost exact artistic reflection of these development, James Baldwin's *Blues for Mr. Charlie* opened on Broadway in 1964. In this play, Baldwin mounted an impassioned and dangerously realistic class struggle between Meridian, the black Dr. King-like figure, and Richard, who seems to embody Malcolm X's disdain for non-violence and passive resistance. (Baldwin has frequently rendered sexual symbolism as social commentary, so the militant's name *Richard* should not be overlooked!)

Blues for Mr. Charlie is one of Baldwin's most impressive and daring works. Its threat to the establishment was that it actually questioned non-violence, with Meridian not only questioning whether his religion has not just been a substitute for his enslaved humanity, but in the climax of this intensely emotional drama raising both the Bible and the gun from the pulpit as symbols of leadership.

My own *Dutchman* opened the next month off-Broadway to a loud, if mixed response. The most striking aspect of this play is not its questioning or dismissal of non-violence but its impassioned proposal of *violence* as a fundamental solution to the oppression of the black nation!

In my mind *Blues for Mr. Charlie* and *Dutchman* are the first double barrel of heat for the Black Theater Movement of the '60s, and *A Raisin in the Sun* must be considered a companion piece, in the same way that the Civil Rights Movement is both companion and precursor of the more militant phases of the Black Liberation Movement.

On the negative side, Baldwin's play earned him the rejection of the bourgeois literary establishment which had lauded him when he criticized Wright's black critical realism or produced merely the perceptive and sensuous writing of *Go Tell It on the Mountain* and *The Amen Corner*. However, Baldwin's Richard is murdered because he gives up his gun to Meridian!

Dutchman earned me eventual praise from many quarters, but its initial fire was attacked as black villainy relatively early. Its hero is also a *victim,* in my own words, who dies stupidly, insisting on the subjective safety of his own self-absorbed isolation.

What became clear to me at this time was that to be an existentialist "victim" or a lionized special — i.e., safe, Negro — was senseless. From the vantage point of a suddenly successful author, I literally vowed that I would use my notoriety not to preach submission or death, but *struggle.* With the jarring focus of the public spotlight came a shattering sense of responsibility to every black slave who ever lived and died here struggling for freedom.

But the Black Theater Movement was part of an entire Black Arts Movement that arose in the '60s, fueled by the same relationship between art and life that the Harlem Renaissance reveals in its connection with the black political eruption of the '20s.

From my own place in America I did pour fuel on the motion of a Black Arts Movement, influenced directly by the Black Liberation Movement and most particularly Malcolm X and also patriots like Robert Williams and the Deacons for Self-Defense. Williams and the Deacons had actually done battle with the Klan and defeated them, even humiliated them.

In my own developing vision, the black artist could do no less. Who were we talking to from our comfortable, self-important enclaves of Bohemia, the academy, or fashionable petty bourgeois salons? Who was our audience? What was it we were saying? There was a national liberation struggle going on, there was an all-out war coming — whose side were we on? Behind whose lines were we living?

In addition to the domestic movement for democracy and self-determination, the forces of the Third World were breaking out of colonial chains at the same time, adding to our inspiration and motivation. We identified especially with the new nations of Africa. Malcolm X had sounded that note clearly. And the assassination of Patrice Lumumba touched the African-American intellectual and artistic community at the point where nerve touched bone.

The Black Arts Repertory School opened in a Harlem brownstone the month after Malcolm X's assassination, although the forming group had been together almost a year in often-heated discussions on the role of the black artist in the black revolution.

The Black Arts was significant because it sought to articulate and structure a black institution that could express and create the committed black art we knew must come to exist, side by side with and as a form of the Black Liberation Movement itself!

As a trendsetter of such organized development, *Umbra* magazine and the Umbra organization predate the BARTS by at least a year. But it remained "downtown" in the East Village, and class struggle inside it sent its members in several directions, some into the BARTS.

What the BARTS group articulated less and less loosely became, in fact, part of the several principles of the whole Black Arts Movement. I think it's not too general to say that a great many of the artists associated with what later came to be the Black Arts Movement wanted an art that was *black*; i.e., that reflected the history and current lives, the lifestyles and aesthetics of the Afro-American nation. We wanted an art that was mass aimed, that could leave the libraries and academies and coffee shops, and speak directly to the people. We wanted poetry that could be chanted from the same places as Malcolm X's speeches, plays that told it "like it was," with that direct revelation of truth and heat.

We wanted an art that was oral, one meant to be listened to, one that could be performed on the backs of trucks, in playgrounds and projects, right out on the sidewalks. A mass art, an anti-elitist art!

And definitely we wanted an art that was revolutionary, that was an expression of the black national revolutionary struggle for self-determination. We spurned the bourgeois critics or "dizzy white boys" in the pay of our peoples' enemies and used whatever media space given us to talk the politics of black revolution!

During the summer of 1965, a year after the Harlem and Jacksonville rebellions that Malcolm X had predicted, the Watts explosion announced to the world the tumultuous seriousness of the Black Liberation Movement. During that summer the BARTS sent theater, poetry, music, painting, and black revolutionary propaganda all over Harlem, night after night, on the backs of trucks with banquet tables for stages.

By the end of 1965, however, the BARTS had folded because most of us did not know how to handle class struggle inside the organization. But what had emerged that was positive from that experiences was the catalyst and inspiration for a replication of BARTS theaters around the country.

At the BARTS, we again did *Dutchman,* now branded as a "racist drama," whereas downtown it had won an Obie as Best American Play! The change of venue was also a change of social context and hence of the play's *meaning!*

We also did my *J-E-L-L-O,* plays by Charles Patterson, including *Black Ice,* and plays by young Ronald Drayton. What was clear was that we wanted black heroes, not black victims. We wanted to create black revolutionaries in the act of destroying a white racist system.

I wrote *Black Mass* at the Arts as well, even while administering the programs. And black artists and intellectuals like director Jim Campbell, writer Harold Cruse, and poets William Patterson, Steve Young, Oji Jiko, Clarence Franklin, and Clarence Reed developed in that context. Joe Overstreet was coordinator of visual arts, with Billy Blayton and Joe Andrews. Andrew Hill, along with Steve Young, was music coordinator. Together these dedicated artists helped us show painters like William White, Vincent Smith, Emilio Cruz, Faith Ringgold, Vivian Brown, and many others through the BARTS. Musicians like Archie Shepp, Sun-Ra, Pharoah Sanders, Albert Ayler, Grachun Moncur, Charles Tolliver, Melford Graves, and John Coltrane played and did benefits and concerts. Poets like Larry Neal and Askia Touré, Ted Wilson, Ed Spriggs, and Sam Anderson were close to the heartbeat of the Movement. A whole group of actors and directors developed out of the Arts.

Part of the developing theory of the Black Arts Movement came from intense discussions with certain black theater people who said that there was no such thing as black art, only art. They would later receive huge grants to be in charge of black theater or even huger grants to be in charge of Negro Ensembles which deny the existence of black theater even to this day.

During the next period, black arts theaters sprang up in different parts of the country. In the Midwest, artists like Ron Milner and

Woody King emerged with their Concept East Theater. Milner, of course, is one of the best known dramatists of the Black Arts Movement, who made a name with his first nationally publicized work, *Who's Got His Own*. He is still a formidable force in American and African-American theater. Woody King is the best known and most respected black producer in this country. He is probably responsible, as producer, for the greater part of the well-known black plays to come out of the '60s.

The Free Southern Theater had developed out of the SNCC student movement. John O'Neal, Gil Moses, and Denise Nichols were some of the best known names. On the West Coast, by 1967, Black Arts West had formed under the aegis of Ed Bullins and Marvin Jackmon, called Marvin X, with support from Jimmy Garrett, then chairman of the Black Students' Union of San Francisco State. When my wife and I came to San Francisco in the Winter of '67 to head a Black Communications Project, Bullins, Marvin X, Jimmy Garrett, Duncan Barber, Hilary Broadus, Carl Boissiere, and we sent a black theater/poetry tour up and down the West Coast that included Bullins' *How Do You Do?*, Marvin X's *Taking Care of Business, The First Militant Preacher* by Ben Caldwell, my own *Madheart, Papa's Daughter* by Dorothy Ahmad, and readings by Marvin, Sonia Sanchez, many young poets, and myself. Carol Freeman was another young playwright and poet whose work we performed as was Joseph White, whose work is still not well-known. Many of our actors, stagehands, and set designers later became part of the Black Panther Party.

Using the Black House in San Francisco, which we shared at first with the newly formed Black Panther Party for Self-Defense, who used to pull security for our readings, we rehearsed, then brought the message of the Black Arts into the black community at large. Later, the artists were driven out of the Black House at the urging of Eldridge Cleaver who had wormed his way into the Panthers, where he also performed his role well as a wormy cleaver!

But from these beginnings a broad expansion of the Black Arts concept was launched: that our art must be a weapon in the struggle for change and liberation, that our art must be open and mass aimed, that it must be as black as our memory and our culture — as positive as our future.

Even before this, in 1965, after being run out of New York by explosions inside the Black Arts, I had set up, with my wife Amina, The Spirit House in my home, Newark, New Jersey. We created a theater company, The Spirit House Movers, named after a group of brothers who actually moved furniture who frequented a tavern near a loft where we had our rehearsals. We wanted to move the black masses. We wanted to move the Earth. And to the Spirit House came many of the artists and musicians, directors and actors, writers and poets who had developed at the Black Arts in New York City as well as some from the local environs. The plays *Black Mass, Slave Ship, Arm Yourself or Harm Yourself, J-E-L-L-O,* and *Home on the Range* were done as were innumerable poetry readings. The Spirit House Movers even traveled to various cities performing and toured various campuses. We performed in bars and in people's homes, in backyards and in parks, on the backs of trucks and on street corners. That was one way the Black Arts message got spread, out of the mouths of the actors.

Amina Baraka, Marvin Camillo, founder of The Family, Charles Barney, Yusef Iman and his family, Carl Boissiere, and Barbara Reilly were among those actors, and I began to learn even more about directing, stage managing, producing, and theater logistics. Some of the work of this period was filmed in a brief work called *The New Ark,* the West Coast aspect in a film we made called *Black Spring.* Some of the work associated with the Black Arts Movement was in the anthology edited by Larry Neal and myself, *Black Fire.* But the whole story of this period has so far not been told.

From out of this brief, generalized catalyst many variations and alternate expressions of the Black Arts impulse moved. But it is safe to say that the main tenet of the Black Arts Movement, and the Black Theater Movement as an aspect of that whole, was that art be a reflection and expression of black people in struggle — that it seek to destroy white racist America and build something beautiful in its place.

A whole host of new plays and playwrights (including Larry Neal, Joseph Walker, Clay Goss, Evan Walker, Richard Wesley, Charles "Oyamo" Gordon, Dorothy Ahmad, Sonia Sanchez, and many others!)

came out of that experience, a whole host of poets and painters and musicians and blackened intellectuals. For once the establishment could not deny that there was such as thing as black art, that since there was French, Russian, Spanish, English, etc. art, perhaps there had to be, even in the establishment's logic, an Afro-American art, an art created by the African-American people. But we also wanted that art to speak to that people's deepest need, which is liberation! So the rulers moved to coopt black theater and black art in general, substituting a theater that was skin black, or atavistic black, or pimp black, or not very black — or even an ensemble of Negroes — with their grants and financial aid and critics and agent provocateurs.

The relative "failure" of the Black Theater Movement and the Black Arts Movement was in their failure to build the political bases that would ensure their continuing life. Either we depended on the rulers' money, and when that failed, we did; or when the organizations which supported revolutionary black arts organizations split, or ran into problems, or were attacked by the state, as they constantly were, the black arts organizations suffered the same fate. And just as the Black Liberation Movement itself bogged down into relative quiescence because of internal contradictions — principal among which were the lack of scientific ideology and organization as well as attacks by the state — so did the Black Theater Movement.

The bourgeoisie continued its cooptation because one thing that the Black Theater Movement did was to prove that indeed there was a large audience for black theater, if it existed. If we look at Broadway today, we will see at least two or three usually sterile and surface products offered to the black theater public, but this weak fare usually has little to do with the most important concerns of the black majority.

So today, just as there is a period of relative quiescence for the Black Liberation Movement, so there is with the Black Theater Movement. But at the same time I see promising signs of a new rebirth. The advent of Reaganism in the general society can be measured by a Reaganism in the world that governs black theater. Yet the news is beginning to come in of new struggles, on higher levels, in the still ongoing struggle for democracy and self-determination for the Afro-American nation. There is word of new organizations, new art groups, new attempts to mount a relevant black theater. But whenever a new black theater movement is mounted, and it erupts with the fire we associate with renaissance, you can be certain that that theater will be a reflection of what the black masses are doing once more, and will do over and over again, in concert finally with the majority of people in this society; that is, smash it and transform it, so that a new age will be ushered in and, with it, a new theater.

* This paper was written for presentation at a Morgan State University theater conference in April of 1983.

Double Mirror: George E. Kent and the Scholarly Imagination

by

R. Baxter Miller

Worldman. Historyman.
Beyond steps that occur and close, your steps are echo-makers.
You can never be forgotten.

     —Gwendolyn Brooks, "Harold Washington"

A thing of beauty is a joy forever: Its loveliness increases; it will never
Pass into nothingness.

     —John Keats, *Endymion*

Discussing the first autobiography of Maya Angelou, George E. Kent writes: "The major function of the imagination . . . is to sustain a vigorous dialectic between self and society, between the intransigent world and the aspiring self. Through the dialectic, the egos maintain themselves, even where tragic incident triumphs. . . ."[1] What he says for the creative writer illuminates the literary scholar as well. While the human spirit is invisibly dynamic, it fills the void between self and other. In facilitating communication, perhaps communion, it informs and transforms existence. Imagination dynamically retains (keeps) the social bond with the present and the past; it maintains (holds) and documents the record for the future. Imagination signifies culture, the humane form through which one generation transmits to succeeding ones the rituals, forms, responses, and values for literary art and folk survival.

For Kent the two contribute equally to the communal rite which embraces reading and literary criticism. The scholar lowers the superficial dichotomy into the deep structure. Awakened to the potential, the folk spirit first emerges, then confronts and finally transcends suffering. Literary scholarship eases the conversation with others. The scholar, like the writer, possesses a double imagination, the fusion of analytic intellect and cultural sensibility.[2] Kent's scholarly world symbolically enacts – structures – varied kinds of doubling. With analytic and philosophical discourse, it bonds communal responsiveness as well as feeling. Informed with erudition, it signifies folk origins, and learned in Western thought, it yet sustains Black American freedom. Kent the private man, who keeps the communal life, looks at once to academic liberty and racial responsibility. In initiating a mental return through cultural history, he detaches himself from the story. His critical mind illuminates what American critical theory has concealed and forbidden.[3]

While the personal signature of George Kent, the man, has passed, the cultural language persists in the communal memory, Black and White, and in the sustained performance of Black folk. Despite physical absence, Kent reinvigorates the spiritual presence of W. E. B. Du Bois, Langston Hughes, and Jessie Fauset as well as that of Zora Hurston and Alain Locke. Kent yet performs in the silent tradition of Black American literary legacy. The social tension, the delimitation of the collective unconscious and conscious discourse, the priority of the imagination as the mediation between folk history and aesthetic voice — all mark the distinction.

Responsive to historical change, Kent leads an advance in critical sophistication, yet doubts the arrogance which would make even critical theory autonomous. Jargon and pomposity hardly suit his style. One of his metaphors concerns the double mirror which both receives and reflects culture: the image exists through the dynamic medium of discursive analysis rooted firmly in the Black self. Another metaphor involves the bullfighter, a highly neglected touchstone to Richard Wright's prose: here Wright concerns himself with the rituals through which Man (humankind), and therefore the artist, exorcizes fear through epiphany in heroic form, the impending confrontation with terror and death.[4] Kent restores dialectic and distancing to the ritual. In a rare effort among discoursers, he demonstrates the scholar's sustained capacity to wonder. It rewards one to examine first the duality in the biography of the personality and of the man, then the critical method of his scholarly communion with major Black American writers, and, finally, his semiotic awareness of the two great traditions he faced.

Without social privilege, Kent achieved scholarly distinction and contributed to public life. Born in Columbus, Georgia, on May 3, 1920, he earned his B.A. from Savannah State College in 1941. He took the M.S. (1948) and Ph.D. (1953) degrees at Boston University. From 1949 through 1960 he was Chairman in the Department of Languages and Literatures and Dean at Delaware State College in Dover. In the years between 1960 and 1969, he was Professor and Chairman in the Division of Liberal Arts at Quinnipiac College in Hamden, Connecticut. At first a visiting lecturer at the University of Chicago in 1969, he remained there as a full professor until his unfortunate death in 1982.

Kent's awards and appointments are doubly telling. Active in the National Council for Teachers of English (1971-1973), the professor became its Distinguished Lecturer in 1972. Later he earned a fellowship from the National Endowment for the Humanities (Center for

African-American Studies, Atlanta University, 1977-1978) to produce
a critical biography of Gwendolyn Brooks, soon to be posthumously
published by the University of Illinois Press. In 1982 he earned the
College Language Association award for distinguished research. Despite
his personal projects he served as an advisory editor for *Obsidian,
Negro American Literature Forum* (the forerunner of *Black American
Literature Forum*), *Black Books Bulletin,* and *Reconstructing American
Literature.*

Though some may equal Kent's professional scholarship, few rival
his dual performance in national life. Once President of the NAACP
in Delaware (1954-1957), he later served on the Board of Directors
for the New Haven Urban League in 1967. Having completed a stint
on a Council for Human Relations (1966-1968), he participated as well
on a council for Black fathers (1968-1969). He was the mentor for
several younger scholars. His former students include David Smith
(Williams College), Jim Coleman (Colorado College), John O. Hodges
(University of Tennessee), and Joanne V. Gabbin (Lincoln University
in Pennsylvania).[5] But his active encouragement transcended the
University of Chicago. When maturing professors directed the conferences "Black American Literature and Humanism" (University of
Tennessee, Fall, 1978) and "Rescuing the Past . . . Securing the
Future" (University of North Carolina, Spring, 1981), he encouraged
them well.

My own awareness of his double performance remains personal.
As a neophyte assistant professor, then at Haverford College, I wote
for his advice about my *Reference Guide to Langston Hughes and
Gwendolyn Brooks* (G. K. Hall, 1978). He responded in a three-page
single-spaced letter. When, seven years later, I submitted a sustained
article on Margaret Walker to *Tennessee Studies in Literature* (the
old series), he remained anonymously in the background. The first
referee, who asked for inquiry into folk forms and metaphorical
processes, wanted the basic readings to include pattern, theme, and
tone. I knew few critics in the United States who so·combined intellectual rigor and cultural responsiveness. Only George Kent came
to mind. When the naive ask why he did not have more books published, one remembers the generously long replies. Often Kent wrote

his scholarship vicariously through the men and women he guided. What Roseann P. Bell said of him in prefacing a 1979 interview still rings doubly true:

> If we are lucky, at some point in our lives, we meet people who make the merger between ontology and epistemology comprehensible; they make the continuous rigor and the mysterious joy of living passionately real. . . . If we call him a critic, we do him a partial disservice, since that designation carries with it some element of negativism: we expect critics to be acerbic and haughty rather than iconoclastic and visionary. The good ones, like Kent, are rarely celebrated because their commodity, common sense, is neither championed nor materially encouraged to the degree it should be. Such is to be expected where propaganda sells well, but logic and a communal understanding of humanity do not.[6]

In the six-hour conversation ("communion") with Kent, Bell superbly reveals his personality. When she inquires about the critic's role, he praises the intelligent reader, the mediator between writer and audience. In revealing customs and conventions, the critic, he observes, places the work tangibly within tradition. Kent confesses he once wanted to write a critical study of Zora Neale Hurston, though feels "that it would be helpful if some thoroughgoing woman would do it first" (p. 222). Some of Hurston's tendencies turn him off fast: "And then I come back and say to myself, how would this look if you thought about it in terms of a woman at that time trying to assert her existence with an almost complete autonomy and without any kind of support, and to really begin to judge her as if she had the little sanction that was given to Black men. And at that point I usually stop. . . ."(p. 222). He wonders if her involvement with patrons gave her time to write. How much did she fit the typical pattern of those who, like Claude McKay, splurged whenever possible, died young, and defected? He would like to know "what went on with those publishers" (p. 225).

Kent's double stance is never patronizing. Neglecting Hurston in
the early commentary, he eventually rethinks the position in a con-
scientious reassessment rather than to an expedient advantage. He
would have ignored the bad short stories anyway, but hardly excuses
his failure to consider seriously the novel *Their Eyes Were Watching
God* (p. 225). Did Hughes and Hurston, he asks, really have a romance?
He suspects intimacy took place during the authors' common odyssey
in the Thirties. Told anecdotes about Hurston's days as a college
teacher in South Carolina, he believes that "she couldn't make it in
any kind of way with the administration. She had to fulfill obliga-
tions in an almost elementary way, and they were after her, I think,
about the boys — the football boys. The woman who was describing
her thought it was all very amusing, and I guess, under a cocktail situation, maybe it is. But I sense a tragic element is there. . . " (p. 227).
   Hurston works within a tradition of writing which extends to Paule
Marshall, Alice Walker, and Toni Morrison, all of whom successfully
hone Black American experience. With rare equilibrium, Kent offers
some hard insights about them. He senses a relative inattention in the
work of contemporary women writers to the way in which their female
personae "look at the world" (p. 228). He inquires about the stories
of Alice Walker, "Where is there a moment in which a man and woman
seem to occupy the same space together?" (p. 229). Whatever an
author's race or sex, Kent would have that individual shape, through
particular awareness, the *range* of human experience. While one might
quarrel with the cryptic judgment, his final assessment of Alice Walker's
writing hardly seems insensitive: "It seems she is always conscious,
always, of exploitation; I don't see much possibility, and I'm not sure
there is always depth" (p. 229). The negative comments will displease
many, but Kent symbolically accords Black women writers the highest
praise. Never patronizing, never paternalistic, he insists upon the
most rigorous scrutiny, a forthright recognition of the problems observed. Truly and honestly, Kent avoids self-serving flattery.
   Elsewhere he doubles as James Baldwin for whom

       . . . the Western concept of reality, with its naive rational-
       ism, its ignoring of unrational [sic] forces that abound

within and without man, its reductivist activities, wherein it ignores the uniqueness of the individual and sees reality in terms of its simplifications and categorizations, is simply impoverishing. He who follows it fails to get into his awareness the richness and complexity of experience — he fails to be. And freedom is unattainable, since, paradoxically, freedom is discovery and recognition of limitations, one's own and that of one's society; to deny complexity is to paralyze the ability to get at such knowledge — it is to strangle freedom.[7]

Freedom is two-way: while one side opens to analytic discourse, the other marks intuition. The cultural formulae which signify freedom imperfectly embody its substance, for freedom stays in dialectic with the language and verbal structure which would contain it. Not the artifact of writing, freedom is the process, the interplay between self and form, the will to articulate the rhetorical space between them. Such doubled freedom implicitly informs Kent's professional life and work. Well-trained in formalism, he liberates himself from the supposed rupture between literature and life. Sensitive to the polemical claims for Black American literature, he frees the approach from rigidly sociological confines.

In valuing literary history from 1789 to 1982, he almost never mistakes the learned record and event, the authorial life, either for the aesthetic response or for the humane meaning. In recognizing that both the creative writer and the critic must have broad freedom, he knows that neither can be completely free. Wright, Brooks, and Baldwin shape their own writings through the culture and history experienced. "At its best," notes Wright, "perspective is a pre-conscious assumption, something which a writer takes for granted, something which he wins in his living."[8] Within limitations, the writer determines independent thought and space. Kent understands the communal rhetoric (myth) which binds race and universalism. While criticism often disguises itself as scientific inquiry, he perceives it truly as an expression of cultural value.

From the epigraph which opens Kent's *Blackness and the Adventure of Western Culture* (1972) to the superior essay on Ellison at its close, the idea of dual freedom recurs. Taken from the title poem in Brooks' volume *In the Mecca* (1968), the epigraph reads: "Sit where the light corrupts your face. / Mies Van der Rohe retires from grace. / And the fair fables fall."[9] In the poet's brilliant epic, the words structure a dramatic situation in which the narrator exhorts her other self and the reader. Yet even the shared performance conceals the rhetorical communion through which it exists. Kent himself seeks an equally double identification. Without rigid allegiance to "high ground humanism," he grasps well the tradition. White writers, he says, have derived values from Greek, Hebrew, and Roman traditions. Well-informed about the assumptions, he isolates them as rugged individualism, illusory truth, democratic freedom, and abstract universalism. In granting the writer independence, Kent pledges personal identification, whatever the ground. He proposes that the bond inevitably leads beyond critical formulae and definitions: "I outsider-insider, insider-outsider follow."[10] Clearly he belongs to the world of the cultural narrative, yet in the critical posture beyond. Complete detachment, he feels, proves as dangerous as complete identification. While the first state provokes illogic, the second provides callousness. The first stance sometimes lacks thought, but the second postion displaces life. The failure to live, to perform within the culture, prevents articulate independence from accepted categorizations. It impedes freedom. Protest would still mean only special pleading. Transcending would yet imply the alleged provinciality of Black American experience. Universalism would be the continued mediation of Western humanism on the high ground. What Kent perceives concerns the rupture between the Western tradition and the humane ideal. For thirty years simplistic notions confined and concealed the literary depths in the world of Richard Wright. While Kent values the human range in literary art, he clarifies that hasty transcendence would mean the expedient effacement of Black American tension. He qualifies that "any universalism worthy of the recognition derives from its depths of exploration of the destiny, complexity, and variety of a people's experience — or a person's. It is achieved by going down deep . . ." (*Blackness*, p. 11). Here he brilliantly reverses Artistotle.

What Kent doubly admires concerns the Black writer's dynamic retracing through cultural time, yet his or her epiphany for a particular situation, object, or period. He subconsciously values lyric narrative or poetic drama. Langston Hughes preserves an unfulfilled fidelity to the folk source. Wright achieves the symbolic truth narratively, but Ralph Ellison makes for a distinguished "performance." Gwendolyn Brooks merits a talented place for mediating between the literary worlds of Wright and Ellison.[11] Hughes might impose more signification upon the blues, spirituals, ballads, and gospel songs, yet he hardly provides the sources with a personal signature. His work marks an advance in the spirit of the folk form but not in the form itself. While Hughes fails to objectify Black life into the deeply polished artifact or poem, he achieves the dynamic "is-ness" of folk tradition. Hughes is both static and dynamic, though the latter aspect wins out. While Hughes may "evoke" the "face twisted in pain," or the laughing mouth, he distinguishes himself by "holding fast to dreams." Hughes, if only momentarily, "maintains" the spiritual self and captures the "strivings" of Black folk (pp. 58-74). The growth of racial consciousness and the attempt to "reclaim the heritage of modern man," especially in Wright's *Black Boy,* deeply concern Kent. Wright marks the double passage, both human and Black, into modernity. Where Southern pastoral had been, Northern urbanism displaces the agrarian world. Wright "faces" and "confronts" existence, the posture toward alienation (p. 99).

Gwendolyn Brooks subsequently faces Black America's turbulent changes between 1945 and 1972 as well as the cultural forms for recording the vibrations. Whereas her poetic narrator takes a double perspective on time, a look backward and forward, the scholar re-performs the cultural drama. The two share "the subject, the tragic struggle for fulfillment without the illusion-giving stage and rituals validated and dignified by tradition" (p. 131). Brooks lacks the facility of Langston Hughes and Margaret Walker "to move" directly into the Southern past (folk spirit), but her intense suggestiveness "makes the past terribly alive in the terrible present" (p. 136). Kent closes his discussion of Brooks where the epigraph began: "Sit where the light corrupts your face. / Mies Van der Rohe retires from grace. / And the

fair fables fall." For both the scholar and poet, the still picture pre-
pares for the advance into new myth and meaning. Both assume the
dynamic spirit ("sit," "retires") of existence as well as the form
("light").

What Ralph Ellison achieves in the folk form, the novelist sometimes
lacks in folk spirit. Ellison's great "performance" provokes Kent's
ambivalent response. In skillfully using folk and cultural tradition,
the source for enlightenment, Ellison connects images to Western
symbols and myths. Kent believes that "Blackness" needs more definition than the West, which has had "innumerable masters." Kent, more
suspicious than faithful, points to Melville and Faulkner. They have,
he says, "whispered" about the death of the West. In Black tradition
Kent discerns "an ambivalence and a questioning of the West that go
deeper than casting a critical eye upon its technology and rationalism"
(p. 161). Ellison, he contends, supersedes Langston Hughes by elevat-
ing the folk source, particularly in the Trueblood scene, to conscious
art. Yet the transformation alone hardly suffices, for ". . . the basic
attitudes [spirit] and *forms* of response to existence evolved by the
folk are abandoned by us only at our peril"(p. 162).

As regards Maya Angelou, Kent discusses the dual movement of
imagination through communal life and racial relations. Here the
former child "faces" the cultural past and the personal present. In
his examination, Kent clarifies the way Black American autobiography,
where semiotic discourse confronts the story, structures cultural
space. Black American life, which faces American institutions,
clarifies an eroded faith as well as a false optimism. While the literary mode bridges rhetorical space, it shapes a profoundly pervasive
irony. Through this unique "stance," Angelou "faces" her own community and, indeed, the universe. In her "communal confrontations"
she balances spiritual beauty with absurdity.[12]

Looking at once to the aesthetic and political worlds, George Kent
naturally assumes that the one influences the other. He roots the
symbolic needs of Western culture and White consciousness in economic motivation as well as in exploitation. So doing he discovers
the endorsement of intense individualism and the extreme self-consciousness leading to alienation. Regarding the West's drive to master

Nature, he perceives a deep uneasiness. He inquires aloud whether
Western assertions about social evolution and progress are true, and
he questions the drive for "massive and intricate organization." Is
even Christianity, he asks, valid "as a status-endowing religion" and
political code (*Blackness*, p. 166)?

Those who would dismiss his double stance as political belief rather
than critical theory suggest their own limitations more than his. The
implicit theory transcends the diverse methods he confronts. He
values the principles of the Black American literary historians who rose
from the 1940s to their apogee in the mid-Sixties. Through an emphasis on biography and history, Saunders Redding, Arthur Davis,
Hugh Gloster, and Richard Barksdale have illuminated social condition as well as mimetic representation.[13] Kent also deepens the concern into formal reading, and philosophic truth. He maintains as well
the cultural awareness partly derived from Amiri Baraka and Addison
Gayle, Jr., two shapers of the critical position for the Black Arts
Movement (1960-1975). While the last two critics explicitly repudiate
Western mythology, Kent, who understands its dangers, believes that
literary criticism intrinsically celebrates culture. Some others may well
promise polemic only, but he attends the restorative imagination
in the Black American literary tradition. Though they may be blind
to his own position, he subsumes and transcends theirs, for theirs
points only outward to the political world. His points inward to the
self as well. When Kent subordinates the monocular to the binocular,
he surpasses many of his colleagues.

Kent prefigures those who seek a holistic aesthetic both for the
cultural metaphor and voice or the deep structure in folk perception.
In this way he looks forward to the generation of Stephen Henderson,
Houston A. Baker, Jr., and Barbara Christian as well as that of Trudier
Harris and others. Finally, Kent theoretically protects the tradition
of Black American literary scholarship from the extreme formalism
of New Mainstream critics Robert Stepto and Henry Louis Gates, who
admittedly surpass him in the highly sophisticated examination of
textuality and structure. Yet theory and form are not all. Kent
endures preeminently for his historical and folk breadth, in his resistance to the exclusion of the folk spirit as the touchstone for cul-

tural authenticity, and for his awareness that the imposed rupture between formal responsiveness and rhetorical communion (reading)
deceives.

The historical Kent imposed a double posture on American literary
tradition. Years prior to his arrival in Chicago, Margaret Danner (poet),
William Couch, Jr. (administrator and scholar), Margaret Burroughs
(cultural historian), and Gwendolyn Brooks (poet) had all honed their
literary skills in a poetry workshop on the city's South Side. Near
there Margaret Walker had researched a highly publicized murder for
Richard Wright's novel *Native Son*. Finally, Kent himself helped
discover a letter in which Wright encouraged Harper's, the novelist's
publisher, to bring out *Street in Bronzeville* (1945), Brooks' first
book of poems.[14]

When Kent arrived at the University of Chicago in 1969, the generation had turned. Though Brooks was still there, Wright had expatriated
to Paris in the mid-Forties and had died in 1960. The newly emerged
novelist Ronald L. Fair had yet to follow Wright's pattern into self-
imposed exile, a path which for Fair would lead eventually to Finland.
While Haki Madhubuti and Carolyn Rodgers still wrote steadily, the
emergence of esoteric theory — its roots in structuralism, semiotics,
or deconstruction — had yet to displace the polemical poets of the
decade. Even many literary scholars were still concerned about the
real world.

George Kent hardly spoke about the double turns which deepened
his critical understanding. Most of his fellows were creative writers,
but he remained the rare scholar. Still, he maintained a dual focus
on literary creativity. Brooks, Walker, Danner, and Burroughs belonged to his own generation — as Wright nearly had — but he spent
considerable time with the young. Through this double perception
on historical time, he helped sustain communal customs.

In his scholarly work, Kent confronts silently the White tradition.
Where Finley Peter Dunne sees humor, he sees tragedy. Surely Kent
understands the historical influence of Frank Norris on Richard
Wright,[15] but he probably reads different cultural spirits as animating
the naturalistic forms. Subconsciously Kent knows that Ernest Hemingway, who was born in Oak Park, wrote about his boyhood summers in

Michigan and that Edgar Rice Burroughs, the author of Tarzan, escaped into exotic fantasies, the figments of the settler's self-interest.[16] For thirteen years Kent lived daily in the literary environment historically determined by Masters, Lindsay, and Sandberg, who was once associated with *Poetry*. He knew, perhaps, about Sherwood Anderson, the native Ohioan who lived in the city during his teens and who later received encouragement there from Robert Moss Lovett as well as from Ben Hecht. When Kent read a review by Kenneth Fearing on Langston Hughes, he encountered once more the White tradition.[17]

Kent's posture displaces telling moments from the city's literary and cultural history. On March 19, 1928, Freeman F. Gosden and Charles J. Correll founded the Amos and Andy show in Chicago. And later, in 1935, those who were too poor to see the Cubs play baseball at Wrigley Field near Clark Street and Addison Avenue followed the descriptions by the announcer Ronald Reagan on the radio. Kent must have known that by the time of Farrell and Wright, the city seemed hopeless and despairing.[18] Professor Kenny J. Williams, the cultural historican, confirms that "when Bigger (Thomas, Wright's *Native Son*) travels the short distance to Drexel Boulevard (Chicago) he psychologically takes a trip greater in scope than any . . . to the moon."[19] At the turnside of Kent's communal criticism remained racial discrimination and the minstrel tradition. Despite his example, greater Chicago had resolidified the monolithic and narrow value some would call right. While Kent had renewed responsiveness to Wright and Brooks, many thinkers doubted that the urban environment could ever facilitate great art, the code word now for highbrow humanism.

Yet the diachronic work of George E. Kent disproves them. Despite his rigorous analytic, the scholarly narrator maintains sensitivity to community and feeling. In his formal essays, often submitted from the University of Chicago, he sustains humble origins in the folk spirit. Skilled in the strategies for Western discourse, he saves a unique place for Black America. And still on the defense for freedom, he fully acts out social commitment. What Kent performs in the communal rite, he readily achieves through the independent mind. In the heroic posture, he doubly mirrors Black folk.

NOTES

1.   "Maya Angelou's *I Know Why the Caged Bird Sings* and Black Autobiographical Tradition," *Kansas Quarterly,* 7, no. 3 (1975), 78.

2.   See Jonathan Culler, *On Deconstruction: Theory and Criticism after Structuralism* (Ithaca, New York: Cornell University Press, 1982) and *Pursuit of Signs* (Ithaca, New York: Cornell University Press, 1981); Kenneth Burke, *Philosophy of Literary Form* (1941; rpt. Berkeley: University of California Press, 1973) and *Rhetoric of Motives* (1950; rpt. Berkeley: University of California Press, 1969).

3.   See Jacques Derrida, *Positions* (1972; trans. Chicago: University of Chicago Press, 1981).

4.   See Wright's *Pagan Spain* (New York: Harper's, 1957).

5.   Richard K. Barksdale, "George E. Kent: A Personal Memoir," *The Langston Hughes Review,* 2 (Spring, 1983), 31-32.

6.   Roseann P. Bell, "Substance: George Kent," an interview, in *Sturdy Black Bridges,* ed. Roseann Bell, Bettye J. Parker, and Beverly Guy-Sheftall (Garden City, New York: Doublday, 1979), p. 217. Future citations from the interview appear parenthetically in the text.

7.   George E. Kent, "Baldwin and the Problem of Being," in *James Baldwin: A Critical Evaluation,* ed. Therman B. O'Daniel (Washington: Howard University Press, 1977), p. 20.

8.   Richard Wright, "Blueprint for Negro Writing" (1937), in *Richard Wright Reader,* ed. Ellen Wright and Michel Fabre (New York: Harper and Row, 1978), p. 46.

9.   *In the Mecca* (New York: Harper and Row, 1968), p. 5.

10.   George E. Kent, *Blackness and the Adventure of Western Culture* (Chicago: Third World Press, 1972), p. 10. Future citations from the book occur parenthetically in the text.

11.   *Blackness,* pp. 79-136; see also George E. Kent, "Aesthetic Values in the Poetry of Gwendolyn Brooks," in *Black American Literature and Humanism,* ed. R. Baxter Miller (Lexington, Kentucky: University Press of Kentucky, 1981), pp. 75-94.

12.   "Maya Angelou's *I Know Why the Caged Bird Sings*," pp. 72-78.

13.   R. Baxter Miller, "Window on the Night: Etymology of Cultural Imagination," *Obsidian,* 6 (Winter, 1980), 68-81, and "The Wasteland and the Flower: Through Blyden Jackson: A Revised Theory for Black South Literature," *Southern Literary Journal,* 16 (Fall, 1984).

14.   R. Baxter Miller, "The 'Etched Flame' of Margaret Walker: Biblical and Literary Re-Creation in Southern History," *Tennessee Studies in Literature,* 26 (1981), 157; Gwendolyn Brooks, *Report From Part One* (Detroit: Broadside, 1972); Kent, "Aesthetic Values," p. 85.

15.   Edward Wagenknect, *Chicago* (Norman: University of Oklahoma

Press, 1964), pp. 132-142; Finis Farr, *Chicago: A Personal History of America's Most American City* (New Rochelle, New York: Arlington House, 1973), p. 385.

16.   Wagenknect, pp. 137-150.

17.   Wagenknect, p. 50; Miller, *Langston Hughes and Gwendolyn Brooks,* p. 9.

18.   Kenny J. Williams, *In the City of Men* (Nashville, Tennessee: Townsend Press, 1974), p. 419.

19.   *Ibid.,* p. 427.

Unraveling a Western Tale:
The Critical Legacy of George Kent

by

Houston A. Baker, Jr.

Thus a Brer Rabbit story is full of the contradictions of experience — an expression of the existing order of the world and Brer Rabbit's unspecific sense of something "other." And there are times in Brer Rabbit stories during which the existing order and Brer Rabbit's "other" have almost equal validity.

—Blackness and the Adventure of Western Culture

The outcome of such uses [of Western literary forms by black writers] can be that the black writer, while making interesting comments about the black experience, seems to be taking care of somebody else's business.

—Blackness and the Advernture of Western Culture

I.

The critical legacy of George Kent is properly sited at the crossroads between post-Althusserian Marxism and a modified, Derridean
post-structuralism.[1] For Kent, like post-Althusserian Marxists, understood that criticism is always an act of political intervention. Re-
jecting a "metaphysic of the text" which postulates an ideal and invariant form lying behind specific historical and materialist appropria-
tions of the practice of writing, Kent sought to intervene in the process
of situating various so-called "literary texts" in relationship to other
cultural practices. Rather than a belief in the discovery of contradictions, fissures, or ideological repressions in texts, Kent knew that the
critic's stance — and that alone — established the very notion *text*
or *literature* in the first instance and, in the second interpretive
instance, was responsible for the placement of such notional processes
within an overall field of cultural practices. He broke decisively,
therefore, in his critical practice with the bourgeois aesthetic theory
that assumes *High Art* as a given. In lieu of such a theory, he adopted
a new problematic, one conditioned by the various energies of a group
of black Chicago writers and critics dedicated to revolutionary creativity.[2]

This new problematic consisted not in revised answers to traditional
questions, but in the formulation of an entirely different set of questions about the practices of black writing and literary study in their
relationship to what Kent labels "High Ground Humanism."[3] One
might claim that Kent would have been in full agreement with the
following assertions drawn from Tony Bennett's *Formalism and Marxism*:

> Any enterprise in criticism is essentially a political under-
> taking. Criticism is not a "science" which has in view,
> as its goal, a day when its knowledge of the pre-given uni-
> verse of literary texts will be complete. It is an active
> and ongoing part of the political process, defined by a
> series of interventions within, and struggles for, the uses
> to which so-called literary texts are to be put within the
> real social process. (p. 148)

The Derridean aspects of Kent's project reside in his recognition that a new problematic can only emerge through solicitation — a rigorously playful "shaking" — of the totality of presuppositions and entailments that constitute the given state of a discursive universe. One must unravel the entire text and texture of High Ground Humanism's tale, or *telling,* of itself in order to come up with a new and resonantly black story. When Kent, in *Blackness and the Adventure of Western Culture* (1972), talks of the "stubborn threads in the warp and woof of white tradition [conceived] as a systematic and *abstract* universalism" (p. 9), he summons, or handles, such "stubborn threads" only in the service of their unraveling.

What he is after — as a critic of a new generation and a representative of a newly-emergent sensibility in the black arts — is a tailored alteration of the fabric and tissue of a Western yarn about "the assumed triumph of the individual, the clarity of truth, the existence of transcendental beauty, the shining virtues of rationality, [and] the glory of democratic freedom" (p. 9). His strategy is, in the tailored sense suggested by the preceding metaphor, to make an end run.

Discussing the practice of literary or artistic criticism, Kent calls such terms as *protest, transcending,* and *universalism* "game names." His designation connotes not only the colloquial and Afro-American vernacular sense of someone "running a game" (engaging in confidence activities to one's detriment), but also the more expansive notion of *play* itself. For Kent knew that High Ground Humanism was but one play in an arena of competing cultural compulsives that constituted the open-ended field of signification in general. To invoke and substitute new signifiers to displace a traditional, Western lexicon was to effect a trick play — a double reverse, for example.

Kent realized that it was necessary to open the ends if a successful play were to be completed. Metaphors of tailoring and play combine in his implicit claim that fludity, openness, a general as opposed to a restricted economy, and a genuine plurality of valorized interpretations of the world will become possible only when the ends of Western wholecloth are made to run, only when the seams are altered and the literary critical universe of discourse becomes polysemous.

Kent was, thus, a tailor, a solicitor, an end runner, an errant wander-

er given to that process the blues people call "movering on." Time
and again, he compels his reader to see that such signs as *man* and
universal in the Western lexicon are marks of an illusory fullness and
presence. They are, in Kent's own reading of the universe, merely
ideological guarantors of motionlessness, of a stolid and abiding status-
quo-ness that seeks to fix "us" (i.e., *the folks,* the vast majority of
Americans) precisely where, how, and as what we (now) are. Stated
philosophically, Kent recognized the tale, the game, the fabric and
yarn of Western High Ground Humanism as the inscription of a *hic
et nunc* (here and now) that maintained a select coterie of white,
Anglo-Saxon, Protestant males at the zenith, awaiting the gradual
ascent, development, emergence of what the Nigerian critic Chinweizu
calls "the rest of us."[4] *The West and the Rest of Us* is a phrase to
which Kent wold have assented as a description of an essential bifurca-
tion in the Western yarn. For the phrase suggests, in truly high-ground
and humanistic fashion, that what resides *outside* a Western total is
but a remainder, a residue, a remnant scarcely salvific in nature.
Against such totalization Kent proposes alterations that find their
clearest pattern in the repertoire of *Blackness* at its American folk
levels.

II.

A topography of Kent's criticism as it appears in the striking collection of essays entitled *Blackness and the Adventure of Western
Culture* reveals peaks of High Ground Humanism juxtaposed to bone-
rattling and sometimes unseasonably-dry valleys of Blackness. In the
Western ranges one finds etched signs of the "timeless and the universal," firm resolutions of "formal logic and rationality," sensibility
and rhythms of a reductively closed "machine culture." In the black
valleys, by contrast, one confronts "topicality" giving immediate
voice to community issues, spirituality that defies rhythms of a
machine culture, irresolute outlawry as a function of an expansively
open-ended and radically contingent universe. In the mountains,
only the romantically-rebellious individual temperamentally governed

by impulses of a revolutionary will can feel free and be heroic. In the valleys, the hero is the communal rabbit, the trickster as embodiment of folk survival strategies and capable of end runs — ludic unravelings, of Western semes.

Kent, as critic, is a denizen of the foothills, a figure of passes and passages where mountain and valley cross. He is a medium of the valley's spirit — "bo-bowed," as the folk would say, under the weight of heavy, existential definitions of *Blackness* derived from cultural traditions and forced (like floating signifiers) to bear as much meaning as he can enforce.

It is not the case that he assumes a *neutral* stance; he knows there can be no such thing as *neutral* ground in the dichotomized geographies of a racist America. Any writer or critic in the practice of writing or criticism finds himself or herself moved by what Kent calls "mythologies." In the mountains, one finds (with appropriate Derridean echoes) white mythologies grouped as High Ground Humanism. In the valleys, one finds defining mythologies of *Blackness* arrayed as always already formalized instances of a culture's *sensibility,* of a group's characteristic intellectual, emotional, and psychic responses to existence.

Kent moves to the valley's (w)hole like a wily rabbit, or an altering "edgeman," and makes his forceful play against high Western closure. His sharpest insights in practical criticism are directed toward black writers who have negotiated the same passages that provoke his own keenest observations.

Claude McKay, Langston Hughes, Gwendolyn Brooks, Richard Wright, James Baldwin, and Ralph Ellison all come under scrutiny. Kent proceeds with a canny deftness equal to the rabbit's most signal trick plays. He discovers in his analyses the peculiar *Black* strengths and the unfortunate Western shortcomings in the work of each writer. Whether isolating the core "niggerhood" of McKay, the instinctual alliance of Hughes with the "is-ness" and "as-ifness' of the folk, or the "feeling sense of form" of Gwendolyn Brooks, he works as a careful appreciative critic, singling out folk resonances and Western leanings with an almost equal share of diplomatic acumen and gritty *sounding* (when he deems it necessary) on the Western entrapments suffered by some of the most valorized Afro-American writers.

In the penultimate essay of *Blackness and the Adventure of Western Culture* he executes a wondrous sortie on the oeuvre of William Faulkner. He does not mince words in denouncing what he perceives as Faulkner's virulent predilection for racist stereotypes of blacks that characterize the cultural compulsive of "white nationalism." Nor does he refuse to grant Faulkner (black nationalist sentiments notwithstanding) the praise he is due for his singular moral engagement with issues of *Blackness* in America.

In the final essay of *Blackness and the Adventure of Western Culture,* Kent points to a newly-emergent sensibility in the black arts, one that finds itself in uneasy tension with such Western-oriented authors as Ralph Ellison. Characteristically, he not only enunciates the strengths of the seemingly opposed parties, but also singles out failings on both sides. An emergent generation can learn to avoid a merely "sloganeering" or "rhetorical" blackness by studying techniques of literary engagement with folk forms manifested in Ellison's best fiction and criticism. Ellison, in turn, might trust the communal vision and hard-line condemnations of white mythology enunciated by a younger generation enough to see the unfortunate exaggeratedness of his own Western postures.

III.

Working the foothills, passes, passages, and crossings between *Blackness* and the adventure of Western culture, George Kent's most impressive accomplishment was his realization of the rooted, Latin meanings of *adventure.* In Latin *adventuras* signifies "unattested." In linguistic descriptions (etymologies, for example) an "unattested" form is one whose existence is not established by documentary evidence but inferred from comparative evidence. Read under the Latin definition, an "adventure of Western culture" would be a speculation, or a sounding of *possible* form — a form, one might say, whose existence can be inferred only through etymologies of "otherness." Kent suggests that the black-and-white texture of discourse between "unattested" forms of white mastery and putative forms of black subservience constitutes the origin and history of an always-to-be-documented "Western culture."

The end-running (ruining) irony of the adventurous situation is that only the attestation of *THE REST OF US* — as "black" on white spaces, as "comparative" others — can give inferrable form to the West. Finally, what Kent calls the "is-ness" (acceptance of life's myriad contradictions) and the "as-ifness" (ceaseless movement of desire) of Black existence constitute the "protowriting" of a white Western cultural adventure.

In his seminal essay "Differance," the French philosopher Jacques Derrida defines the deferral (temporal delay) and difference (spatial gapping) that enable signification as follows: "It is this constitution of the present as a 'primordial' and irreducibly nonsimple, and therefore, in the strict sense nonprimordial, synthesis of traces, retentions, and protentions . . . that I propose to call protowriting, prototrace, of *différance.* The latter [*différance*] (is) (both) spacing (and) temporalizing."[5] George Kent knew that there could exist such a thing as "legitimate universalism" (*Blackness,* p. 112). But he knew that it would only exist in a world in which a "complete projection of a situation or experience's *space* and *vibrations"* can occur. The prototypical writing required to inscribe such an experience can be achieved, Kent claims, only by "going down deep, not transcending" (p. 112).

Translated in terms of the overall topography of *Blackness and the Adventure of Western Culture,* one might read Kent's formulations as a suggestion that it is in the "otherness" of Brer Rabbit's experience, in the rabbit (w)hole, as it were, in the Black valley's rattling contingency and depths, that Western culture finds its severest test and most valid *attestation.* Kent, of course, was always honest enough to know that despite his repeated avowals of the value of a defining *Blackness,* he was yet conditioned by the virtues of Western High Ground Humanism. He writes: "Despite the strained condition which I have attributed to high ground humanism, I am after no simple conclusion that it was worthless. For it was wielded by gifted Blacks with a certain Brer Rabbit wiliness, and some of the spirit and wit of

High John de Conqueror. And it has its notched scoreboard of half loaves, which one can ignore only if he insists upon rigidly holding his back to the past and his face to the front — a posture involving a petrified presentism" (p. 192).

Neither "presentism" nor myths of presence constrain the criticism of George Kent. He seems instinctually to know that taking care of Black business is, at one and the same instant, a prototrace and a seam-running attestation to the adventure of Western culture. He was ever a man correct in his spatial and temporal coordinates, and his strategically political interventions and mappings of critical territory encompass us all in extraordinarily alluring ways.

NOTES

1.   For an account of the development of Marxist literary study after the seminal contributions of Louis Althusser, one might turn to Tony Bennett's *Formalism and Marxism* (London and New York: Methuen, 1979).

2.   Led by such senior figures as the late Hoyt W. Fuller (Editor of *Negro Digest,* which became *Black World,* which, in turn, became *First World*) and the current Poet Laureate of Illinois, Gwendolyn Brooks, a group of young black writers in Chicago christened themselves The Organization of Black American Culture (OBAC). One of the most influential members of this group was Don L. Lee (now, Haki Madhubuti), a young poet who wrote in an accessible vernacular style and distributed his books in the black community. Kent was much moved by the activities of OBAC, and his most productive years as a critic coincided with this Midwestern extension of the general Black Arts Movement in the United States.

3.   My citations of Kent's criticism are all drawn from his major work entitled *Blackness and the Adventure of Western Culture* (Chicago: Third World Press, 1972). The Third World Press is an ongoing enterprise that was established primarily through Don L. Lee's energies in the early 1970s. OBAC not only talked of "cultural revolution," but also built institutions in the service of that ideal.

4.   *The West and the Rest of Us* (New York: Vintage, 1975).

5.   In *Speech and Phenomena* (Evanston: Northwestern University Press, 1973), p. 143.